Romantic Nationalism and Liberalism: Joachim Lelewel and the Polish National Idea

❦

Joan S. Skurnowicz

EAST EUROPEAN MONOGRAPHS, BOULDER
DISTRIBUTED BY COLUMBIA UNIVERSITY PRESS
NEW YORK

1981

EAST EUROPEAN MONOGRAPHS, NO. LXXXIII

This book has been published with the help of a
grant from The Kościuszko Foundation.

*Winner of the Kościuszko Foundation Doctoral
Dissertation Award, 1972.*

Printed in the United States of America

❀ For my parents

Contents

Preface

The dominant intellectual currents of early nineteenth century Western Europe shaped the historical writing of the age. Philosophical idealism stimulated the study of the philosophy of history and found prominent exponents in Johann Gottfried von Herder and Georg Wilhelm Friedrich Hegel. Romanticism and nationalism spurred, on the one hand, the collecting, editing, and publishing of documents on the national past, and on the other, the study of language and the origins of peoples, and the writing of romantic national history which found its greatest masters in Jules Michelet and Thomas Carlyle. Liberalism inspired the study of the past for the lessons it taught the present and for the justification of the political power of the middle class. Liberalism's most famous spokesmen were Thomas Babington Macauley and François Guizot. Finally, historical criticism brought forth the ideal and method of objective history and found its greatest master in Leopold von Ranke.[1]

In the partitioned Polish lands, philosophical idealism, romanticism and nationalism, and liberalism, together with ideas of the Enlightenment, influenced the emerging Polish intelligentsia. From its ranks emerged one of Poland's foremost scholars of the nineteenth century.

Among Polish scholars, Joachim Lelewel was the supreme authority in the field of history for half a century, and the influence of eighteenth century enlightenment and nineteenth century philosophical idealism, romanticism, nationalism, and liberalism permeated his works and actions.

His *Historyka* (*The Art of History*) was one of the first in Poland which established criteria to be followed "in pursuit of historical truth," and his analytical approach in his treatment of historical materials far surpassed the efforts of earlier Polish historians whose traditional chronological approaches were subjected increasingly to criticism. Lelewel's *Historyka* remained the only comprehensive theory in the Polish language until the twentieth century.

Lelewel collected and edited documents and manuscripts of his nation's past, wrote treatises on historical-geography, and before he became preoccupied with national history and politics, produced commentaries on antiquity.

In his studies of the origins of peoples, he formulated a unique theory of "dual development of the nations of Europe." The southwestern nations and states, according to Lelewel, developed on the foundations laid by the ancient and despotic Roman Empire. The nations and states of northeastern Europe, beyond the reach and influence of the old Roman Empire, formed directly from very primitive but freer social and political traditions than those inherited by the southwestern nations and states of Europe. Accepting this as the basic premise of his theory of dual development, Lelewel proceeded to endow the prehistoric Slavs of northeastern Europe with unique virtues of *wolność* (freedom) and *obywatelstwo* (a sense of citizenship) and contrasted them with the characteristics of those nations influenced by Rome where feudalism and its social hierarchies developed.

In his lectures in history at the universities in Warsaw and Wilno, Lelewel emphasized these unique virtues of the Slavs. In the romantic national histories of Poland which he wrote, he portrayed the Polish *Rzeczpospolita* (Commonwealth) as the foremost representative of the Slav spirit of freedom and sense of citizenship in northeastern Europe.

Joachim Lelewel, the scholar and author of the first modern national history of the Polish state and its people, also played a significant role in the politics of the November uprising of 1830. Resigning his position as a deputy in the lower house of the Sejm when the uprising erupted, he participated in the series of revolutionary national governments created between 29 November 1830 and 18 October 1831. During this period, he also wrote several political commentaries which reflected his republican political beliefs and his democratic social principles.

In the decades of his subsequent exile, he resumed his scholarly activities; continued his political tracts on behalf of the Polish cause. The latter, with the commentaries he wrote during 1830–1831, contributed significantly to the development of republican-democratic political and social thought among the Poles.

Despite his significant contributions to modern scholarship and to the development of liberal political and social thought, Joachim

Lelewel and his work are known chiefly by those familiar with the Polish language. Although many of his works have also appeared in the leading European languages, few studies of this man, his scholarship, or his political activities have been published by Western or émigré scholars. The author of this brief study proposes to contribute, in a small way, to historical scholarship by introducing Lelewel's works to a wider audience, by discussing his contributions to the development of Polish historiography, his contributions to the writing of Polish history, and his tireless efforts on behalf of Poland. His scholarly contributions in the fields of numismatics and geography which gained for him an eminent place among European scholars will be alluded to briefly in the text, but emphasis is on Joachim Lelewel, the first modern historian of Poland and the individual most responsible for the foundation of the cult of the Polish nation, i.e., Polish romantic nationalism.

As an historian, Joachim Lelewel joined in the movement of his epoch and his nation — intellectual, moral, social, and political. He intermingled his histories with ideology as did his eminent contemporaries — François Guizot, Jules Michelet, Karl von Rotteck, Thomas Macauley, and František Palacký. His legacy to future generations included not only an abundance of information concerning Poland's past but also a unique interpretation of that past — an interpretation based on his personal republican-democratic ideals.

The present volume is a revised version of my doctoral dissertation which I completed at the University of Wisconsin, Madison, under the supervision of Professor Alfred Erich Senn. I am grateful to him and to my other mentors at the University of Wisconsin and the Pennsylvania State University for their encouragement, criticisms, and helpful suggestions in the evolution of this study. I also want to express my appreciation to the editors of *Laurentian University Review* for their permission to draw on my article: "Joachim Lelewel: A Polish Émigré's Anti-Tsarist Politics (1831–1833)," *Laurentian University Review* (Sudbury, Ont.) X, no. 1 (Nov., 1977) and to the Kościuszko Foundation for subsidizing the publication of my manuscript. It is with particular gratitude that I acknowledge the patient and perceptive assistance of Professor Thomas E. and Mrs. Theresa Auge in the preparation of the final draft of this manuscript.

Joan S. Skurnowicz
Loras College
Dubuque, Iowa

I   Introduction

Among Polish historians, Joachim Lelewel generally has been accorded a place of high esteem, with a brief exception in the latter part of the nineteenth century when Józef Szujski and Michał Bobrzyński, representatives of the Realist School of Polish history, in their opposition to the romanticism of the pre-1863 generation, sought to discredit him. In the twentieth century, however, when nationalism reasserted itself so profoundly throughout Europe, Joachim Lelewel regained his former place of eminence.[1] This was not only because of a resurgent interest in his contributions to library science, geography, numismatics, and to the development of modern historiography in Poland, but also because of his romantic-national approach to the study of Poland's past. His radical republican political beliefs, his democratic social objectives, and his revolutionary political activities on behalf of the Polish national cause also aroused the interests of numerous scholars and writers.

The late Professor Marceli Handelsman, noted historian and biographer of Prince Adam Jerzy Czartoryski, praised Lelewel as an innovator and an initiator of ideas which future scholars could not neglect. Evaluating Lelewel's work as an historian, Handelsman wrote:

> His works are the first scholarly — in today's understanding of the word — synthesis of Poland's past; his monographs fundamental researches in the immense field of history; his methods — the first accurate and critical probe of scholarly researches among us. His creations mark the beginning of the further development of history as a great scholarly movement in Poland which eventually matured into an organized totality.[2]

Handelsman's contemporaries concurred. In the interwar period,

Helena Hleb-Koszańska and Maria Kotwiczówna began collecting and cataloguing in chronological order a record of all printed books and articles by Joachim Lelewel. This task, interrupted by the outbreak of war in 1939, was resumed only when the war ended. In 1924, Janusz Iwaszkiewicz published Lelewel's *Pamiętnik z roku 1830–31* (*A Memoir of the Year 1830–31*). This publication is based on a copy by Leon Chodźko of Lelewel's manuscript which was found quite accidentally among other papers in the *Archiwum Akt Dawnych* in Warsaw.[3] The work of collecting Lelewel's correspondence in emigration also began in the interwar period, and Ignacy Chrzanowski, professor at Kraków, announced a proposed biography of Lelewel. In 1941, the year of Chrzanowski's death, the first part of his biography of Lelewel appeared in *Great Men and Women of Poland*.[4]

Like Marceli Handelsman, Ignacy Chrzanowski, too, praised the nineteenth century scholar-revolutionary for his prolific contributions to the study of history in Poland. In particular, Chrzanowski noted Lelewel's work in historiography. He described Lelewel as "the first in Poland to apply strictly scholarly methods of criticism to historical sources and the first to give deeper meaning to the idea of historical pragmatism by searching for the true causes of the course of national events . . . in the particular national character and in the spirit of the time."[5] He recognized that Lelewel's approach was influenced frequently by idealistic and romantic notions and that Lelewel considered it a sacred duty to instill in his young students patriotic feelings, but in an age of nationalism, Chrzanowski proposed that this was not a grievous shortcoming.[6]

An expanded version of Chrzanowski's biographical sketch entitled *Joachim Lelewel: człowiek i pisarz* (*Joachim Lelewel: The Man and the Writer*), edited by Stanisław Pigoń, was published posthumously in Warsaw in 1946. In this study of Lelewel, a literary portrait of the protagonist emerged. In discussing Lelewel's personal characteristics, Professor Chrzanowski sympathized with the austere romantic intellectual who led a life of work and heroic abnegation for many years and who eloquently called on Poles everywhere to continue their struggle for the independence of their homeland.[7] Describing and analyzing the writer and scholar in the latter pages of his biography, Professor Chrzanowski praised Lelewel's contributions to methodology and his interpretations of Poland's national history, and he extolled the histories for their literary value. Although brief, this biography remains an excellent introduction to Joachim Lelewel the intellectual.

Since the end of World War II, considerable attention has been paid by scholars and historians in Poland to the works and correspondence of Joachim Lelewel. Several volumes of his collected correspondence in emigration have been published in Kraków.[8] Since 1950, scholars such as Marian Henryk Serejski, Helena Więckowska, and Nina Assorodobraj have edited collections of Lelewel's works. These volumes have been published individually in Warsaw and Kraków by the Institute of History of the Polish Academy of Sciences under the general title *Dzieła* (*Works*). A comprehensive bibliography of works written and published by Joachim Lelewel, compiled by Helena Hleb-Koszańska, Director of the National Library in Warsaw, and Maria Kotwiczówna, appeared in 1952.[9]

In addition to the publication of the bibliography of Lelewel's works, his collected works, and correspondence in emigration, many secondary studies have appeared since 1945. In 1958, Marian Henryk Serejski published his *Koncepcja historii powszechnej Joachima Lelewela* (*Joachim Lelewel's Conception of General History*).[10] The following year, a detailed evaluation of Lelewel's *Bibliograficznych ksiąg dwoje* (*Two Bibliographical Volumes, 1823-1826*) by Witold Nowodworski appeared.[11] In this monograph, Nowodworski devoted most of his attention to the origin and evolution of Lelewel's *Bibliograficznych ksiąg dwoje,* the significance of the two volumes for the development of library science in Poland, and the significance of the two volumes relative to comparable studies by Western European contemporaries of Lelewel. The author also discussed the influence of Polish scholars such as Czacki, Bentkowski, and the Bandtkie brothers on Lelewel the bibliographer, and he devoted a considerable number of pages to the history and organization of the Public Library at the University of Warsaw — where Lelewel served as a curator and bibliographer from 1818 to 1821.

Numerous commemorations signalled the centenary of Lelewel's death in 1961. For example, an entire volume of the prestigious *Kwartalnik Historyczny* (*The Historical Quarterly*) was devoted to relevant questions posed by this nineteenth century scholar's contributions to Polish intellectual thought and to critical reviews of new studies of the man and his many faceted work. Notable scholars, including the editors of his collected works, dealt with such diverse topics as Joachim Lelewel's contributions to the contemporary study of history and Lelewel's idea of *gminowładztwo* (a form of communal democracy); Lelewel as a scholar of the history of the peasants and their rights; his contributions to archeology and numismatics; and the *Historyka* (*The Art of History*). Other topics included

Joachim Lelewel's relations with the *Towarzystwo Przyjaciół Nauk* (Society of Friends of Learning) and his rapport with Bohemians and Slovaks from his initial contacts with them to the Slav Congress held in Prague in 1848.

Jerzy Czacki's *Ojczyzna, naród, rewolucja* (*Fatherland, Nation, Revolution*) also appeared in 1961. In this, the author's doctoral dissertation, he analyzed Lelewel's ideas and assessed their impact on the development of Polish national thought.

Although a definitive study of the life of Joachim Lelewel remains to be written, several biographies of him appeared in Poland in the decade of the sixties. In addition, one by Abram M. Basevich, a young Soviet scholar, was published after its author's death. Basevich's *Ioakhim Lelevel': Pol'skii revoliutsioner, demokrat, uchen'ii* (*Joachim Lelewel: Polish Revolutionary, Democrat, Scholar*) included a biography of Lelewel to 1831 and an interpretation of Lelewel's concepts of historico-sociology. Franciszek Bronowski, a reviewer of Basevich's study, praised it as an original contribution to scholarship. Despite the fact that Basevich had only limited access to Polish sources, the young Soviet scholar effectively utilized archival materials available in Leningrad and Vilnius, and he included, in his study, the reactions of Russian society and tsarist censors to Joachim Lelewel and his work.[12]

In 1966, the memoirs and diary of Prot Lelewel, Joachim's younger brother, was published, and a romanticized, fictional version of the life of Lelewel, by Karol Koźmiński, appeared in Torun. An excellent scholarly study of Lelewel was published in 1969. A monograph based on extensive archival materials, *Działalność polityczno-spo-łeczna Joachima Lelewela na emigracji w latach 1831-1861* (*The Political and Social Activities of Joachim Lelewel in Emigration, 1831-1861*) by Bogusław Cygler is a carefully researched and lucid account of Lelewel's activities in emigration in France and Belgium.

As the decade of the seventies opened, new studies of Joachim Lelewel appeared in Poland and in the Soviet Union.[13] In contrast to the continued interest in him which is expressed by scholars in Poland, and more recently in the Soviet Union, references to this nineteenth century intellectual-revolutionary by Western scholars are almost non-existent. There are some exceptions, e.g., Peter Brock and R. F. Leslie deal marginally with Lelewel's political activities in their studies. The major interests of Marian Kukiel and Oscar Halecki, prominent émigré historians, do not include Joachim Lelewel, his political activities, or his scholarship. Few articles devoted to this nineteenth century figure have appeared in scholarly Western journals. These include the contributions of the late William J. Rose which were published in the interwar period and Peter Brock's references to Joachim Lelewel in his numerous studies of Polish socialism which appear in various journals in the West. Most recently, the American scholars Frank Mocha and Kenneth F. Lewalski have focused on specific incidents in Lelewel's life.[14]

Despite the enduring concerns of Polish scholars with all facets of Joachim Lelewel's scholarly and political career, the interests of Western scholars remain nominal. The present writer believes that Joachim Lelewel's fundamental contributions to the modern development of history and, more specifically, his contributions to the history and political traditions of his nation, deserve a larger audience.

2 Family Background and Formative Years

The Lelewel Family

Joachim Lelewel's family background represents a mixed ethnic heritage. He referred to his polonized gentry roots in a letter to Karol Sienkiewicz, a fellow émigré and intellectual, in 1859. His mother, Ewa Szelutta Lelewel (1764–1837), belonged to a Polish-Ruthenian landowning family that settled in Mazovia (*Mazowsze*), one of the three provinces which constituted Great Poland (*Wielkopolska*) in the sixteenth century.[1]

His paternal roots were primarily Germanic and Swiss.[2] According to oral family tradition, the Lelewel family were Huguenots who were forced to emigrate to Austria some time after the Saint Bartholomew Day Massacres of 1572.[3] Written records indicate that in the eighteenth century, the family settled in East Prussia (*Prusy*), and in 1713 obtained a diploma of nobility (*indygenat*) from Frederick I Hohenzollern. In the latter part of the eighteenth century, Joachim Lelewel's paternal grandfather, Henryk Loelhoeffel, married and settled in Warsaw where he practiced medicine and served as physician to Augustus III.[4] In 1768 and 1775, Joachim's father, Karol Maurycy Lelewel (1748–1831), received *indygenaty* from the Polish Sejm. These diplomas conferred Polish citizenship and gentry (*szlachta*) status on the Lelewel family and acknowledged as permanent that spelling of the family surname.[5]

Karol Maurycy Lelewel, Joachim's father, was educated by the Theatine priests in Warsaw and attended the university in Goettingen. Upon his return to Poland in 1768, he served briefly as a Captain in the Royal Dragoon Regiment. Between 1772 and 1794, he served as Treasurer of the National Education Commission (*Komisja Edu-*

kacji Narodowej) until the third partition of Poland. After the partition, the elder Lelewel resigned from public office, declining Prussian requests to continue to serve.[6] In the Napoleonic era, Karol Maurycy Lelewel resumed his career as a public servant. In the autonomous Grand Duchy of Warsaw, he worked in the Chamber of Deputies and in the Directorate of Education. In the post Napoleonic era, in the Congress Kingdom, he was appointed Councillor of State and served on the Commission of Public Education.[7]

A competent public servant who was praised by the Great Sejm (1788–1792) for his contributions to the *Rzeczpospolita,* Karol Maurycy Lelewel maintained close ties with the reform minded Polish intellectuals of the late eighteenth and early nineteenth centuries. According to his sons' accounts, Karol's circle of intimate friends included Szymon Malewski, Jan Śniadecki, the Reverend Marcin Poczobutt, and other prominent figures.[8] He developed a close working relationship with Hugo Kołłątaj, the greatest reformer of the late eighteenth century renaissance in the Polish lands. He also maintained close ties with the reform elements at the Court of Stanisław August Poniatowski. These latter included numerous members of Karol's own family. For a long time his brother-in-law, Adam Cieciszowski (d. 1783), was head of the King's Cabinet. Pius Kiciński and Józef Deszert, married to the daughters of Ignacy Cieciszowski, worked in the king's Chancellery. Between 1783 and 1792, Pius Kiciński served as head of Stanisław August's Cabinet.[9] Most members of the Cieciszowski family favored political reforms of the state. This was especially characteristic of Pius Kiciński whose speeches as Deputy from the Liw lands of Mazovia during the sessions of the Great Sejm made him a leader in the reform movement.[10] Kiciński also belonged with Karol Lelewel to the stockholders of the woolen manufacturing company in Łowicz and was a friend of the Bishop Jan Albertrandy — a noted historian and a prominent member and first president of the Warsaw *Towarzystwo Przyjaciół Nauk* (Society of the Friends of Learning), and the bibliographer of Stanisław August's library after 1790.[11] When Joachim Lelewel wrote the first draft of his history of the reign of Stanisław August, he cited as one of his major sources of information, his conversations with his father and his uncles Pius Kiciński and Józef Deszert "who knew the Poniatowskis."[12]

His father's distinguished and dedicated service and relations with the progressive elements in the Court of Stanisław August Poniatowski and in public life certainly influenced the formation of the young future scholar's attitudes toward service for his fatherland and progressive reform.

🌼 Joachim Lelewel: The Formative Years

Among the nine progeny of Karol and Ewa Lelewel, Joachim was the eldest, born on 22 March 1786 in the family home on Długa Street in Warsaw. Until the age of ten, Joachim lived with his parents and family in the city of Warsaw. As a result of the political crises of 1794–95, i.e., the failure of Kościuszko's uprising and the third partition of Poland, the Karol Lelewel family experienced serious difficulties. Karol Lelewel lost his title and position in the National Education Commission. He also suffered serious economic reverses, with his property located in territory annexed by Austria and his real estate in Warsaw placed under Prussian jurisdiction. His savings in banks, which were not totally lost in the course of these rapid political changes, declined in value. This placed a considerable strain on his ability to maintain his Warsaw household which consisted of his wife with child, several young children, a tutor, and his wife's mother.[14] Given this difficult situation, Karol Lelewel decided to move from Warsaw to the countryside. In the latter part of 1796, after the birth of his youngest son Jan Pawel (April 26, 1796), he moved his entire family to Wola Cygowska, the country estate which he had purchased almost eight years earlier.[15]

In the years from 1796 to 1801, Joachim lived in the country, first with his parents in Wola Cygowska, then with his paternal aunt in Wola Okrzejska. Karol Lelewel's sister, Teresa Cieciszowska, helped to raise and to educate her brother's children. Her eldest nephew, Joachim, especially benefitted from the opportunities she provided. In Wola Cygowska, the Piarist priests Antoni Dąbrowski and Aleksander Karol Konkowski tutored the Lelewel children, but inadequate living quarters and other factors limited the opportunities for learning, causing the aunt to take the fourteen year old Joachim to Wola Okrzejska to be educated with her sons Jan and Adam. Joachim spent two years at his aunt's estate where he was tutored by the Reverend Leopold Moroz, the pastor in Okrzeja.[16]

During his stay in Wola Okrzejska, Joachim found chronicles and historical works readily accessible and frequently listened to discussions of literary and political issues. He recorded his early experiences in the numerous letters he wrote to his family in Wola Cygowska. His brief and affectionate letters to his younger brother Prot were especially enlightening. In these, he expressed an avid interest in history. He reported his progress in writing a history of Poland and brief histories of Spain and France, and he promised to forward copies to his brother as he completed these projects. He also demonstrated an interest in art.[17]

In Okrzeja he displayed artistic talents which he developed further at the Piarist boarding school in Warsaw and at the University of Wilno where, in addition to other pursuits, he studied the history of engraving. Joachim's artistic talents and his studies of the art of engraving benefitted the scholar throughout his career, for Lelewel personally illustrated his works of history, frequently including detailed maps which he drew skillfully.

At the age of fifteen, Joachim entered the *Collegium Nobilium Scholarum Piarum,* a respectable boarding school in Warsaw, for the young Polish gentry. The school was organized by the Piarist educator and reformer Stanisław Konarski in 1740.[18] It boasted of a progressive curriculum and a faculty dedicated to working closely with the National Education Commission (established in 1773) for the improvement of the national educational system in Poland.

Joachim's teachers at the Piarist school included the rector, Reverend Kajetan Kamieński, and the Reverends Stefan Saśicki, Gwalbert Bystrzycki, and Onufry Kopczyński (1735–1817) — authors of Polish school textbooks.[19] The grammarian Father Onufry Kopczyński is of special interest because of his knowledge of library science — one of the disciplines Joachim Lelewel helped to develop in his homeland.

The Reverend Kopczyński acquired a wide reputation among educators as a result of organizing and cataloguing library materials in the *Collegium Nobilium,* using Bacon's methods of classification. Named Assistant Bibliographer (*podbibliotekarz*) of the Załuski library in 1783 by the National Education Commission, Kopczyński assisted the Reverend Jerzy Kozmiński in reorganizing the future National Library (*Biblioteka Narodowa*) of Poland. The major tasks which Kopczyński faced included the repair of the buildings in which the library was housed and the conservation and preservation of the materials in the library. He frequently worked long hours and paid aides with personal funds because of lack of governmental financial resources.[20]

The young Joachim Lelewel studied at the Piarist boarding school for three years. Here he found just what he needed: little structured instruction and much encouragement and guidance. He was slowly introduced to the great world around him, whose past excited him from the outset. The Piarists had an extensive library, and they encouraged their students to study independently. Each student had his own carrel (*privato studio*) in the main salon in which he could pursue his studies. In addition to encouraging independent study, the Piarists stressed participation in intellectual and cultural activities outside the boarding school. The development of the idea of service to the fatherland and the nation represented, for the Piarists, significant educational objectives, and they pursued these in a progressive manner.[21]

Guided and encouraged by his Piarist tutors, Joachim rapidly developed his interests in geography and history, and reading intensively, he compiled copious notes. At the Rector's suggestion, the young student prepared a Polish translation of the eighteenth century English historian John Blair's chronological tables and a chronology of the history of Poland based on the eminent eighteenth century Polish historian Adam Naruszewicz's work. Although these assignments were merely exercises to determine Lelewel's capabilities, they intensified his interest in history and his determination to become a writer.[22]

Student participation in intellectual and cultural activities outside the boarding school included attending the public sessions of the newly established *Towarzystwo Przyjaciół Nauk*. The Warsaw *Towarzystwo Przyjaciół Nauk* began its activities when Joachim was a student at the Piarist boarding school. Organized in 1800 at the initiative of Stanisław Sołtyk, a group of intellectuals which included aristocrats, high ranking clergy, ex-clergy, representatives of the military, and others, gathered in Sołtyk's salon once or twice each month to discuss cultural and scientific topics. Adhering to the progressive traditions of the Enlightenment, i.e., to the ideals of rationalism and scholarly criticism, with overtones of patriotism, the *Towarzystwo* periodically announced competitions and encouraged long range projects in numerous fields.[23] These projects included Linde's *Słownik języka polskiego* (*A Dictionary of the Polish Language*) and completion of Naruszewicz's *Historia Polski* (*History of Poland*).

In addition to the private gatherings, members of this learned society organized public sessions. The early public meetings were held in the salon of the Piarist school in Miodowa Street. These sessions were ceremonious occasions in which Poland's cultural and scientific contributions to civilization and the significance of a knowledge of the Polish language and Polish history for the administration of the state (which ceased to exist in 1795) were stressed.[24] Many residents of Warsaw attended the public sessions, including the students of the Piarist boarding school, and among the latter, Joachim Lelewel. Undoubtedly, in the environment created by the *Towarzystwo Przyjaciół Nauk*, an aura of national consciousness developed and impressed the young student.

At the age of eighteen, Joachim went from the Piarist school in Warsaw to the newly reorganized University of Wilno, where his father, as Treasurer of the National Education Commission, knew many of the professors. In his autobiography and letters, Lelewel mentioned several, including Tomasz Hussarzewski and Józef Mickiewicz.[25]

The influence of his family background and of the environment created by the Piarists and the *Towarzystwo Przyjaciół Nauk* manifested themselves in Joachim's choice of a university. In his autobiography, Lelewel recalled a conversation with his father where Karol Lelewel asked the young aspiring scholar about his plans for the future. He told his son that he could attend the German university in Königsberg or the newly reorganized university which was opening in Wilno as a result of the educational reforms of Tsar Alexander I. Joachim responded: "I did not want to go to the German university. I was repulsed by the idea that I would involuntarily become Germanized."[26] He also chose the teaching profession — the only way in which one could serve the fatherland and the nation in the uncertainties of the Napoleonic era. The chief motive which influenced his decision was that in learning to be a teacher he would find an environment conducive to becoming an author — a goal he had set for himself as a child of ten.[27] With the Bishop Cieciszowski as his patron, Joachim Lelewel was accepted by the university authorities in Wilno as a candidate preparing for a teaching position.

The beginning of his university studies marked the inauguration of a new and important period in his life. His student years at Wilno represented a time in which the world of scholarship gave form to his interests and direction to his researches. It was also a time in which his national consciousness first crystallized.

The University of Wilno was established in 1803 by order of Tsar Alexander I. A school of higher education had existed in Wilno since Stefan Batory encouraged the Society of Jesus to establish an academy there in the late sixteenth century (1579). In 1780 the Jesuit Academy had been replaced by the Principal School of the Grand Duchy of Lithuania (*Szkoła Główna Wielkiego Księstwa Litew-*

skiego). In 1797 the school was reorganized as the Principal School of Wilno-Lithuania (*Szkoła Główna Wileńska-Litewska*). In 1803, the school was renamed the University of Wilno and reorganized on the German model with four faculties (theology, philosophy, law, and medicine). Prince Adam Jerzy Czartoryski, an eminent Polish magnate, was appointed curator by the tsar.

The new university quickly attracted reputable foreign scholars, including the physician Frank, the naturalist Bojanus, the philologist G. E. Groddek. In addition, Czartoryski invited distinguished Polish scholars to Wilno. Among these latter were the Śniadecki brothers and Euzebiusz Słowacki. These men and others like them helped to make Wilno the intellectual center of Polish culture which nurtured Adam Mickiewicz, Juliusz Słowacki, and Joachim Lelewel.

When the young Lelewel began his studies in 1804, the University of Wilno, in the initial stages of its development, lacked prestige. He remembered years later that "the newly organized university had something incomplete and inadequate about it."[28] But in less than thirty brief years (1803–1831), the University of Wilno surpassed the university in Kraków, Poland's oldest seat of learning, and the university in Warsaw, created in 1816 as the Congress Kingdom's center of learning and national culture.[29] Joachim Lelewel played a leading role in the development of the University of Wilno as a student and when he returned there as its first professor of history.

As a candidate for teacher, Joachim studied the natural sciences and mathematics; Latin, Greek, and other languages; drawing and engraving. History was not taught as a separate discipline when Joachim Lelewel was a student at Wilno. The theologian Tomasz Hussarzewski (1732–1807) directed Lelewel in his studies of history. Professor Ernest Groddek, a distinguished philologist, introduced the young student to ancient history and classical Greek literature and stimulated his interests in geography, numismatics, and the critical analysis of texts. At the university in Wilno, Lelewel enthusiastically resumed that independent course of studies which he so diligently pursued at the Piarist boarding school in Warsaw.[30]

The young Lelewel read in philosophy and in the history of England and France. He became familiar with the Greek, German, and French languages, and he collected historical source materials. He wrote papers on the origins of nations. In these papers he frequently exhibited boldness and creativity and expressed a healthy irreverence for established authorities.

Under the guidance of Hussarzewski, he began to work on the

theoretical and methodological problems of history from which eventually emerged the *Historyka* (*The Art of History*) — the basic and only study of its kind in Poland at the time.[31] Even as a student, Lelewel emphasized the need for an accurate art and science of history and criticized those who did not comply with these criteria.[32]

He boldly challenged the German scholar August Ludwig von Schlözer and Adam Naruszewicz, the most eminent historian in Poland prior to Lelewel, in his student essays. In part one of his *Rzut oka na dawność litewskich narodów i związki ich z Herulami* (*A Glance at the Antiquity of the Lithuanian Nations and Their Relations with the Heruli*), Lelewel invalidated Schlözer's theory of the Germanic origins of the Lithuanians. In the second part of his essay, Lelewel contradicted the well known Polish scholar's theory of the Germanic origins of the Lithuanians. Lelewel argued that because their primary settlements were between the Volga and the Don Rivers and not along the Niemen, they were not Germanic. The critical observations by a young and inexperienced writer of the work of a widely recognized and respected scholar — Naruszewicz — aroused the indignation of Jan Śniadecki, the Rector of the University of Wilno. He criticized the young student for his "indecent and affected daring."[33]

In addition to his *Historyka* and *Rzut oka,* Joachim Lelewel published anonymously his first book, *Edda czyli księga religii dawnych Skandynawii mięszkańców* (*Edda: Or the Book of Religion of the Ancient Inhabitants of Scandinavia*). First presented as a paper during a meeting of a student society, *Edda* represented Lelewel's revision of a study by a Swiss historian Paul Mallet to which he added an introduction. In his introduction, Lelewel fallaciously deduced that the Scandinavians originated from the Scythians.[34]

As a university student, Joachim Lelewel actively participated in the *Towarzystwo Doskonalącej się Młodzi w Naukach i Umiejętnościach* (The Society for the Improvement of Youth in Learning and Science). Established at the end of 1805, this student club was reorganized two years later as the Society of Philomaths (*Towarzystwo Filomatów*).[35] This secret society of university students, also known as the Society of the Lovers of Learning, was similar to a group in Russia in the 1820s, the Lovers of Wisdom. The Society of Philomaths also shared common characteristics with the German League of Virtue (the *Tugenbund*). Also known as the Moral and Scientific Union, this patriotic organization of German youth formed in Königsberg one year after Prussia's defeat by Napoleon. It proposed to uplift the German nation and to protect the fatherland.

Student groups such as these shared a belief in the necessity of developing national feelings and generally discussed literature, art, and philosophy with the purpose of elevating their members, their colleagues, and all of society. Their objective was to stimulate national consciousness, and they proposed to achieve this goal by taking an active interest in their roots and their cultural traditions. Their interest was a cultural nationalism which the Poles called *narodowość*. It differed significantly from the state and power oriented integral nationalism (*nacjonalizm*) of the twentieth century. In spite of their seemingly innocent objective, these student organizations allegedly threatened established authorities and protectors of the Vienna state system established in 1815. As a result, most of these societies were forced to disband in the 1820s. Members of the University of Wilno's Society of Philomaths were arrested and exiled by the tsarist government in 1823-1824.

Lelewel studied at the University of Wilno until mid-1808. Taking examinations in several areas, e.g., languages, history, and geography, he left without receiving the title of Magister from the University. Nevertheless he had established a reputation as a promising scholar. Artur Śliwiński, one of Lelewel's biographers, observed that the background Lelewel gained at Wilno sustained him throughout his life as a scholar dedicated to the service of his fatherland and nation.[36]

Upon completion of the courses required for the status of teacher, Lelewel accepted a position to teach history and ancient geography at the Lyceum in Krzemieniec in Podolia on the Ukrainian border. When he arrived there late in 1809, he found someone else teaching the history course, and only four students enrolled in his course in ancient geography.[37]

Disappointed, he lingered in Krzemieniec for a short time. During his brief stay, Lelewel hoped to take advantage of the opportunity to utilize Tadeusz Czacki's library in nearby Poryck. The library of the Rector of the Lyceum in Krzemieniec housed a rich collection of medieval manuscripts and coins. However, Lelewel found it inaccessible because the building in which the collections were housed was being renovated.[38] The young Lelewel nevertheless availed himself of the opportunity to discuss with Czacki the latter's study of Lithuanian and Polish law. Czacki theorized that Polish and Lithuanian law originated with the Norman sources. More than a decade later, in reviews written in 1825 and 1826, Lelewel criticized Czacki's interpretation, arguing that Polish law originated with the Slav.[39] In most of his researches, Lelewel sought to discredit Germanic and other foreign influences on the development of Slav, and most especially Polish, civilization.

At the time of his stay in Krzemieniec, Lelewel also visited his maternal uncle, the Bishop of Łuck, and gained access to the latter's rich library which included Gallus' *Chronicles*. Thus, deprived of the opportunity to teach, he became familiar with new source materials and studied intensively old Polish Chronicles and other documents and manuscripts at his disposal.

These endeavors resulted in publications which included the pamphlets *Wzmianka o najdawniejszych dziejopismach polskich* and *Uwagi nad rozprawą Bohusza o Litwie* (*A Mention of the Oldest Polish Chronicles* and *Remarks on Bohusz's Discourse on Lithuania*). In the introduction to *Wzmianka*, Lelewel again sharply criticized Schlözer. In the second pamphlet, he expressed his opinions on Xavier Bohusz's discourse on the origins of the Lithuanian nation and language. He attacked, in writing, the Reverend Xavier Bohusz, Prelate of Wilno Cathedral, a distinguished member of the *Towarzystwo Przyjaciół Nauk* and an honorary member of the University of Wilno. Bohusz, the accepted authority on Lithuanian affairs at the time, suffered the same fate at the hands of the young scholar as did Naruszewicz and Schlözer — authorities in their fields.[40] Lelewel, in criticizing established authorities, indicated that he submitted to the opinions of no one but based his conclusions on the results of his own researches. Although some of Lelewel's interpretations have been invalidated by later scholars, his critical approach to specific historical problems such as the origins of peoples and laws paved the way for his successors and was a significant factor in stimulating new interpretations and in invalidating older, frequently erroneous positions.

Arriving in Warsaw in June, 1811, Lelewel discovered that the administrative position promised to him in the Grand Duchy was filled by another applicant. His career plans were further disrupted with the outbreak of war and the ultimate collapse of Napoleon and the Grand Duchy. Uninterested in politics, unmoved by the formidable events which loomed on the horizon in the fields of battle and diplomacy, and disappointed in the lack of opportunities in Warsaw, Lelewel returned to the privacy of the family estate — to Wola Cygowska. There he soon wearied of his scholarly endeavors as well.[41]

Despite his weariness, by the spring of 1813, according to his own narrative, he wrote the first draft of *Historia Polski aż do końca panowania Stefana Batorego* (*The History of Poland to the end of the Reign of Stefan Batory*) which was published for the first time a half century later, in 1863 — two years after its author's death.

This first larger work of the twenty-seven year old scholar was sketchy and lacked originality. It was a narrative of events, with special emphasis on domestic political affairs, placed in a framework of general European history and culture. The book ended abruptly with the year 1588. Portions of this work, specifically the sections dealing with the reigns of Bolesław Chrobry and Bolesław Śmiały, were read by Lelewel at the May 2, 1815 session of *Wydział Nauk*, a division of the Warsaw *Towarzystwo Przyjaciół Nauk*.[42]

Although he participated in the sessions of the Warsaw *Towarzystwo Przyjaciół Nauk* which intellectuals such as Stanisław Staszic had transformed into a kind of Polish academy, Lelewel was not elected to full membership in that august body until 1831. Neither were his writings readily accepted for publication. In fact, his father subsidized the publication of his study, *Pisma pomniejsze geograficzne-historyczne* (*Minor Historico-Geographic Writings*) in 1814.[43]

In February, 1815, Lelewel received a letter from Jan Śniadecki, the Rector of the University of Wilno, requesting that Lelewel lecture in history there.[44] A new phase of his life was about to begin. In these his early adult years, the scholarly Lelewel had shown no interest in politics, but his national consciousness began to find concrete expression in some aspects of his scholarship. His diverse intellectual interests demanded most of his time. He laid the foundations for his theory and methodology of history in the *Historyka*. His criticism of known authorities Naruszewicz, Schlözer, and Bohusz indicated that Lelewel planned to pursue an independent course in his researches. He preferred not to rely on established authorities and experts but chose to pursue a systematic, methodological quest for truth, according to criteria he established in his pioneer work, the *Historyka*. In his works, he attempted to discount foreign influences on Slav — and Polish — development. He proposed to find and to emphasize those qualities which were unique to the Slavs but which also contributed to the progressive perfection of humanity.

In this his formative period, he also wrote the first draft of a history of Poland to the end of the reign of Stefan Batory. His national consciousness was vague, cultural. It found expression in his acceptance of the idea of service to the fatherland and nation (*ojczyzna i naród*), the ideals and goals which the Piarists had instilled in him and the ideals and goals of the Philomaths and the *Towarzystwo Przyjaciół Nauk*. His national consciousness also found expression in his interest in writing a national history of his fatherland. When he accepted Śniadecki's invitation in 1815, a new phase in his intellectual evolution began. He devoted the next decade of his life to scholarship.

3   The University Professor and Productive Scholar

Wilno: 1815–1818

Joachim Lelewel began his ten year career as a university professor when he accepted the position of lecturer in general history at the University of Wilno in 1815. At the time, history was not a major subject at the university. In fact, the chair of history had remained vacant for eight years following the death, in 1807, of the theologian and Professor Emeritus Tomasz Hussarzewski who had taught Lelewel.[1] The position remained vacant mainly because Jan Śniadecki, Rector of the University of Wilno (1807–1815), considered history as a discipline of minor importance, useful only for the purposes of moral instruction, and since only an insignificant number of students at Wilno planned careers in law or administration, he concentrated on the more practical development of science facilities at the university.[2] The majority of students attending the University of Wilno prepared for careers in medicine, theology, or teaching in the lower schools of the western provinces of the Russian Empire. The university in Wilno administered all lower schools in the Educational District of Wilno which encompassed all of Lithuania, Byelorussia, and the Ukraine.[3]

The study of history as a distinct and distinguished discipline at the university in Wilno developed during Lelewel's first Wilno period (1815–1818). His basic contribution to the study of history during this brief period was the completion of his work on the fundamental principles of a modern theory and methodology of history.[4] These principles, discussed below, placed the study of history at Wilno — and elsewhere in the Polish lands — on a respectable, scientific basis.

Lelewel expressed his ideas concerning the theory and methodology of history in his *Historyka* (*The Art of History*) and in a short, complementary work, *O łatwym i pożytecznym nauczaniu historii* (*On the Convenient and Useful Lessons of History*).[5] He completed the manuscript of the *Historyka* during the first weeks after his arrival in Wilno in April 1815. An abbreviated version, carefully adapted from his manuscript, was published before the start of the new academic year, but he used the longer, uncensored manuscript as the basis for his lectures in history at the university. The short complementary work was Lelewel's inaugural lecture in 1815 and was published with the *Historyka* that same year.[6]

In the *Historyka*, Lelewel developed the following ideas which clearly paralleled the ideas of German idealists and historicists. In a broad sense, according to Lelewel, history comprised all circumstances of time and space; in a more limited sense, it presented the activities of people (*lud*) in a given time and place.[7] The former referred to universal history, the latter to national history. He developed his concept of national history as a subcategory of his concept of *Etiologika* ("Etiologics"). This aspect of his theory of history will be discussed in greater detail below because of its pertinence to the study of Lelewel's national ideas.

Lelewel divided the study of history into three categories: *Krytyka* ("Criticism"); *Etiologika* ("Etiologics"); and *Historiografia* ("Historiography"). For the historian, "Criticism" discovered what happened. "Etiologics" determined why events occurred and dealt with cause and effect relationships. "Historiography" concerned the manner of telling the tale. A critical approach to history, Lelewel believed, was necessary in examining sources and in seeking truth. All the endeavors of the scholarly historian obviously rested on gathering and becoming familiar with sources; in these, the historian sought truth.[8]

Proceeding to discuss what he meant by source materials, Lelewel divided them into three categories: traditions, e.g., narratives of past events and epic poetry; nonverbal records, e.g., buildings, medals, monuments; and finally, written records, i.e., documents, manuscripts, and other materials. He continued, stating that the first task of the scholar must be to gather all the sources necessary for his endeavors, to authenticate them, and to select from those authenticated the ones most necessary for the recognition of truth. Historical truth, according to Lelewel, must always be sought pragmatically and can be achieved only through the disciplined use of reason. Ability to interpret source materials presupposed a knowledge of man and the processes of history. He discussed the relative value derived from various sources and then indicated that the interpretation of these sources depended upon the skill and disposition of the historian. He concluded by stating that although one "critic," i.e., historian, labored to develop a specific interpretation or point of view, it was possible for another one to propose a different but equally valid interpretation.[9]

In the *Historyka,* Lelewel expressed that traditions could be utilized as source materials by the historian. His discrete approach to the uses of "traditional sources" was obvious in some of his comments on folk tales and fables concerning the origins of the Polish nation and some Polish cities. In his introduction to his children's history of Poland, Lelewel narrated several fables and advised his readers that they were interesting but should not be considered historical truth.[10]

The second aspect of the three categories of Lelewel's *Historyka* was "Etiologics" which he defined as the means by which one determined the causes and effects of historical events. In this category he discussed the circumstances of time, place, events, historical man, social relations and the interrelationship of these factors. He emphasized the search for those relationships between causes and effects which led to the progressive perfection of man.[11]

In discussing man and his relationships to society, Lelewel stressed that *wolność* (freedom) and *pomyślność* (well-being or welfare) encouraged man to strive for perfection, for the full development of his genius. Conversely, oppression and adversity engraved on man "a stamp of gloominess and debasement" and hindered the full development of man's genius.[12]

According to Lelewel, "Etiologics" must take into consideration anthropology, statism (statistics), and politics. Anthropology included "ethnology, the physical aspects of man, the nature of language, religion . . . and the national character which enabled one to recognize the strength and disposition of a particular nation. . . ."[13] Discussing statism (statistics), Lelewel claimed that the historian must determine the components of a nation's economic potential and what emphasis was placed on each component, e.g., on agriculture, commerce, industry, trade, and handicrafts. The internal order of a country must also be considered: in fulfilling assurances of peace and justice; in meting out justice to everyone; in the handling of finances. It was also necessary for the historian to consider in what ways general funds were gathered and for what ends they were used and to assess whether funds were used reasonably for the maintenance of internal stability and for purposes of defense from external threats.[14]

Referring to politics, Lelewel stated: "National circumstances are observed in a nation's external and internal affairs."[15] He then focused his discussion on the internal affairs of a nation, concentrating on the significance of constitutions: "In considering constitutions, two observations must be made: first, the relations between the nation and government [which he equated with authority]; secondly, relations of the various social strata within a given community. . . ."[16]

In his analysis in 1830 of three Polish constitutions, Lelewel considered such relationships, and the conclusions he reached were based not on simple cause and effect relationships but were arrived at by application of the criteria he established in the *Historyka*.[17]

Continuing his commentary on politics, Lelewel proceeded to discuss his theory of the general effects of relations among nations. The primary goal of a nation, according to Lelewel, was to secure its safety and independence. A nation's security was assured best when and where *wolność* (freedom) existed. Again he emphasized the significant relationship between the existence of freedom and the progressive perfection of mankind or humanity. Freedom enhanced the development of the various nations and the internal evolution of each.[18]

In elaborating on his third category, "Historiography," Lelewel proposed that the historian should present "sincere truth, without exaggeration and sarcasm, in a serious manner."[19] The task of the historian was difficult, if only because of the wealth of materials which he must command. The historian, dedicating himself to his subject, must aim to broaden the outlook for others — to create a horizon through which a synthesis can be found.[20]

Lelewel introduced his theory and method of history to the one hundred students who attended his inaugural lecture on Easter Sunday, 1815. The inaugural lecture, first published in 1815 in *Tygodnik Wileński* (*The Wilno Weekly*), complemented those ideas which he expressed in the *Historyka* and set the tone for his future lectures at the University of Wilno. Ultimately, Lelewel's inaugural lecture was published as part of the *Historyka*.[21]

Defining history as that which considers what happens to people in a given time and place, he warned his students that history was more than a narrative of facts.

> It also encompasses the study of the general and particular perfection of the human kind (*rodzaj ludzki*), its variations in customs, religions, talents, and inclinations. History also considers

to what extent it [humankind] knows how to benefit from its given location and local resources. Considering the variety of life's opportunities, history also determines how to render pleasant its existence [i.e., the existence of the humankind] and how to achieve its welfare by diligence and labor; and how societies, nations, and states rise, expand, and decline, influencing greatly the destiny of mankind.[22]

He informed his students that history included social and cultural, as well as political, aspects; that the historian's purpose was to recognize in general history the existence of a total, all encompassing process leading to the ultimate perfection of man; in studying history, it was necessary to know the auxiliary sciences and to explore various source materials. In accenting the intellectual meaning of history, he did not neglect its more pragmatic objectives — the encouragement of responsible political activity and the elevation of social consciousness.

A knowledge of history instills in the individual a sense of service, the fulfillment of unimpeachable obligations. History provides beneficial advice for state and national governments; in administering governments for common advantage, assuring security and internal peace and order for the general welfare. It revives a spirit of industry and progressive thought. . . . History also inspires society to great deeds. . . . Awakens a social consciousness.[23]

A brief commentary by Lelewel on the moral and social uses of history completed the important foundations and guidelines for the modern study of history at the University of Wilno. Lelewel discussed the purposes of history and the obligations of the historian in considerable detail. A knowledge of history, he explained, was basic for the education of the individual and for the benefit of mankind.

History is a beloved and seldom adequately studied storehouse of memories of past times; in it, each individual reads of his ancestors, his forefathers, and his nation's accomplishments; each area, each country records the transformations to which it succumbed, recalls the times in which its inhabitants enjoyed good fortune and excelled, and leaves a storehouse of memories for future generations.[24]

The study of history must be approached critically and morally, warned Lelewel, for the historian's goal was the truthful presentation of relations among peoples in general, and more specifically, the relations of nations in a given time and place. In addition, the responsibilities of an historian were such that he must have a thorough knowledge of man, languages, and auxiliary disciplines such as diplomacy and numismatics. The historian must be aware of the nature of human societies, of political economies, of statism (statistics), of nations and peoples, and although these may be impossible criteria, the historian was obligated to strive to attain them, if he intended to present historical truth based on reasoned observations and an understanding of humanity.[25]

In his closing words, Lelewel expressed his ideas about the useful lessons of history:

> . . . In truth, each man who desires to respond to his kindred (*rodu*) worthily, to expend his life for his own and society's benefit, who is interested in the study of nature and man should look to history as a guide; avidly apply himself to the truth history embodies; and participate in historical studies, enthusiastically and eagerly acquiring a basic knowledge of history.[26]

In addition to laying the foundations for the modern study of history at Wilno, Lelewel wrote the first textbook on ancient history in the Polish language for the university students there. He also participated in the creation of a new periodical, *Tygodnik Wileński* (*The Wilno Weekly*), and was its first editor.[27] The articles he wrote for this periodical in 1816 and 1817 were basic contributions to Polish literary criticism and historical literature.[28]

Lelewel also contributed articles to *Pamiętnik Warszawski* (*The Warsaw Journal*), a liberal periodical affiliated with Polish Freemasonry. This periodical was published between 1815 and 1823 in Warsaw, in the Congress Kingdom.[29]

During the first Wilno period, Lelewel introduced the study of history as a separate discipline. He actively engaged in a variety of scholarly pursuits and made numerous contributions to knowledge. Among the contributions which date from this period, the *Historyka* was the most significant. He not only introduced new concepts and new approaches to the study of history to his students, but he also provided the criteria for his own future studies of Poland's history.

❀ Warsaw: 1818–1821

The young scholar resigned his position at the university in the spring of 1818, effective at the end of that academic year. But he remained in Wilno throughout that summer awaiting the publication of his textbook, *Dzieje starożytne* (*Ancient History*).[30] On September 22, 1818, he arrived in Warsaw, having accepted a position as professor of bibliography at the newly created University of Warsaw and curator of the library located at the University and housed in Kazimierowski Palace.[31] The Government Commission (created on 31 January 1818) responsible for Joachim Lelewel's appointment recommended that the library be separated from the University of Warsaw effective 24 March 1818 and be developed as a centralized national public library which would serve the entire Congress Kingdom.[32] Lelewel, in the course of his three year association with the University of Warsaw, played a significant role in the development of the national library in the Congress Kingdom.

As curator of the newly organized national library, he faced the formidable task of taking inventory of and cataloguing all the manuscripts, books, and volumes deposited there.[33] These included various materials from the Warsaw Lyceum, the Library of the Appellate Court in Warsaw, the ancient and medieval manuscript collections acquired by Adam Czartoryski, and the library of the Archbishop of Gniezno which was acquired after Krasicki's death. With the help of a colleague, Pawel Zaroski, and the Director of the Library, Bogumił S. Linde, Lelewel completed this task within a year.[34]

In 1819, the number of monasteries and abbies in the Congress Kingdom was reduced, and their assets, i.e., funds, libraries, and other possessions, were placed at the disposal of the Government Commission and the Minister of Education.[45] The government agencies, in turn, made the libraries available to schools and seminaries in the Congress Kingdom, and to the public library in Warsaw. As a result, the new national library acquired an additional 50,000 volumes. Lelewel's responsibilities included taking inventory of these new acquisitions and cataloguing the volumes as they were delivered to the library.[35] In addition to these acquisitions from Cistercian and Benedictine abbeys and Pauline monasteries, numerous other books were purchased annually in Regensburg, Reissach, Vienna, and Leipzig for the national library. Lelewel managed also to catalogue these. Only the theological collection remained to be catalogued by his successor, Adam Tomasz Chłędowski, but even here Lelewel left detailed instructions for the latter. When Lelewel resigned his position at the University of Warsaw three years after his arrival (June, 1821), the library housed approximately 100,000 volumes, inventoried and catalogued by him. The library's director, Linde, opened a museum as part of the national library, having acquired the art collection of Stanisław August from the Poniatowski family.[36]

Lelewel played an important role in the organization and development of the national library in Warsaw. He also wrote the first of his seminal two volume study of the libraries and printing in Poland. He based his study on the materials available to him in the library in Warsaw.[37]

Joachim Lelewel's *Bibliograficznych ksiąg dwoje* (*Two Bibliographic Books*), published in 1823 and 1826, was the most comprehensive work on the history of libraries and library science in Poland at the time. A landmark in the development of Polish national culture, the two volumes by Lelewel surpassed the formidable works of Jerzy Samuel Bandtkie and Felix Bentkowski and placed modern library science in Poland on a firm foundation.[38] It is not the purpose of the present author to evaluate this work, only to present a brief description of it.[39]

In the first of his two extremely detailed volumes, the author commented on the art of printing in the fifteenth century and described the codexes and bulls printed at that time. He presented a detailed historical sketch of printers and printing in Poland from the earliest native printers, e.g., Świętopołk Fiol who printed Slavic works in the cyrillic alphabet and Jan Haller who was primarily a merchant and winemaker but also a bookseller in Kraków, to the numerous printers of the late eighteenth century Polish renaissance. Among the latter, he included Gröll, Dufue, Tyzenhaus, and others who printed works in Polish, Latin, Greek, and Hebrew. Lelewel devoted the last one-third of his first volume to a comparative analysis of the various texts of the Polish statutes of the fifteenth century. These statutes included the Charter of Jan Albert, the Piotrkowski Charter of Casimir Jagiello, and the Wiślicki Charter.[40]

In his second volume, published in 1826, Lelewel discussed a variety of subjects related to printing and library science. Most important were his historical descriptions of the public and private libraries in Poland, Lithuania, Volhynia, and Galicia from their origins to the second decade of the nineteenth century. The public libraries he included in his volume were the libraries in Krzemieniec,

Wilno, Kraków, and Warsaw. Among the numerous private libraries he described, he included the famous Czartoryski library at Puławy and the Zamojski library in Zamość.[41]

He also devoted a large portion of his second volume to the problems of library techniques and methodology, basing his observations on his personal experiences at the library in Warsaw.[42] Both volumes played an important role not only in the evolution of modern library techniques and methodology in Poland but also contributed to the development of Polish culture in the early nineteenth century.

Although he spent most of his time in the library organizing the various collections and compiling materials for his *Bibliograficznych ksiąg dwoje,* Lelewel also found time to publish several short papers on history. Among these was his review of Izabela Czartoryska's *Pielgrzym w Dobromilu* (*Pilgrim in Dobromil*), a popular pedagogical work intended for the peasant class. In his brief commentary on Czartoryska's book, first published in 1819 in the liberal periodical *Pamiętnik Warszawski,* Lelewel discussed the gradual subjugation of the peasants in the Polish lands and the need to awaken their consciousness by improving their condition, and especially their education.[43] He praised Czartoryska for her efforts on behalf of the peasants and complimented her *Pielgrzym w Dobromilu* as the first text for peasants "for their daily use so that they become familiar with national concerns."[44] Lelewel showed an interest in peasant conditions early in his life, notable in his correspondence with his parents, but it was not until the spring of 1831 in the course of the imminent failure of the war against tsarist Russia that he became seriously interested in the peasant class as potentially decisive for the Polish political cause. In exile, he called for action by the traditional "nation," i.e., the active and politically conscious szlachta class, united with the traditionally "passive" peasant class and other social classes. Only such a unified effort could bring about the recreation of an independent Polish state.

Although he found time to write short reviews for the public, Lelewel's responsibilities as Curator of the Public Library prevented him from lecturing at the University. Only during his third year in Warsaw did he prepare lectures in the general history of the sixteenth and early seventeenth centuries and also planned several lectures on bibliography. These lectures attracted scant attention. Attendance was not required. Lelewel later recounted that very few students heard his lectures, and eventually only three attended. However, his popularity as a lecturer improved near the end of the academic year when the lecture topic was the history of Spain and Poland in the sixteenth, seventeenth, and eighteenth centuries.[45]

Concentrating on these three centuries, Lelewel prepared notes on the comparative history of Poland and Spain — a topic of current interest in the Congress Kingdom because of political and diplomatic developments in Europe which threatened the Vienna settlement of 1815. Not active in the politics of the Congress Kingdom at this time, the young scholar-lecturer took this opportunity to analyze why Spain and Poland, both great political powers in the sixteenth, seventeenth, and eighteenth centuries, declined. In his lectures, later published as *Historyczna paralela Hiszpanii z Polską w XVI, XVII, XVIII wieku* (*A Historical Parallel of Spain and Poland in the Sixteenth, Seventeenth, and Eighteenth Centuries*), Lelewel expressed succinctly his concepts of nationality (*narodowość*) for the first time to an academic audience in the capital of the Congress Kingdom. Comparing the histories of Spain and Poland, he proposed the thesis that the same effects, i.e., decline, can be created by diametrically opposed causes, and given the creation of a proper environment, revolt was inevitable, even justifiable. He compared the situation then current in Spain, i.e., the Spanish revolt against their oppressors, with Poland's national revolt against autocratic Russia in 1794 led by Kościuszko.

The reasons for the decline of Spain and Poland differed, according to Lelewel. However, in both cases, internal factors, aggravated by external forces created an environment for the overthrow of the existing order, for revolution — for Poland in 1794 and Spain in 1820. The situation in Spain did not differ greatly from Congress Poland's in 1820. After the Vienna settlement, the situation in the Congress Kingdom had stabilized. Now, in 1820, a foreigner, a Romanov, sat on a truncated Poland's throne. Alexander's promises to extend the Constitution of the Congress Kingdom to Russia's western provinces, former Polish lands, remained unfulfilled. In his final address to the third Polish Diet (Fall, 1820), Alexander had even hinted at the withdrawal of the promises he had made earlier.[46] In addition, Alexander named his brother, the Grand Duke Constantine, as viceroy *de facto* of the Congress Kingdom before his departure from Warsaw.[47]

Alexander's actions in Warsaw in 1820 aggravated the growing discord among the Poles regarding the administration of the Congress Kingdom. In July, 1819, censorship of the press had been imposed in the Kingdom in violation of constitutional guarantees.[48] Progressive and liberal dailies and periodicals, e.g., *Gazeta codzienna i obca* (*The Daily Home and Foreign Gazette*) and the *Orzeł Biały* (*The White Eagle*), were curtailed by the government. In November, 1819, prefects (monitors) were introduced into the Warsaw Lyceum to supervise the students more closely. By 1820, such repressive policies also affected Lelewel.[49] The censors soon focused their attention on Lelewel's lectures. Displeased with the political implications which inhered in the lectures on the comparative history of Spain and Poland delivered by Lelewel in 1820, they censored the manuscript he had prepared for publication. Lelewel's work was not published until the relaxation of censorship by the revolutionary National Government in 1831 — eleven years later.[50]

The publication of *Historyczna paralela* during the national insurrection provided a justification for the revolt — a justification based on historical precedents, enunciated and clarified by a respected scholar and member of the revolutionary National Government.

Finding that his responsibilities and preoccupations at the national library hindered his interests in research and scholarship, Lelewel declined the offer of a professorship at the University of Warsaw (8 June 1821).[51] Instead, he accepted the Chair of General History at the University of Wilno. In the fall of 1821, he left the capital of the Congress Kingdom to return to Wilno. "Because of Lithuania's good will," he wrote, "I left my somewhat inconvenient position in the land of my birth."[52]

❀ Wilno: 1821–1824

Lelewel returned to Wilno, one of the largest towns in the western provinces of the Russian Empire. This town, with its predominantly provincial characteristics, nevertheless took pride in its professional intelligentsia (largely university faculty), several printing houses and bookstores, the professional societies, and the variety of periodicals which were published there. The latter included *Tygodnik Wileński* (*The Wilno Weekly*) which Lelewel helped establish in 1815, *Dziennik Wileński* (*The Wilno Daily*), *Gazeta Literacka* (*The Literary Gazette*), and *Kalendarzyk Polityczny* (*The Political Calendar*).[54] Wilno's cultural and intellectual development was also enhanced by the progressive growth of the university in the decade of the twenties.

Under the protective tutelage of its curator, Prince Adam Jerzy Czartoryski, a personal friend and adviser to Tsar Alexander I, the University of Wilno rapidly developed as the most important center of learning in all the lands of traditional Poland. The university's competent native and foreign faculty included Jan Śniadecki (1756–1830), a former Rector of the University of Wilno (1807–1815). Śniadecki represented the Enlightenment traditions of Europe's age of reason. In the early eighteen twenties, he served as professor of mathematics and taught rational philosophy. Writing occasionally on literary subjects, he defended classical rules in literature. Because of men such as Śniadecki, the Enlightenment influence lingered longer in Poland and Imperial Russia than in western Europe. Its influence was especially great in Wilno in the years 1815–1825.

However, the appointment of Józef Gołuchowski (1797–1858) as Professor of Philosophy and Joachim Lelewel as Professor of History in 1821 marked the eclipse of Enlightenment influence at Wilno. Gołuchowski, a student of the German philosopher Friedrich von Schelling of Erlangen, introduced that German philosopher's idealist philosophy to Wilno, despite Śniadecki's persistent opposition.[55] In Lelewel's works of this period, one finds a blend of rational Enlightenment thought and of the new ideas of Romanticism.

Upon his arrival, Lelewel found that the intellectual climate at Wilno was still influenced primarily by the rational and classical traditions of the Enlightenment, but he also discerned newer social and intellectual trends, with national overtones. He discovered this new intellectual and social ferment among those students at the University of Wilno who organized and participated in the Society of Philarets (Lovers of Virtue) in the years 1820 to 1824. Non-students such as Adam Mickiewicz also participated in this society for the moral up-lifting of the Polish nation and the continued enhancement of Polish-ness (*polskość*).[56] During his second Wilno period, Lelewel influenced significantly the outlook and ideology of this group.[57]

The Society of Philarets was the latest in a series of student associations at the University of Wilno. Its predecessors included the *Zwią-zek Przyjaciół* (The Association of Friends), organized in 1819, and the *Promieniści* (The Radiants), organized in 1820.[58] Rimskii-Korsakov, the military governor of Wilno, and Szymon Malewski, successor to Śniadecki as rector of the university (1816–1822), per-mitted such groups to function. The statutes of the *Promieniści*, for example, were published, and the university administrators looked on this organization as a positive means by which to engage students in constructive activities. The favorable status enjoyed by the *Pro-mieniści* sharply contrasted with the status of its counterparts in the student movement in the Germanies, especially as a result of the "Sand situation."[59]

In 1819, Karl Sand, a mentally unbalanced theological student from Jena who was a *Burschenschaft* member, assassinated the journalist August von Kotzebue, a known political reactionary formerly in the tsar's service. Sand was condemned to death, and Metternich, supported by King Frederick William of Prussia, introduced repressive measures against the *Burschenschaften*. Acting in concert with the nine most important German states, Metternich drew up the celebrated Carlsbad Decrees which the Diet of the German Confederation promptly ratified. These decrees dissolved the *Burschenschaften* and created an elaborate system for controlling the German universities and for rooting out subversive individuals there. Undaunted, the nationalist student societies reappeared in the latter part of the 1820s and met clandestinely to avoid the secret police.[60]

In Wilno, the Society of Philarets functioned without restrictions in the early 1820s and continued in the traditions of its predecessors. Both the Philarets and their predecessors encouraged the moral, intellectual, and physical development of Polish youth, especially the gentry, so that they might utilize to the fullest extent their talents on behalf of the fatherland in a nonpolitical manner.[61] The leaders of these Wilno organizations made extensive plans for serving their nation in the cultural and social areas. In sharp contrast, their counterparts in the Congress Kingdom, i.e., the Warsaw youth, notably the young military cadets and officers, organized for political purposes.[62]

The Society of Philarets at Wilno consisted of approximately two hundred members in the years 1821–1823.[63] Like its precursors, it was organized and guided by the secret and elite literary and scholarly association called the Society of Philomaths, i.e., Lovers of Learning, (*Miłośniki Nauki*). This elitist group consisted of twenty members and was the first significant organization of intellectuals at Wilno.[64]

Named after the French eighteenth century learned *Société Philomatique de Paris,* the secret society of Philomaths was established on October 1, 1817, by students Józef Jeżowski, Tomasz Zan, Adam Mickiewicz, Onufry Pietraszkiewicz, Brunon Suchecki, and Erazm Poluszyński. Suchecki and Poluszyński left the organization, and Franciszek Malewski and Jan Czeczot, two prominent leaders, joined later.[65] Józef Jeżowski was the guiding spirit of the Philomaths. The young Mickiewicz was its official poet, and Tomasz Zan, the leading exponent of the mystical doctrines of the Russian Martinists and Jewish cabala lore.[66]

The members of this small and closely knit elitist circle were seriously interested in a variety of subjects, especially literature and poetry. They met regularly to read and to discuss their own poetry and/or Polish and foreign works of history, politics, literature, and criticism.[67] They also arranged informal excursions, and in general, spent much time together.

Each Philomath vowed to devote his entire life for the good of the fatherland, to education and virtue, and pledged to influence by example and leadership the young students, first at the university in Wilno, then in the various other educational institutions in the western provinces of the Russian Empire. In order to fulfill their vows, the Philomaths created the various filial societies mentioned above, e.g., *Związek Przyjaciół, Promieniści,* and Philarets. They also drew up detailed rules and regulations by which these societies were governed.[68]

The first of the filial groups organized by the Philomaths was the *Związek Przyjaciół.* Established on 10 April 1819, its charter members were Mickiewicz, Czeczot, Łoziński, Kowalewski, and Pietraszkiewicz. On 30 January 1820, these individuals organized a *Związek Naukowy* (Study Circle). Selected members of the *Związek Naukowy* received invitations to join the Philarets when this organization superseded the *Promieniści* in the spring of 1821.[69]

The elitist Philomaths also played a significant role in the creation of the *Promieniści* at the University of Wilno.[70] This popular student association of "friends for constructive leisure" received approval from the Rector of the University of Wilno, Szymon Malewski (1816–1822). Its members, under the guidance of the Philomaths, enjoyed various social activities, e.g., May Day outings. At such group outings, poetry was read and patriotic songs were sung.[71] The *Promieniści* disbanded in the spring of 1821 at the request of the university authorities, and the organization's most active members joined the new, secret society of Philarets.[72] By 1823 branches of Philarets had been established by the Philomaths in most of the gymnasia and provincial schools administered by the University of Wilno.[73] By extending their organization of Philarets throughout the western provinces of the Russian Empire, the Philomaths proposed to serve their nation socially and culturally. They aspired to educate Polish gentry youth to be worthy sons of the fatherland and responsible citizens of society.[74] Inadvertently, they also undermined the autocratic, imperial authority of the Russian tsar.

Although undercurrents of romantic nationalism and patriotism were discernible in the ideas and actions of the Philomaths, they were primarily influenced by the cultural climate which prevailed in intellectual circles in Wilno at the time, i.e., that of the eighteenth century Enlightenment. The Philomaths firmly believed in reason, in the spread of education, and in the progressive development of mankind with freedom and liberty as its goals.[75]

In December, 1821, the Philomaths joined university authorities, faculty, and students to welcome Joachim Lelewel — the embodiment of these ideals — to Wilno. The most articulate spokesman of the Philomaths, Adam Mickiewicz, expressed their feelings in his long, discursive poem written especially for the occasion.[76]

In his poem "To Joachim Lelewel," Mickiewicz praised Lelewel for his dedication to historical research and to the search for truth, for his erudition and his love of fatherland. Because of Lelewel's contributions to the theory and the methodology of history, his studies of antiquity, and his work in the national library in Warsaw, he deserved the praise. In the three years that followed his arrival in Wilno, Lelewel enhanced his reputation as a scholar of history in the traditions of the Enlightenment. He also contributed to the development of Romanticism at the University of Wilno. Lelewel's writings, lectures, and debates with other scholars during his second Wilno period were a curious blend of Enlightenment and Romantic ideas.

This blend of Enlightenment and Romantic ideas developed gradually in Lelewel's works, and it first appeared in *O Historii jej rozgałęźieniu i naukach związek z nia mając* (*On History, Its Branches and Related Disciplines*). This addition to Lelewel's *Historyka* marked the completion of his major writings on the theory and methodology of history. In *O Historii,* Lelewel added a new dimension to his concept of the purpose of the historian.

In the 1815 edition of the *Historyka,* Lelewel stated that the historian's major goal was the pursuit of truth:

> Pure in itself; without the need to apply it to practical usages or to prove its maxims.[77]

The historian arrived at truth by the rational selection and appraisal of historical source materials, and by criticism and familiarity with the philosophy of the nature of man and society.[78] In 1822, he added that this did not mean that the historian was to be dull and devoid of any moral, patriotic, or humanitarian feelings, for these characteristics were assets which enhanced the historian's ability to appraise the material sources at his disposal. Within this framework, Joachim

Lelewel presented his lectures in general history at Wilno in the years 1822–1824.[79]

The first year, Lelewel concentrated on chronology, the art of history, and on the origins of civilization in the eastern Mediterranean basin and Asia Minor. He also lectured on Greece and the sixteenth to the mid-seventeenth centuries. The second year, his subjects included the history of Rome, the Middle Ages, and the history of the second half of the seventeenth century. The third year, i.e., 1823–1824, he resumed his lectures on the civilization of the eastern Mediterranean basin, focusing on Asia Minor, Syria, Mesopotamia, and Egypt. He also introduced the history of the eighteenth century, and in his general history, he included Polish history, statistics (statism) or the study of contemporary states, and supplementary topics, e.g., on the useful study of history.[80]

The lectures in general history which Lelewel delivered (9 January 1822 – Summer 1824) were incorporated into four small volumes first published in Wrocław in 1850 and as the third volume of his collected works (*Dzieła*) in 1959. They are important in assessing Lelewel's contributions to historical studies during his second Wilno period, especially in determining the degree of originality of his interpretations of general European history, his growing interests in Poland's history, and the place his early interpretations occupy in the evolution of his own historical thought and Polish historical writing. The published lectures reflect his didactic activities and his concept of history.

The author divided the text of his general history into ancient (to 565 A.D.), medieval, and modern history (to 1786). Viewing history as a dynamic, organic process, he interpreted each period in terms of the progressive perfection of man. In dealing with the ancient era, Lelewel concentrated on the processes of history as they affected the Mediterranean basin and India. For him, India and the Mediterranean basin were the East, and he omitted references to the Far East and Central Asia. He portrayed the Mediterranean, in the course of 2500 years, as an arena of rivalries where the peoples and cultures of East and West, Asia and Europe, intermingled and reacted with each other to produce new ethnic and cultural admixtures.

The ancient East, the cradle of the perfection of man, represented a culture which failed to develop beyond a fairly primitive phase, and especially beyond intuitive-mystical thought (exemplified by Zoroaster). According to Lelewel, this aborted development resulted because of the esoteric nature of knowledge (*ezoteryzmem wiedzy*), the caste system, the despotic monarchy, and above all, the peculiarly Eastern "spirit of theism" which pervaded all life and hindered the free development of those vital strengths which would lead to the progressive perfection of man.[81]

Lelewel observed that classical Greek civilization, in contrast to the older Mediterranean civilization, developed universal values which contributed to the progressive perfection of man. This enabled Greek civilization to surpass the static civilization of the East. The progressive development of Greek unity was rather spontaneous. Cultural ties, e.g., customs, language, religion, and Homeric poetry, and not politics provided the firm foundations for the unity and progress of Greek civilization.[82]

A socially free and active citizen emerged in classical Greece. This citizen freed himself from external authorities and from "theism" and developed cultural, educational, and artistic assets available to all.[83] Certain negative aspects of her political life, e.g., her particularisms and certain domestic and foreign struggles, brought about the disintegration of Greece and the decline of her "political spirit" and citizens' virtues. Nevertheless, Greece, by her cultural values, exerted a permanent influence on East and West, and especially on Rome.[84]

In turn, in Lelewel's interpretation, Rome played a significant historical role because she politically integrated the ancient world. He based his interpretation of the history of Rome primarily on the extant writings of the Greek historian Polybius (204?–122? B.C.) who portrayed Rome sympathetically and tried to influence his fellow Greeks to accept imperial Roman rule. However, Lelewel also perceived the seeds of Rome's decline in her conquests, in forcing her government upon nearly the entire known world, in her imperial despotism, and in the discredited *Pax Romana.* Circumstances which fostered the *Pax Romana* changed, and Rome's power and the strength of her subject peoples atrophied. The decline of Rome which followed marked the end of ancient history for Lelewel; however, he did not view ancient history as a closed period. For him, two major events in the ancient era, the victory of Christianity and the appearance of the barbarian states, i.e., the rise of the Goths and the Vandals, in the West greatly influenced the history of medieval Europe.[85]

Lelewel dealt most comprehensively with the Middle Ages in his general history, and his interpretations of this period were, for the most part, original contributions to historical scholarship. As in his ancient history, Lelewel interpreted the history of the Middle Ages in terms of the progressive perfection of man. He viewed this period as one in which the Europeans with their dynamic freedoms and ethnic variety (*swobodami i różnorodnością*), their encouragement of nationality (*narodowość*) and the sovereignty of states quickly surpassed the original cultural superiority of the Arabs whose development was restricted by their "Asiatic" unity and despotism.[86]

In the history of the early Middle Ages, Lelewel concentrated his attention and observations on the fusion in the West of the ancient heritage of the Mediterranean, classical Greece, and Rome with northern barbarism. This fusion, he found, was accompanied, for various reasons, by an intellectual and moral decline. As a result, the primacy of civilization passed temporarily to the Arabs.[87] Nevertheless, during the "dark and gloomy" Middle Ages in the West, there developed a new alliance (*wspólnota*). In this new alliance, the Papacy and the Empire played decisive roles.[88]

Lelewel's presentation and conceptualization of the two powers, i.e., the Papacy and the Empire, in his medieval studies differed somewhat from those of his European contemporaries. Observing the existence of close political ties between the Emperor and the Pope, Lelewel stressed the development of feudalism and the subjugation of peoples in western Europe as a consequence of their conversion to Christianity and the close alliance between the Church and the Emperor.[89] He explained the stubborn resistance of the Slavs to Christianity in terms of their apprehensions concerning the possible loss of their independence and their primitive democratic institutions through their subordination to the German emperor and to their own Germanized aristocracy of the ninth century.[90] He specifically focused on the Poles' conversion to Christianity and the resultant, though abortive, efforts of the German emperors to subdue the Polish kings.

In 1000 A.D., the German Emperor Otto III (983–1002) sanctioned the establishment of the Archbishopric of Gniezno and the independent organization of the Church in Poland. Otto III recognized the independence of the Poles and permitted Bolesław the Brave (966–1025) to assume the title of king. This German emperor encouraged Bolesław to appeal to Rome for the Pope's consecration. However, there were several delays in Rome, and Otto III failed to win the support of the German lords in his endeavors to bring Poland into the universal empire. Ultimately conflict between the German emperors and the Polish kings resulted. Under Otto III's successor, Henry II, the first of a series of wars between Bolesław and the Holy Roman Empire erupted. Bolesław was acknowledged as Poland's king only in

1025, the year of his death. Poland's relations with the German Empire remained precarious, and Bolesław's successor, Mieszko II, faced a new series of conflicts.[91]

Lelewel's interpretation of these early medieval developments, especially the christianization of the northern tribes, e.g., the Slavs, was related to his "theory of dual development." He theorized that the peoples settling in Northeastern Europe, the Slavs and the Scandinavian tribes, were affected by the civilizing influences of the West rather late and retained much from their primitive communal democracy (*gminowładztwo*), especially attributes of *wolność* (freedom) and *duch publiczny* (a sense of public responsibility). Those peoples of Southwestern Europe within the range and influence of the old Roman Empire yielded to the decadent culture of the late Roman Empire and quickly lost their ancient characteristics. Feudalism, based on servitude and ties of individual interdependence, and the antithesis of freedom, justice, and the idea of public responsibility and national spirit, triumphed among them.[92] Conversely, attitudes and conditions sharply opposed to feudalism developed in Northeastern Europe in the early Middle Ages, according to Lelewel, especially among the Slavs in Poland and Russia with their deeply engrained characteristics of freedom, independence, and ideas of public responsibility and nationality.

Feudalism in Western Europe declined in the period of the Crusades (1073–1294). It was during this period that Western Europe experienced the growth of trade, the development of towns, an increase in monarchical authority, and the evolution of culture. In addition, other manifestations of progressive development appeared. All these factors led to a growing "striving for perfection" in the West in intellectual and economic spheres.[93] The situation in Eastern Europe differed. The number of towns declined and weakened, and as the number of alien peoples increased, the peasants were gradually subjugated.[94]

Lelewel's interpretation of the more recent period of history was his least original and was based almost entirely on the German historian Arnold H. L. Heeren's (1760–1842) *The European State System* (1809). Lelewel used Heeren's periodization, nomenclature, and interpretations. Dividing the modern period (1492–1796) into the political-religious (1492–1660) and the mercantile-military (1660–1780), he interpreted the history of Europe to 1660 in terms of developments which were the result of religious wars between Protestant and Catholic Europe. The guiding political motives in the period between 1660 and 1780 were the military and traditional interests, especially of the ascendant Protestant states which exhibited more vigor, elasticity, and dynamism than the countries associated with the Counter Reformation, i.e., Spain, Austria, and Poland. By 1786 the diplomatic politics of absolutism took over the incentive, and the politics of self-interest of the states laid the bases for the revolutions of the late eighteenth century.[95]

Lelewel became increasingly involved in the history of Poland, notably in the medieval period, during the decade of his association with the universities in Wilno and Warsaw. In the studies he wrote during this period, Lelewel sought new interpretations of such vital questions as the beginnings of the Polish state and of social stratification, the development of law, reasons for Poland's decline and fall, and others.[96]

In Poland, at the dawn of her history, he saw the freedom (*wolność*) of the peasant (*kmieć*) and equality of citizenship (*obywatelstwo*) which declined and disappeared under the influence of the growth of the power of the state, the church, and of other foreign, non-Slav influences on the Poles.[97] He saw the influence of Western civilization as a factor which stimulated the decline of Poland in the seventeenth and eighteenth centuries — especially in the degradation and subjugation of the lower estates and in the religious intolerance introduced by Western influences.

The Polish state remained strong only while the spirit of citizenship (*obywatelstwo*) and the nationality (*narodowość*) remained strong. Lelewel accounted for the re-emergence of Poland as an independent kingdom under Łokietek after its breakup and division in the early fourteenth century by attributing to Łokietek these virtues of citizenship and nationality.[98]

Lelewel's sincere fondness for the progressive ideals of freedom and humanitarianism — whose sources he suggested were in his nation's unique past — and his faith in the nation (*naród*) and his belief in a better future were the aspects of his lectures and publications which endeared him to his students. His ideas especially influenced the Philarets and Philomaths, the secret, nationalistic, and patriotic student organizations at the University of Wilno. His ideas also made him suspect to government authorities. Influential when first expressed in his lectures, when incorporated into his published works, the ideas he expressed had more far-reaching political implications because they reached a wider audience. In the realm of historical scholarship, the thoughts Lelewel expressed in his monographs concerning his nation's past provided the foundations for the first national history of Poland — a history in which the finest traditions of enlightenment and romanticism-historicism blended.[99]

During his second Wilno period, Lelewel's reputation as a scholar extended beyond the confines of Polish university circles. Several works by Lelewel were published in Germany. And he gained the respect of Russian scholars and intellectuals as a result of submitting a critical review of *A History of the Russian State,* the multivolume work by Imperial Russia's first national historian Nicholas M. Karamzin (1765–1826), to the St. Petersburg periodical *Severnyĭ Arkhiv* (*The Archive of the North*).[100]

In "Uwagi nad historią Karamzina" ("Observations on Karamzin's History"), Lelewel evaluated Karamzin's grandiose undertaking on the basis of four criteria. These included the Russian author's contemporary approach to history and his national, religious, and political feelings. Lelewel also made several comparisons between Karamzin and Adam Naruszewicz (1733–1796), the prominent Polish historian.

In comparing the two scholars, Lelewel characterized both as "men of their times" who sought historical truth by critical approaches. He observed that both disagreed with and corrected the ancient chroniclers, and both wrote the history of kings, princes, and states. In this manner, both men wrote their histories under the banners of autocracy.[101]

In December, 1821, Faddie V. Bulgarin (a transplanted Pole, Tadeusz Bułharyn), the editor of *Severnyĭ Arkhiv,* informed Lelewel that his initial review of Karamzin's history was enthusiastically received by Russian intellectuals, specifically Golitsin, Speransky, and Olenin, who were already acquainted with Lelewel's studies of primitive Slav culture.[102] Shortly after the publication of his review in *Severnyĭ Arkhiv,* Lelewel was elected an honorary member in several Russian professional societies. These professional societies included the Society of Friends of Learning in St. Petersburg, the Moscow Society for the Study of Russian Antiquities, and the Kharkov Scientific Society. "These honors," he wrote, "I willingly and cheerfully accepted."[103]

Lelewel's academic career and his contacts with fellow literati in the Russian Empire, including Bulgarin (Bułharyn), ended abruptly at the end of the 1823–1824 academic year.[104] In the fall of 1823, an investigation of Polish student organizations began. In charge of the investigation was Imperial Senator Nicholas Novosiltsev, the Tsar's

Extraordinary Commissioner at the Viceroy's Court in Warsaw. Philomaths and Philarets at the University and throughout the Wilno Educational District were arrested and imprisoned on the charge of conspiratorial, anti-Russian activity. The allegation stemmed partly from developments in Warsaw where the case of a young military officer, Walerian Łukasiński, Grand Master of National Freemasonry, was to come before the courts in the Congress Kingdom.[105] Police anticipated ramifications of Łukasiński's activities in Wilno, and the investigation was launched beyond the borders of the Congress Kingdom.[106] Historians and others writers on the subject, e.g., Weintraub, Domejko, believed the charge was only a pretext used by Novosiltsev to extend his investigation to Wilno.[107] They argue that the real cause of the persecution which followed the arrests in Wilno was the personal antagonism between Novosiltsev, an extremely influential representative of the Tsar, and Prince Adam Czartoryski, the Curator of all the schools on traditionally Polish territory incorporated into the Russian Empire. In order to compromise Czartoryski in the eyes of the Tsar, Novosiltsev decided to prove to Alexander that the latter's Polish friend sanctioned deliberately the patriotic, anti-Russian activities of Polish youth. Czartoryski had attempted to protect the young Polish students and their organizations.[108]

A minor incident provided Novosiltsev with the opportunity to initiate the investigation in Wilno. The critical event occurred in May, 1823, on the anniversary of the promulgation of the Constitution of 3 May 1791, the constitution that marked an attempt to modernize the Polish state and to free it from foreign (and Russian) intervention. Cezary Plater, one of the pupils of the fifth form of the Wilno secondary school, wrote on the blackboard, "Long live the Constitution of May 3. What a sweet remembrance for fellow compatriots."[109] Three other boys added their slogans. The allegedly seditious inscriptions were discovered by the Polish school authorities who promptly punished the culprits. The representatives of the Grand Duke Constantine, the adjutant Frederick Nesselrode, reported this isolated incident to his superior, the General-Governor Korsakov.[110]

Korsakov decided that the punishment by the school authorities was too lenient. As a result, not only was the assistant director of the school arrested, but also his superior Józef Twardowski, the Rector of the University of Wilno (1822–1824). Korsakov held Twardowski personally responsible since all the secondary schools of the district were administered by the University.[111]

Shortly after the incident involving the students of the gymnasium,

Novosiltsev arrived in Wilno (1 October 1823). He promptly established a Commission of Inquiry under his control and began a widespread investigation. He aimed to prove that the entire school district teemed with conspiracies.[112] There were numerous arrests, and the methods of the investigation were capricious and cruel. One of the arrested students, Jan Jankowski, admitted that he was a member of the Society of Philarets. On the basis of Jankowski's testimony, members of the Philomaths, notably Tomasz Zan, Adam Mickiewicz, and others, and its affiliated organizations were arrested on October 23 and 24.[113]

The Philomaths were interned in an old Basilian monastery which had been transformed into a prison. They were treated rather leniently during their confinement and were permitted to meet and to communicate with each other.[114]

Meanwhile the secret investigation spread to the secondary schools throughout the district administered by the University of Wilno. By January, 1824, more than one hundred persons had been arrested.[115]

Several secondary school pupils who had been guilty of childish patriotic gestures were punished extremely severely. They were condemned to hard labor or inducted into the army. Here they were forced to serve long terms.[116] Conversely, the verdict against the Philomaths was relatively mild, although unjust. The Commission of Inquiry discovered no connections between the Philomaths and the Warsaw National Freemasons.[117] Nevertheless, the Philomaths received punishments. Tomasz Zan was confined for one year; two others received six-month sentences and were interned in the Basilian monastery. The seventeen other Philomaths were to be deported to more central provinces of the Russian Empire, e.g., to Kazan or Siberia, or to St. Petersburg, where they were to be put at the disposal of the Minister of Education to serve as teachers. This group included Adam Mickiewicz who left Wilno for St. Petersburg on 25 October 1824. The Philomaths were not allowed to remain in the Polish provinces because, according to the verdict of the Commission, "by teaching, they were spreading unreasonable Polish nationalism."[118]

The dissolution of the Philomaths marked the end of their organized activities among youth at the University of Wilno and in the secondary schools of the provinces administered by the university authorities. Novosiltsev's investigating committee uncovered no evidence of conspiratorial anti-Russian activity in Wilno or its educational district. Yet, the findings of the Commission were used not only to disperse the Philomaths but also to put an end to Polish educational self-government in the western provinces of the Russian Empire. Novosiltsev replaced his antagonist Prince Adam Jerzy Czartoryski as Curator of the University of Wilno.

In 1824, Novosiltsev's appointment as curator was accompanied by the introduction of regressive changes into the curricula of the University and the gymnasia. For example, restrictions were placed on the study of poetry and debate, and more emphasis was placed on subjects such as Greek, Latin, and the Russian language. All political subjects were eliminated.[119] Attendance at the university lectures was closely supervised as a result of the events of 1823-1824. All student correspondence was subjected to strict censorship, and the students were restricted to their quarters or to the lecture halls.[120] The new rector of the University of Wilno, Wacław Pelikan (1826-1831), and the deans were chosen on the basis of their loyalty to the tsarist government and to its representative Novosiltsev.[121] In addition, certain Polish language textbooks were prohibited, and Gołuchowski's philosophy course eliminated because of its dangerous and anarchistic content.[122]

Alexander I's decree of 14 August 1824 also affected four young faculty members of the University of Wilno who were found guilty of "contributing to the spirit of unrest at the University of Wilno."[123] Gołuchowski, whose philosophy course had been canceled, was among the four. Joachim Lelewel who influenced and supported the young student "nationalists" was also among the four. Although he had not participated actively in anti-governmental activity, the content of his lectures and his printed works, especially those dealing with Poland's past, caused much consternation among the tsarist officials. The government found Lelewel's support of the Philomaths and Philarets during the inquiry intolerable, and by order of the autocratic tsar, he was forced to leave the University of Wilno. The order stated:

> Because of their opposition to university authorities, the Full Professors Lelewel, Gołuchowski, Bobrowski, and Daniłowicz are relieved of their responsibilities at the University of Wilno, and their continued stay in Wilno cannot be permitted. Therefore, the first of these, Lelewel, whose birthplace is the Congress Kingdom, is ordered to return to his fatherland.[124]

He never again lectured before an academic audience or associated officially with a university after 1824. In this respect, 1824 marked a turning point for Joachim Lelewel, the university professor and scholar. The year 1824 was also a turning point for the University of Wilno, for it marked the beginning of its liquidation. With the introduction of restrictions in 1824 and the expulsion of its most dynamic faculty members, the prestige of the University declined and obscurantism set in.[125]

Upon his return to Warsaw in 1824, Joachim Lelewel engaged in private research, notably in numismatics; completed his second volume of *Bibliograficznych ksiąg dwoje*; and gradually entered politics. By 1830–1831, totally and actively involved in the politics of the insurrection, he found little time for his scholarly pursuits.

4 Lelewel in Warsaw Before and During the November Uprising

Prelude: 1824–1828

೫ ೫ During his professionally active, second Wilno period,
Joachim Lelewel and his colleague Ignacy Daniłowicz
had embarked on an ambitious scholarly project. This
involved collecting all extant documents of Polish-Lithuanian laws,
collating the various Polish, Lithuanian, Ruthenian, and Latin texts,
writing appropriate commentaries, and systematically publishing
their completed work. The published materials would serve many
useful purposes. Ultimately Lelewel proposed to use them as a significant source for a history of Lithuanian law.[1]

At the time of their summary dismissal from the University of
Wilno in 1824, Lelewel and Daniłowicz had barely begun their work.
In fact, on the eve of their reluctant departure from Wilno (Daniłowicz was ordered to St. Petersburg; Lelewel to Warsaw), only the
first of the numerous projected volumes had appeared in print. Nevertheless, Lelewel resumed work on this project shortly after he resettled
in Warsaw.[2]

In the Congress Kingdom, Lelewel also devoted much time and
energy to numismatics and archeology. His studies of the ancient
coins, excavated near Płock, and of the gravestones in the Ruszczy
cemetery in Sandomir resulted in the publication of *Stare pieniądze w
roku 1824 blisko Płocka w Trzebuniu wykopane* (*Ancient Coins
Excavated in Trzebun near Płock in 1824*) in Warsaw two years
later. In 1829, on the eve of the insurrection, he catalogued the entire
numismatics collection, consisting of 4,000 coins, of the *Towarzystwo Przyjaciół Nauk*. These endeavors in numismatics helped to
establish Lelewel's reputation as a pioneer in that field.[3] Lelewel's

interests and researches included finding and identifying coins from the Piast period. These discoveries proved significant for his studies of trade relations during the Piast period which he later included in his national histories.

In addition to his preoccupation with law, numismatics, and archeology, Lelewel also prepared the second volume of his *Bibliograficznych ksiąg dwoje* (*Two Bibliographic Books*) when he returned to Warsaw in 1824.[4] It was published by Józef Zawadzki in Wilno in 1826. Lelewel never completed a proposed third volume which was to include a catalogue of incunabula of Polish printers, largely because of his increasing interest in writing a national history of Poland.[5]

His association with the Warsaw *Towarzystwo Przyjaciół Nauk* after 1824 stimulated his interest in this subject. The *Towarzystwo Przyjaciół Nauk* had been very interested in the popularization of Polish history since the creation of this organization in 1800. Its members frequently contributed monographs on various aspects of Polish history, and they periodically proposed plans for a comprehensive national history at various meetings.[6] For example, at the meeting of 12 January 1801, Tadeusz Czacki (1763–1813), one of the founders of the *Towarzystwo*, proposed to continue the study begun by Adam Naruszewicz (1733–1796) of the history of earliest Poland and to add to it a section on the Jagiellonian period in addition to correcting and clarifying the Bishop's work. On 20 January 1805, Czacki informed the *Towarzystwo Przyjaciół Nauk* that he was working on the Jagiellonian period and had completed several chapters.[7]

Other *Towarzystwo* members were also involved in the history project and in projects in related fields. The latter included Polish laws and charters, geography (notably the preparation of atlases), and various subjects dealing with antiquity. Because most of the active members of the *Towarzystwo*, e.g., Jan Potocki, Ksawery Bohusz, and Jan Albertrandy, were interested in such diversity of topics, no general popular history of Poland, encompassing all aspects of Poland's past, resulted until the publication of Joachim Lelewel's studies.[8]

Two years before the outbreak of the uprising in the Congress Kingdom, Lelewel wrote a small historical sketch, *Historia: Obraz dziejów polskich* (*History: An Image of Polish History*), in which he expressed vaguely formulated elements of his interpretation of Poland's political and social history. The following ideas which he expressed in his *Historia*, he expounded more fully and reiterated in his later histories.

The political structure of primal Poland, according to Lelewel, rested on the foundations of brotherhood, *gminowładztwo* (a kind of communal democracy), equality before the law, and public owner-ship of land.[9] By the mid-eleventh century, a serious conflict devel-oped between the two segments of primitive Polish society, the *kmieć* (peasants) and the *lechites* (*Lechowie*).[10] The *kmieć* defended the indigenous bases of their polity; conversely, the *lechites,* influenced by the politics introduced by the West, especially by the Holy Roman Empire and its ally the Church, favored westernization of politics and wanted changes in the polity.

Within this framework, Lelewel explained sharp social conflicts such as those which emerged after the death of Mieszko II (1025–1134) and during the reigns of Bolesław II (the Bold, 1058–1079) and Bolesław III (Krzywousty, 1102–1138). The struggles ended with the victory of the *możnowładcy* (magnates) — the upper strata of the szlachta — and the subjugation of the peasants.[11] As a result of these social developments, the Polish state weakened. For two hundred years following the death of Bolesław III Krzywousty, the Piast princes ruled Poland with the magnates. During this period of Po-land's history, the Polish state declined further with the influx of Ger-mans from the west. Polish law, the autocratic magnates, and the princes yielded to Germanization.[12] After more than two centuries of dynastic squabbles, Władysław Łokietek, the father of Casimir the Great (1333–1370), restored stability.[13] The period of "*Polska kwit-nąca* — of *gminowładztwo szlacheckie*" ("A Flourishing Poland under Local Gentry Rule") commenced. Differences between the princes and the szlachta declined. Affluence characterized Poland during this era of her history. However, by the late fifteenth century, this prosperity proved ephemeral, as Poland precariously faced seri-ous external and internal problems. The Tartars and the Turks ap-peared in the east, creating a serious threat to Poland's prosperity and stability. Moreover, certain domestic issues emerged, undermining further Poland's stability.[14] These latter included the imposition of new restrictions on the rights of the *kmieć* and the townspeople as well as serious limitations on the king's powers.[15]

Nevertheless, during the reigns of the first Zygmunts, which spanned most of the sixteenth century, Poland survived, experienced a renais-sance, and became the center of culture and freedom. The situation worsened, however, during the reign of Zygmunt III (Vasa, 1588–1632) when Poland again faced foreign threats and succumbed to the influences of the Jesuits and the Hapsburgs. Attempted resistance to these foreign influences failed. The revolt of Mikołaj Zebrzydowski

(1606–1607) who rose to defend the integrity of the Republic in opposition to Zygmunt III's insistence on a marriage alliance with Austria, ended in defeat.[16] The consistent oppression of the people (*lud*) by the aristocracy culminated in the Cossack uprisings in the seventeenth century.[17] These Cossack uprisings invited the interference of Muscovy. As foreign influences from west and east increased in Poland, prosperity and stability declined, and the szlachta lost their civic spirit (*duch obywatelski*).

Turning to a more recent historical period, Lelewel then expressed his thoughts on the inadequacies of the reform movement which began in Poland in the mid-eighteenth century. He indicated that even a reformed Poland was unable to sustain her independence given the interference of her eastern and western neighbors. In spite of the inadequacies of the reform movement, Lelewel praised the reformers and creators of the 3 May 1791 Constitution. These reformers, according to Lelewel, intended to minimize foreign intervention by creating a strong, hereditary monarchy. Concomitantly they recognized the rights of the szlachta and peasant estates, attempted to establish closer relations between the two, and recognized the *sejms* (diets) as legal authorities with responsibilities which included providing ministers for the government.[18]

In the *Historia*, Lelewel accepted the idea of a hereditary constitutional monarchy for Poland. He also enunciated his republicanism and his idea of *gminowładztwo*, and he glorified the *Rzeczpospolita*. He continually worked and reworked these themes in his national histories and in his political essays.

A more complete sketch of Poland's history is found in his *Dzieje Polski potocznym sposobem opowiedziane* (*A History of Poland Related in a Colloquial Manner*). Written as a popular history for children, this publication appeared in 1828 and included not only political but also social and cultural history. In *Dzieje Polski*, Lelewel again expressed his beliefs in primitive Slav virtues, his republicanism, his sympathy for the people and the petty szlachta, and his bias against the aristocracy, whom he blamed for the fall of the *Rzeczpospolita*.

For many years, *Dzieje Polski* served as a textbook (nine editions were published by 1859), and it influenced many generations of Polish youth. The immediate effect of this popular history was that Lelewel's reputation as a liberal grew, and when the insurrection erupted in Warsaw in November 1830, he was appointed a member of the government and simultaneously elected as president of the revolutionary *Towarzystwo Patriotyczne* (The Patriotic Society). In the course of 1830–1831, he became increasingly involved in the government and in the patriotic society and found little time to devote to scholarship until after he settled in Belgium.

Lelewel first expressed his vaguely formulated ideas of republicanism, his sympathy for the lower classes of Polish society, and his biases against the Polish aristocracy in the national histories he wrote for popular consumption in the decade of the twenties. His increasing involvement in politics in the latter part of that decade contributed to the further evolution of his republican-democratic ideas and provided him with the opportunity to transform these ideas into action.

His participation in the politics of the Congress Kingdom after 1828 took three forms: legal — as representative of the Żelechów *powiat* (district) in the Chamber of Deputies; extra-legal — as president of the *Towarzystwo Patriotyczne* (Patriotic Society) in 1830–1831; and revolutionary — as a member of the National Government in 1830–1831.

Lelewel's active participation in politics began in 1828 when he declared his candidacy for the Sejm (Diet). As a squire from Wola Okrzejska, the estate owned by his relatives the Cieciszowskis, he secured a mandate on 11 February 1828, and replaced Adam Cieciszowski as the representative in the Chamber of Deputies from the district of Żelechów. Between 1829 and 1830, he headed the Commission on Organization and Administrative Laws in the Sejm.[19] But he played no significant role in this deliberative assembly until it met in extraordinary session in 1830.

At the suggestion of his brother Prot, Joachim Lelewel joined the extra-legal *Towarzystwo Patriotyczne* in 1824.[20] When relations between this organization and the revolutionary Russian Southern Society were exposed in 1826, Joachim's brother Prot was among those arrested and interned in the Carmelite monastery near Warsaw. But Joachim, who appeared before the Commission of Inquiry, was released for lack of evidence concerning his participation in the allegedly subversive activities of the *Towarzystwo*.[21] Although he did not actively participate in this patriotic society at the time he joined, by 1830–1831 he was elected its president.[22]

Until the insurrection erupted, Lelewel's membership in the Sejm did not prevent him from continuing his scholarly pursuits. Just two weeks prior to the uprising of 29 November 1830, he accepted his first official position in the *Towarzystwo Przyjaciół Nauk,* replacing Fryderyk Skarbek (who left Warsaw on a mission to St. Petersburg) as

Inspector of the Library of that society.[23] His brief tenure in the *Towarzystwo Przyjaciół Nauk* had no profound effect on the development of this national institution, but it had a political consequence.

In the library of the *Towarzystwo Przyjaciół Nauk* on 21 November, the young conspirators Piotr Wysocki, Józef Zaliwski, and Ksawery Bronikowski met with Lelewel to inform him that the outbreak against Russian imperial authority in the Congress Kingdom had been decided upon.[24] Lelewel expressed his opposition to the timing of the outbreak, but he promised his moral support. Thus he assured his involvement in the revolutionary politics of the uprising, in spite of his initial opposition to it.

The outbreak in Warsaw in the latter part of November marked another turning point in the life of Joachim Lelewel. Throughout 1830–1831 and the three years of exile in France which followed, politics took precedence over scholarship in his life. The national-republican ideas he expressed vaguely in *Historia: Obraz dziejów polskich* and in *Dzieje Polski potocznym sposobem opowiedzane* found concrete expression in his political works and actions during those critical ten months of the insurrection and war with imperial Russia. In exile in Western Europe after the failures of 1831, he became the foremost representative of the Polish democratic left and the most vociferous and eloquent spokesman of anti-tsarism.

⊛ From the Congress of Vienna to 29 November 1830

There is general agreement among historians that the immediate cause of the revolt which erupted in the capital of the Congress Kingdom on 29 November 1830 was the outbreak of the July Revolution in France and the Belgian revolt in late August of that year.[25] The additional, deeper causes can be traced back to the Vienna settlement of 1815.[26]

The Kingdom of Poland, a creation of the Congress of Vienna, included an area of 128,500 km[2] and a population of 3.3 million people (in 1816), but it did not satisfy totally the national aspirations of the small number of politically articulate Poles who looked forward to the unification of the Congress Kingdom with the western provinces of the Russian Empire and ultimately with the former Polish lands held by Prussia and Austria.[27] Nevertheless, in 1815, the Poles accepted the decisions of the great powers and the liberal and enlightened constitution of Tsar Alexander I, now the hereditary monarch of Congress Poland. The constitution granted by Alexander I contained a number of provisions of the earlier constitution of the Grand Duchy of Warsaw. In the fifteen years which followed the Vienna settlement, the tsar-kings of Congress Poland either neglected or ignored this royal charter. The Poles, increasingly dissatisfied, disappointed, and frustrated, resorted to violence. In the late fall of 1830, a serious insurrection against the tsar-king erupted in the Congress Kingdom.

The Constitution (which consisted of seven titles and 165 articles) granted to the Congress Kingdom was prepared by Alexander's Russian and Polish advisers, revised by the Tsar, and promulgated in November, 1815. According to its provisions, the Kingdom of Poland was an hereditary monarchy. Its king was also the Russian Emperor. Thus the fate of the Poles was, after 1815, indirectly linked for a century with the fate of the Russian Empire. Except for foreign relations, the conduct of which was reserved for the imperial government, the Congress Kingdom was granted a broad and comprehensive autonomy. It had its own army; only Polish citizens were eligible for public office; and the Polish language was used in the army, the administration, and in the courts.

The Crown in Congress Poland was represented by a viceroy who acted with the assistance of an appointed state council (*Rada Administracyjna*). Members of this executive council were the heads of five central executive departments — the Departments of Finance, War, Education, Public Worship, and Home Affairs and Police.

The Diet (Sejm) consisted of the king and two houses. The upper house, i.e., the Senate, consisted of not more than one-half of the number of members of the lower chamber. The Senators (*wojewody, kasztelany, biskupi*) were appointed for life by the Crown. The Chamber of Deputies, the lower house, consisted of seventy-seven representatives of the szlachta and fifty-one other deputies. All were elected by the landed nobility and burghers. Both the franchise and eligibility for membership in the Diet were restricted by property qualifications.[28] The poorer classes, the peasants, and the Jews were denied the right to participate in the government of the Congress Kingdom. The Diet was to meet every two years for a thirty day period, but the Crown retained the power to postpone its convocation, and actually only four sessions were held between 1815 and 1830.[29] The Diet was denied legislative initiative but was entitled to petition the Crown.

In addition to their participation in the lower chamber of the Diet, the landed nobility and the wealthy townsmen were granted effective participation in local government, and they elected the judges of the local courts. The Constitution also provided for the abolition of serfdom and the establishment of equal rights before the law. These provisions, however, remained a dead letter.

Although the Congress Kingdom consisted of only approximately one-sixth of the area of pre-partition Poland, many Poles optimistically looked forward to the expansion of their state by unification with or annexation of at least part of the Lithuanian-Byelorussian lands and the extension of the 1815 Constitution to those areas which had been part of the old Polish Commonwealth (*Rzeczpospolita*). The optimism of the Poles concerning the future of the western provinces of the Russian Empire was based largely on the promises and actions of Tsar Alexander I at the Congress of Vienna and in the years immediately following.

At the Congress of Vienna, Alexander expressly reserved to himself in the treaties and in the Final Act the right of making such additions to the Polish state as he might think fit. Taken in conjunction with the recent precedent of the annexation of old Finland to the Grand Duchy of Finland (1811), Alexander's actions in Vienna concerning the Polish question helped to conciliate public opinion in the Kingdom.[30] The expectations of the Poles were encouraged further in the spring of 1818 when Alexander, in his speech from the throne to the first Diet, assured the Poles of his intention to unify the Lithuanian lands with the Congress Kingdom.[31] In his decrees of 1817 and 1819, he extended the military authority of Grand Duke Constantine, the Commander-in-Chief of the Polish army, to five of the eight Lithuanian provinces by establishing a separate Lithuania corps.[32] These actions also contributed to the rising expectations of the Poles in the Congress Kingdom.

However, when the second Polish Diet met in the fall of 1820, its proceedings were not acceptable to Alexander, and in his final address to that body, he rebuked the deputies and hinted that he seriously considered withdrawing the promises he made earlier. Before he left Warsaw on 14 October 1820, Alexander named his brother Constantine viceroy *de facto* in the Congress Kingdom, rather than appointing a Pole to the position. This indicated to many Poles that Alexander contemplated a policy contrary to his initial promises, a policy opposed to unification of the Congress Kingdom and the Lithuanian-Byelorussian lands and to the extension of the Constitution to the latter areas.[33]

In the five years between the meetings of the second and third Diets

(1820–1825), a period of increasing restrictions and violations of the Constitution ensued. This resulted in the continuous growth of resentment of the Poles in the Congress Kingdom. They especially resented the Grand Duke Constantine's abuses of power. As viceroy *de facto,* Constantine frequently decided fundamental questions, meddled in the administration of state under the pretext of controlling funds for the military, and ignored the advice of the Minister of War. Erratic, rude, and a ruthless military disciplinarian, he ignored the traditions of the Polish legions and the army of the Grand Duchy as well as the strategy and tactics developed during the period of the Napoleonic Wars. He replaced these with Prussian drill, garrison duty, and day-long dress parades.[34] He created a widespread spy system and established a special commission of inquiry for the purposes of investigating the most prominent members of Polish society. Members of his organization searched for conspiratorial plots for independence, interrogated those persons suspected of revolutionary activity, and arbitrarily imprisoned those accused. Constantine, the personification of tyranny, became a living symbol of tsarist oppression to those who grew to despise him. Among the latter were the young military officers and cadets, many of whom openly expressed their discontent with him.[35]

The Poles also resented the restrictions of their civil liberties imposed by the high commissioner of the imperial government in Congress Poland, Nicholas Novosiltsev. They especially resented his spy system (separate from Constantine's), his imposition of censorship in the Kingdom in violation of constitutional guarantees in 1819, and his influence over the obscurantist Minister of Education Stanisław Grabowski who replaced the progressive Stanisław Kostka Potocki on August 14, 1821.[36]

Two trends of organized opposition developed in the Congress Kingdom between 1815 and 1830: one legal and one clandestine. Both at first shared the goal of defending the Constitution against the encroachments of the tsar's representatives.

The legal opposition consisted of a group of Kalisz deputies to the Diet led by the brothers Wincenty and Bonawentura Niemojowski. They first voiced their criticism of the government at the first Diet in 1818. In the following session in 1820, their criticism of the government grew more vociferous, and Wincenty Niemojowski demanded the indictment of two government officials for endorsing the decree on censorship. The 1820 session of the Sejm, influenced by Wincenty Niemojowski and the Kalisz group, rejected most of the government's bills. As a result, Alexander I gave vent to his annoyance publicly.[37] As preparations were made for the third Diet (1825), the opposition leaders in the Sejm were forbidden to attend. Wincenty Niemojowski, the head of the government opposition, was forbidden to travel to Warsaw, and the election in the Kalisz province in which he had been elected a deputy was cancelled.[38] Under these circumstances, the legal opposition to the government was unable to play a decisive political role in the Congress Kingdom. The illegal opposition which developed rapidly in the form of secret organizations took the incentive.[39] These clandestine groups were responsible for the violent outbreak of 29 November 1830.

Clandestine associations flourished in the Polish lands after 1815 as they did in other parts of western and eastern Europe (e.g., the *Burschenschaften,* the *Carbonari,* the Decembrists) among the intelligentsia who had no influence on the affairs of state. The first secret society in the Congress Kingdom, the *Panta Koina* ("Everything in Common"), was created at the University of Warsaw in 1817 by a small group of students led by Ludwik Mauersberger. This group confined its activities to theoretical instruction and was discovered belatedly, i.e., several years after it had discontinued its meetings in Warsaw. Its successor, *Związek Wolnych Polaków* (The Union of Free Poles), founded in 1820, included among its members the prominent future revolutionaries Tadeusz Krępowiecki, Wiktor Heltman, and Maurycy Mochnacki. The Union of Free Poles prepared students for the struggle for liberation and for rousing the masses of the population when the revolution came. The Union published a legal monthly journal *Dekada Polska* (*The Polish Decade*). However, several months after its inception, the Union of Free Poles was discovered by the police, and its members were placed under arrest. The Polish student organizations in the western provinces of the Russian Empire existed longer than those in Warsaw largely because their goals differed from those of their counterparts in Warsaw. The Philomaths and the Philarets at the University of Wilno, for example, aimed at self-improvement and the eventual transformation of the nation and society by education, and they flourished until their collapse as a result of Novosiltsev's investigation in 1823–1824.[40]

Independent of the student organizations, young Polish military officers created an important underground movement. One participant prominent in this movement was Major Walerian Łukasiński of the Fourth Infantry Regiment. Taking advantage of the government's initial tolerance of freemasonry, he founded, in 1819, an independent organization called National Freemasons.[41] The humanitarian phraseology and symbolism of the freemasons was replaced in his lodge by patriotic slogans. Łukasiński's aim was the reunification and liberation of Poland. There was no statement on how these objectives were to be achieved. Nevertheless a considerable number of Polish gentry who sympathized with the Kalisz group joined this organization of National Freemasonry.[42]

In 1821, Łukasiński dissolved the National Freemasons and founded the Patriotic Society with branches in the Russian Empire — in Lithuania and the Ukraine. Again his goals were vaguely formulated, although in general he called for the unification of the western provinces of the Russian Empire with the Congress Kingdom without armed conflict.

The following year, Łukasiński was arrested and court martialed. Eventually sentenced to prison, he died in the Schlüsselburg Prison in the Russian Empire after a confinement of thirty-eight years. By 1824 Łukasiński's organization was rapidly reorganized by Lieutenant Colonel Seweryn Krzyżanowski. Opposition to tsarist authorities in the Congress Kingdom gained momentum until the arrest of Krzyżanowski and other members of the Patriotic Society in 1826 after their alleged collusion with the Russian Decembrists.[43]

A special Commission of Inquiry (*Komisja Sledcza*) interrogated Krzyżanowski and the other suspects for one year. The defendants were accused of high treason but were tried neither by a military court, as the Grand Duke desired, nor by Russian criminal procedure, as Novosiltsev desired.[44] Instead, Nicholas, according to the Constitution of 1815, created a Court of the Diet (*Sąd Sejmowy*) by imperial decree (18 April 1827). This Court of the Diet, composed of members of the Polish Senate, met in Warsaw and acquitted all those accused from the charge of high treason.[45] The accused were given lenient sentences for their participation in clandestine organizations and for failing to disclose the Russian conspiracy to the authorities.[46] Krzyżanowski was sentenced to three years imprisonment, and his companions received minor sentences.[47]

Nicholas took the actions of the Court of the Diet as a personal defeat and censured the Court. Nevertheless, he ordered the release of all the defendants except two Polish officers who were Russian subjects. One of these was Krzyżanowski who was born in the Ukraine. Nicholas then invalidated the Court's decision regarding Krzyżanowski and ordered his exile. Krzyżanowski died in Siberia ten years later.[48]

In the two years that followed the conspiracy trial, Nicholas treated the Poles with consideration and avoided a direct confrontation. However, the trial and its aftermath were a prelude to the critical events which began 29 November 1830. The breach which developed between the Poles and their king could not be overcome without violence.[49]

After the exposure of the Patriotic Society and the proceedings of the Court of the Diet, small conspiratorial groups continued to meet secretly in Warsaw and throughout the Congress Kingdom. In December, 1828, a new, clandestine association was organized by the cadets of the Infantry Officers' School in Warsaw (*Szkoła Podchorążych Piechoty*) under the leadership of a young instructor Piotr Wysocki. This new patriotic society, led by the son of an impoverished szlachta family, consisted of young officers from Warsaw and the provinces who kept in touch with literary circles and university students. Among the latter was the poet Seweryn Goszczyński and his colleagues Ludwik Nabielak, Ksawery Bronikowski, Maurycy Mochnacki, Tadeusz Krępowiecki, and Jan Żukowski.[50] Responsibility for the November 29 outbreak rests primarily on these young men and on the cadets of the Infantry Officers' School.

Members of these most recently reorganized conspiratorial groups and literary circles vowed obedience to the Constitution of 1815 and called for the union of the Congress Kingdom with Lithuania. Beyond these, they proposed no specific goals.[51]

Wysocki's small group planned a Polish rising during the Russo-Turkish War (1828-1829), plotted the assassination of Nicholas I at the time of his coronation as King of Poland (May, 1829), and sought to disrupt the meeting of the fourth Diet (May 28 - June 28, 1830). None of these ambitious plans materialized, however, because of the indecisiveness of the leaders and the weakness of the organization itself.[52] Nonetheless, the organization of cadets, seeing no prospect of being commissioned and weary of the military parades and drills, thrived in the environment of growing political and economic discontent.[53]

The eruption of the July Revolution in France in 1830 gave a powerful impetus to the conspirators and helped to decide the future of Congress Poland. The revolution in France, followed by the upheaval in the Netherlands, made a European war seem quite probable and stimulated Nicholas I to embark on a potentially aggressive foreign policy. The concurrence of conspiratorial activities in the Congress Kingdom with warlike movements in St. Petersburg brought the discontent to a head in Warsaw.

The tsar, upon hearing the news of the Paris revolution one month after the adjournment of the fourth Polish Diet, immediately prepared for war against France, expecting Prussia to join him in the campaign.[54] On 18 August 1830, he informed the Grand Duke Constantine of his intentions and plans to use the Polish army and finances of the Kingdom for action against France. On the same day, his Secretary of State sent a confidential communication to the Polish Minister of Finance Franciszek Lubecki with an injunction to have funds ready both for mobilization and for the campaign. Constantine informed the tsar of his personal opposition to the war on August 25 while Lubecki confined his response to a report (September 3) showing the cash at his disposal and available for initial expenses. Despite the opposition of the Grand Duke and the vague response of Lubecki, Nicholas proceeded with his plans.[55]

On 31 August, Field Marshal Dibich (1785–1831), who was selected as Commander-in-Chief of the projected campaign, was dispatched to Berlin by Nicholas to induce Frederick William III to take up arms and to adopt the plan of campaign elaborated by the Russian Minister of War Chernyshev. The Prussian ruler, however, was anxious to avoid war because Austria and England had already recognized Louis Philippe's government. He replied evasively to the Russians, but simultaneously concentrated some of his troops on the Rhine.

Meanwhile the Polish conspirators learned of the secret instructions of Nicholas to Constantine and Lubecki. Anticipating the outbreak of a war which would involve the departure of the Polish army to the west, they reasoned that they must begin their struggle before the army was sent abroad.[56]

The conspirators then approached General Józef Chłopicki, a popular figure who had served in Napoleon's legions but had retired as a result of a dispute with Constantine, the head of the Polish armed forces in the Congress Kingdom. Chłopicki, however, refused to head the intended revolt. Disappointed with Chłopicki's refusal to cooperate and uncertain of Nicholas's ultimate intentions, the conspirators hesitated. The rising, originally fixed for October 20, was postponed until the spring of the following year.

The outbreak of the revolt in the Netherlands in the latter part of August confirmed Nicholas's intentions to take the offensive.[57] In October, Dibich was again sent to Berlin with instructions that upon arriving at an understanding with Prussia he was to return to Warsaw as Commander-in-Chief. In a letter of November 13, Nicholas informed Dibich that the opening date for the French campaign was

December 22. The Polish army and the Lithuanian Corps were to form part of the vanguard. The conspirators in Warsaw, again informed of the confidential communications, decided to speed up the insurrection in an effort to paralyze Nicholas's intended offensive.

On the nineteenth and twentieth of November, the first mobilization orders appeared in the Warsaw press, and the police, informed of the planned conspiracy, began arresting students.[58] On November 21, the military leaders who planned the rising sought Lelewel's advice and confided in him. Lelewel, the scholar and historian and recently chosen deputy to the Sejm, became increasingly involved in the politics of insurrection in the Congress Kingdom from this point forward.

&⁸ Joachim Lelewel and the Politics of Insurrection

Lelewel, who did not participate in planning the conspiracy, opposed the timing of the insurrection when informed of it.[59] He argued that the high ranking officers and civilian officers, not informed of the plans and intentions of the young, junior officers and cadets, would not risk their positions to support a small group who were not even certain of the support of the military ranks.[60] In spite of Lelewel's cautious warning, the outbreak was set for 29 November 1830. The young conspirators aimed to eliminate those Russian forces already stationed in the Kingdom and to redeem the Polish provinces from the Russian Empire.[61]

On the evening of November 29, two separate attacks occurred in Warsaw: one on the Belvedere Palace, the home of Constantine, and the other on the barracks of the Russian cavalry near Łazienki Park.[62] Both attacks, however, proved unsuccessful. The assault on the Belvedere Palace was made by eighteen cadets and university students led by Ludwik Nabielak and Seweryn Goszczyński. They killed the officer on duty and wounded two other persons who came to warn the Grand Duke, but they failed to capture Constantine. The assault on the Russian barracks was made by 160 cadets led by Piotr Wysocki. Overwhelmed, the cadets quickly abandoned their attempt to seize the barracks and ran through the city calling on the people to rise. Initially they met with little response, and there were few casualties.[63] At this stage, Constantine, who commanded approximately 7,000 Lithuanian and Russian troops, undoubtedly could have stifled the outburst for which neither the city nor the army was prepared. But he failed to take any decisive action. Instead, he withdrew to Wierzbno — a suburb of Warsaw located south of the capital.

That night the situation changed when some inhabitants of the city responded to the insurgents' calls and stormed the arsenal. Arming themselves, they engaged some Russian detachments, and by morning, they occupied Old Town (*stare miasto*). Under these circumstances, the executive Administrative Council met and authorized Prince Adam Jerzy Czartoryski, Senator and member of the Administrative Council, and Franciszek Ksawery Lubecki, Minister of Finance and the most prominent member of the government, to meet with Constantine at the latter's encampment at Wierzbno to discuss the tenuous situation. The Grand Duke, in answer to the inquiries of the Poles, declared his refusal to intervene and left the pacification of the capital to the Poles themselves.[64]

In dealing with the imminent crisis, the Administrative Council endeavored to keep within its constitutional limits. On November 30, it issued a proclamation in the name of Nicholas calling on the people to remain calm.[65] However, the actions of the crowds of laborers (*wyrobniki*) and workmen from Old Town (*stare miasto*) who joined the insurgents during the night gave the insurrection an aura of popular revolution in Warsaw, and the movement soon spread to other parts of the Congress Kingdom.[66]

The following day, December 1, Maurycy Mochnacki reorganized the revolutionary club, the *Towarzystwo Patriotyczne* (The Patriotic Society). At a stormy meeting, he demanded vigorous action, including disarming the Grand Duke's forces and the establishment of a new government. The government responded by making some concessions to these demands. Unacceptable members of the Administrative Council were dismissed, and popular deputies of the Diet were appointed to the vacated positions. Two representatives of the "revolutionary left" — Joachim Lelewel (the newly elected President of the Patriotic Society) and Władysław Ostrowski — were admitted, and an executive commission with Czartoryski as president was appointed.[67]

On December 2, Czartoryski and Lubecki again conferred with the Grand Duke. Joachim Lelewel and Władysław Ostrowski accompanied them to Wierzbno on the outskirts of Warsaw.

The Polish delegation met with the Grand Duke and his Polish wife, the Countess Łowicka, to discuss the latest developments in Warsaw and the Congress Kingdom and to determine how the situation was to be handled.[68] In an atmosphere of legality and compromise, an agreement between the Grand Duke and the representatives of the Administrative Council was reached. The Administrative Council was to act to put down all unrest in Warsaw. Again Constantine emphasized that the outburst was a quarrel among Poles and was to be handled by them. He agreed to withdraw from the Congress Kingdom with his forces. He also promised neither to order the military at his command into the Congress Kingdom nor to take any military action against the rebellious Poles without giving forty-eight hours' notice of his intentions. In addition, he promised to intercede on behalf of the insurgents with his brother Tsar Nicholas I, King of Congress Poland, and to urge Nicholas to grant amnesty to those responsible for the trouble. However, he refused to intercede with the Emperor in reference to the question of the annexation of Lithuania by the Congress Kingdom. Those present agreed to the pacification of the insurrectionists, prevention of further eruptions of violence, avoidance of a rupture with the tsar, and above all, avoidance of a revolution.[69]

Lelewel concurred with the compromise solution, but not until he expressed his opinions concerning the outbreak to the Grand Duke and to the latter's Polish wife, the Countess Łowicka. Although he had opposed the timing of the insurrection when first notified of the plans by the cadet leaders Piotr Wysocki and Józef Zaliwski, in the course of the meeting in Wierzbno, Lelewel realized the opportunity created by the recent events for a national revolution against tsarist oppression — in reality a revolution he believed was justified by the repeated, flagrant violations of the Constitution of 1815 by Poland's Romanov kings — the Russian Emperors Alexander and Nicholas.[70] He expressed himself in the following manner.

Speaking with the Grand Duke in Wierzbno, Lelewel averred that surely the *tsarevich* could see that the events at the Belvedere Palace the night of November 29 were but a prelude to a national rising:

> . . . That even now a higher objective unfolds, that a great and inextinguishable enthusiasm for the extension of rights and the Polish constitution to the Poles in the Polish provinces of the Russian Empire and their union with the Kingdom is being asserted; that the first outbreak was only the stimulus; now the general will of the nation manifests itself.[71]

Such a radical statement was not taken seriously by anyone at the Wierzbno meeting except by Lelewel. The other members of the Polish delegation, determined to act only within the limits of their delegated authority, ignored Lelewel's comments. The Grand Duke listened quietly.

In his conversation with the Countess Łowicka, Lelewel expounded on this idea of a national political rising further:

> I perceive in the development of this national rising not a rising against the king or against the Russian nation (*naród*) which, if it so desired, could be called brothers of the Poles; but against Russian politics, which has been oppressing the Poles for a long time.[72]

He reminded the Countess of Alexander's broken promises and of the worsening conditions since the accession of Nicholas to the throne; having lived in the Polish provinces for many years, and travelling annually to Volhynia, he had observed personally the deteriorating conditions of the inhabitants. Everything had worsened during the reign of Nicholas: "Intolerance of nationality (*narodowość*), intolerance in religion and in administration intensified . . . and the Poles cannot tolerate this."[73]

Lelewel, given the opportunity to express his opinions at the meeting, impressed no one with his remarks. The Countess assured him that she intended to repeat his arguments to her husband who in turn would repeat them to the king. She asked Lelewel to be patient. The meeting ended at eight that evening. Lelewel and the other representatives of the Administrative Council returned to the capital to await further developments.[74]

The situation grew more serious while the delegation met with Constantine at Wierzbno. Polish regiments still under the Grand Duke's orders grew restive, and some joined the insurgents and succeeded in enforcing upon the government the decision to request immediate release of those Polish troops still under Constantine's command.

On the day following the Wierzbno meeting (December 3), Constantine issued a proclamation as Commander-in-Chief of the Polish forces, authorizing the Polish troops who accompanied him to return to Warsaw. That same day, he departed in the direction of the Lithuanian border, and on December 12, he crossed the frontier of the Congress Kingdom.[75] The day following Constantine's proclamation to the Polish forces at his command, the Administrative Council, now the only legal authority in Warsaw, formed a provisional government (*rząd tymczasowy*). Its seven members (Supreme Council) included Adam Czartoryski, Michał Kochanowski, Ludwik Pac, Julian U. Niemciewicz, Władysław Ostrowski, Leon Dembowski, and Joachim Lelewel. Its first task was to call for an extraordinary meeting of the Sejm, and in the absence of the Commander-in-Chief, they gave complete control of the armed forces to Józef Chłopicki, the old Napoleonic general and Constantine's antagonist.[76]

Chłopicki, an implacable adversary of revolution and popular government, refused to act as commander-in-chief under the collective authority of the provisional government. Supported by the army, he declared his loyalty to Nicholas I and proclaimed himself dictator. He assumed dictatorial powers on December 5 and announced that the Supreme Council would assist him in an advisory capacity.[77] He planned to serve as dictator until the meeting of the Extraordinary Diet, scheduled to convene on December 18. To assure his loyalty to Nicholas, Chłopicki sent an emissary to St. Petersburg with conciliatory proposals.[78] Meanwhile, heads of the various government departments, i.e., the Supreme Council, were named. Joachim Lelewel was named Minister of Education.

In his brief tenure as Minister of Education (December 5 to mid-January) during the Chłopicki dictatorship, Joachim Lelewel accomplished little. He proposed certain reforms of the university and presented projects for the organization of other schools in the Congress Kingdom.[79] However, within two months, the Sejm, in the process of reorganizing the government, temporarily eliminated the Ministry of Education, and Lelewel's proposals were aborted.

During the period of the dictatorship, Lelewel chose to remain isolated from the revolutionary groups in the capital, although he was the nominal head of the *Towarzystwo Patriotyczne,* the most active radical organization. Instead, he spent his time either at home or at the Ministry of Education. He sometimes sat in on the meetings of the Supreme Council, i.e., the council of Chłopicki's advisers.[80] Its major concern was to find a means of dealing effectively with the continuous unrest in Warsaw. Lelewel unofficially expressed his opinions about the unrest in the capital and predicted that a revolution was inevitable in the Congress Kingdom unless war was declared against the tsar.[81]

Chłopicki felt differently. He did not believe in the success of the insurrection and considered it madness for the Poles to hurl themselves against a power to which even Napoleon had yielded. He placed his sole hope in fruitful negotiations with the tsar.[82] While waiting for his emissary's return from St. Petersburg, Chłopicki rejected plans for a military offensive against the Russian forces submitted by his aides-de-camp. Finally, Chłopicki decided on purely defensive military preparations in the event of war with Russia.[83]

On December 18, the Extraordinary Diet convened under the presidency of Władysław Ostrowski.[84] It proposed to deal with the crisis which now spread to the provinces of the Congress Kingdom and to decide future actions. On the following day (December 19), the Chamber of Deputies unanimously declared the insurrection a national rising, and on December 20, it confirmed the two week old dictatorship of Chłopicki. He would now be responsible to a Sejm committee.[85]

The dictator's envoys to St. Petersburg returned on January 6. They informed the Polish government that Nicholas received them as private individuals rather than as representatives of the Congress Kingdom, and he refused categorically to make any concessions to the rebels. He demanded their unconditional surrender and promised a general amnesty only on condition of immediate surrender. In addition, they confirmed that Nicholas had issued mobilization orders to Dibich's Russian forces to move against the Congress Kingdom.[86]

Disheartened, Chłopicki submitted his resignation to the Sejm on January 17. Warsaw was in ferment. The *Towarzystwo Patriotyczne* used the press and street demonstrations to influence members of the Sejm to take firm and positive actions against the tsar's position.[87]

The Extraordinary Diet assembled again on January 19; this time as the highest authority in the Congress Kingdom.[88] In the midst of preparations for a war with Russia, the Diet appointed the Lithuanian Prince Michał Radziwiłł as the commander-in-chief of the armed forces in the Congress Kingdom. With the appointment of this Lithuanian prince as commander-in-chief, the question of extending the uprising beyond the borders of the Congress Kingdom and into the western provinces of the Russian Empire gained momentum.[89]

Representatives from Lithuania, Volhynia, Podolia, and the Ukraine organized the *Towarzystwo Braći Zjednoczonych* (The Association of United Brothers) and named Joachim Lelewel president. When the insurrection had erupted in Warsaw in November, Lelewel had been named president of the *Towarzystwo Patriotyczne* — to gain support for that organization and its cause. Now the Polish representatives from the western provinces of Imperial Russia believed that his name would attract support of their cause beyond the borders of Congress Poland. On January 24, 1831, a deputation of the *Towarzystwo Braći Zjednoczonych* presented an address to Lelewel which he, in turn, read at a joint session of the Sejm the following day.[90]

In the address, the *Towarzystwo Braći Zjednoczonych* proposed that the Polish question was one and indivisible to the Dvina and Dnieper Rivers and that all Poles represented one Poland.[91] Lelewel assured the delegation that the Sejm would do all in its power to help the subjugated Poles and that the union of the Congress Kingdom with Lithuania and Ruthenia (*Rus*) would be achieved.[92] This assurance by Lelewel came after the dethronement of Nicholas I and the exclusion of his heirs from the throne of Poland by the Sejm on January 25.[93] The Sejm dethroned Nicholas because he had proclaimed war on the Congress Kingdom. Until this time, Lelewel favored a negotiated, compromise solution with Nicholas.[94] Accepting the Act of Dethronement, Lelewel now supported fully the idea of expanding the revolt into the western provinces of the Russian Empire.[95]

Several days after the formal declaration of the Act of Dethronement, a new executive body, the National Government (*Rząd Narodowy*) was formed. On January 30, Lelewel was elected by the Sejm (now the National Assembly) as a member of the National Government. He reluctantly resigned his position in the Chamber of Deputies, the lower house of the Sejm. Lelewel served in the National Government with Adam Czartoryski, Wincenty Niemojowski, Teofil Morawski, and Stanisław Barzykowski until the military capitulation of the Poles to Paskevich and his imperial army in the late summer of 1831.[96]

With the dethronement of Nicholas on 25 January 1831 by the Sejm, the revolutionary National Government faced war with the formidable Russian Empire and the related problem of gaining diplomatic recognition from the major European powers. The crucial task of constructing a viable government also confronted it. Joachim Lelewel was especially concerned with the latter.

His *Trzy konstytucje polskie* (*Three Polish Constitutions*), conceived of during the period of revolt against foreign domination, is important as a political document and as an example of Lelewel's perceptiveness as a scholar.[97] In 1830–1831, the historian dedicated his study of the three Polish constitutions of 1791, 1807, and 1815 to his compatriots in the Sejm. He proposed that it serve as a guide for them in their task of establishing an effective government. In his introductory speech to the Extraordinary Sejm which convened on 18 December 1830, he indicated that it was unfeasible to return to the Constitution of 1791, no matter how attractive the idea appeared at the time. Times and conditions in 1830, he cautioned, differed considerably from those of 1791. For Lelewel, the 3 May 1791 Constitution was the best of Poland's three constitutions because it was not imposed on or introduced by external forces as were the constitutions of 1807 and 1815, but was the product of a national spirit (*duch narodowy*). Although it called for a constitutional monarchy, the 1791 constitution provided, nevertheless, for a republic — a *Rzecz-pospolita* — with an independent Sejm, in contrast with the Sejms of the Grand Duchy and the Congress Kingdom which were subservient to the king.[98] He now hoped that a knowledge of the historical documents, i.e., the constitutions, would serve the present assembly as a guide to action.[99] Here, as in his popular history for children published in 1828, he emphasized the didactic purposes of history. *Trzy konstytucje polskie* had little practical effect on the Sejm which met from December, 1830, until June, 1831. However, after 1833, translated into French and other languages, it served not only to popularize the Polish cause among liberals in western Europe but also as a critique of the aristocratic faction of Polish émigrés led by the monarchist Adam Czartoryski in exile after 1831.

Joachim Lelewel's primary concern in *Trzy konstytucje polskie* was the striving for the nation's full freedom and rule, political equality, representative authorities, responsibility of officials directly to the nation from the lowest to those holding highest office. He stated this in the preface to the French translation of his study of the comparison of three Polish constitutions which he wrote for the 1833 French edition when he was a political exile enroute from France to Belgium.[100]

In Lelewel's introduction to the French translation of *Trzy konstytucje polskie,* the political and social implications of the material are evident. He stated that in Poland the szlachta (gentry) alone enjoyed political privileges. He continued: "In place of the szlachta put the common inhabitants, the people; eliminate all differences based on caste and discover . . . the foundation of our fatherland is the people."[101] His comparison of three Polish constitutions, equally significant as an example of Lelewel's scholarship, reflected especially his perceptive analysis of Polish society and the adverse effects of the political privileges guaranteed to certain segments of that society. In his study, Lelewel sought rational explanations for the partitions of Poland as well as reasons for Poland's weaknesses. He compared the period in which the Constitution of 3 May 1791 was promulgated with the period of the 1807 Constitution of the Grand Duchy of Warsaw and the period of the Congress Kingdom and its Constitution.[102] Lelewel discussed what the Pole is capable of politically. The conclusions he reached were based on his reflections on several major problems: the historical bases of the various principles incorporated in the three constitutions; the validity of the principles at the time they were incorporated; the extent to which the principles were applicable in 1831.[103]

He was particularly concerned with the 1791 constitution, a document inspired by a national renaissance, a national spirit (*duch narodowy*) which guaranteed the principles of republican government and the freedom and authority of the szlachta. Lelewel found precedents for these principles of republicanism, freedom, and the authority of the szlachta deeply rooted in Poland's past (a common theme in his histories). He told his readers that Poland was a republic which dated back to the days of Władysław Łokietek, i.e., to the mid-thirteenth century. The Polish nation was the politically conscious szlachta. Poland had a king, but the szlachta had a unique position. They shared a *gminowładztwo,* a communal authority. Eventually the power of the nation declined, but in 1791 a reversal occurred. The nation prepared a constitution in 1791 which would revive its past virtues. In this constitution of 3 May 1791, the szlachta preserved its freedoms and authority. Among other things, the szlachta allowed the townsmen political citizenship and thus added new strength to the *Rzeczpospolita.*[104] The aristocracy, i.e., the magnates, were not satisfied. "Thinking only of improving their own status with the help of foreign powers, they brought about the loss of the Republic, the nation, and the state."[105]

The question arises: how did Lelewel define a nation? In the text, he stated that the nation was the politically conscious gentry class — the szlachta. Thus, when he called for the nation's full freedom, republicanism, responsibility of officials to the nation, and political equality, it is plausible to assume that he was referring to the szlachta who lost these attributes as a result of the growth of the power of the magnates in the eighteenth century. But he also spoke of people's rule. This implicated all other social strata (*lud*) — the townsmen, peasants, and Jews. These elements had been excluded from political participation by the 1815 Constitution. Yet, they all shared a potential love of the fatherland (*ojczyzna*), and if embued with a national spirit (*duch narodowy*), they, too, would participate actively and productively in the political life of the fatherland. For Lelewel, equating the nation with the szlachta was no longer adequate. It was the broader definition of nation which was essential to him.

Discussing the causes of the partitions of Poland, Lelewel cited foreign interference, including the meddling of the Jesuits in the period of the Counter-Reformation. But these were not the only contributing factors. The traditional Polish nation, i.e., the szlachta, was

also responsible for Poland's downfall. Above all, the unwise administration of the laws by those in responsible positions resulted in the
weakening of the internal structure of the Polish state. This made the
Rzeczpospolita susceptible to foreign domination. The downfall of
Poland was not caused by the fact that for five hundred years she had
republican institutions but that they degenerated from abuse.[106] He
continued, stating that although there were no slaves in Poland as
there were in America, all Polish people did not participate in the
political life of the nation because these privileges were held only by
the gentry.[107] He intimated that it was again time to extend political
rights to other segments of the population. The implications of his
study and comparison of three Polish constitutions for Western
Europe and the Polish émigrés after 1831 has been alluded to. The
meaning for the Sejm in the Congress Kingdom in 1830–1831 was
clear. The Sejm must establish a government encompassing all strata
of society, for the basic tenets on which the *Rzeczpospolita* had been
established were fundamentally sound. Although the Sejm could not
expect the 1791 constitution to work now, its members could adapt
its principles to contemporary conditions and include all segments of
society, all strata of the population.

Analyzing the effects of the partitions of Poland, Lelewel proposed
in the text of *Trzy konstytucje polskie* that, as a result of the partitions, all classes which had existed in the Republic were levelled
because

> . . . the szlachta and nonszlachta completely lost their rights,
> were equally deprived of their political life, were made equally
> servile. For an entire generation, the Polish nation, deprived of
> its rights and freedom, in servitude, forgot about its national in-
> stitutions, about its citizenship in the *Rzeczpospolita*. . . .[108]

Now he emphasized the need for the unity of all classes in society. The
day the Extraordinary Diet convened (18 December 1830) became
the signal for regaining political independence and national autonomy.[109] Lelewel's belief that man is a political animal and that unity
would result only if the *lud*, i.e., the people, would support the traditional leaders, the szlachta, led him to advocate that all social and
ethnic groups had to be considered as members of the nation. He
repeated this in the preface to the 1833 edition:

> . . . As long as the peasants and all townsmen do not return to the

complete rights of citizenship, as long as they are not called to political life . . . , as long as their needs are not met, one cannot expect the freedom and independence of Poland.[110]

The constitutional question was never resolved by the National Assembly in 1831 because of military defeat, but it became a preoccupation of the Polish émigrés in exile after the defeat of the insurrection. However, important deliberations concerning the status of the peasants in the Polish lands commenced in the National Assembly in the winter of 1831 — when it became a matter of utmost significance to attract the generally apathetic and apolitical peasants to the national movement. In the debates which followed, the resolution passed by the Great Sejm in May, 1791, giving peasants legal rights and protection, and Kościuszko's proclamation of emancipation in May, 1794, were mentioned as precedents. The land question was also considered, and the National Government proposed to allot lands to the peasants on the national domains and to make the peasants rent-paying tenants on the private estates.

In the course of the deliberations, Alojzy Biernacki, a representative of the Kalisz group, presented a project for discussion which aroused heated debate. He emphasized those national benefits which would accrue with peasant emancipation and proposed that peasants not be given the "right of ownership" of the land, but instead, that they be permitted to pay rent (*oczyńszowanie*). Lelewel participated in these debates and supported Biernacki.

In "*Nadanie własności ziemskiej włościanom*" ("Granting Property Rights to the Peasants") which appeared in *Nowa Polska* (*New Poland*), the organ of the *Towarzystwo Patriotyczne*, on 18 March 1831, Lelewel appealed to public opinion to support the proposal to make peasants on the private estates rent-paying tenants. He also favored granting land to those peasants who served in the military.[111]

Ultimately it was decided (April 18) to postpone a decision on the peasant question until the recovery of the western provinces by the Congress Kingdom. However, the deliberations of the Diet attracted the attention of the Tsar Nicholas I. As a result, he issued a decree (May 18, 1831), lessening the burdens of the peasants in the western provinces. This opportunistic, imperial Russian policy set the peasantry against the predominantly Polish nobility, and eliminated the possibility of the insurgents gaining the crucial support of the peasants.[112]

Lelewel again spoke of the need for social reform on 29 May 1831 at a meeting of the *Towarzystwo Patriotyczne,* called to commemorate the six-month anniversary of the November uprising.[113] According to Lelewel, the 29th of November was memorable for two reasons: first as the date of a national uprising in which the Sejm and the nation in the Congress Kingdom and the Poles in Lithuania, Volhynia, Podolia, and the Ukraine joined the political struggle; second, November 29th marked the renewal of the social revolution which began with the Great Sejm when that august body drafted the 3 May 1791 Constitution. This social revolution continued during the period following the partitions and the current Sejm, i.e., the National Assembly, supported it. He added that the social revolution must be completed by the time of the restoration of Poland.[114]

The timing of the speech was unfortunate. Considerable internal conflict had developed among the Sejm members between April and June of 1831, and when the Diet assembled in Warsaw on May 31, in an aura of great dissatisfaction with the government, a debate on the organic nature of the state commenced. This debate took precedence over the more imperative issues of peasant emancipation and military reorganization.[115]

By early May, the conflict between two political systems — represented by Niemojowski's Kalisz group and the monarchist Czartoryski's supporters — crystallized. The clamor for a change in personalities in the National Government followed. As a result of his speech of May 29 to the *Towarzystwo Patriotyczne,* Lelewel's critics from both camps called for his removal, emphasizing the incompatibility of his position in the government with his new radical position in the patriotic society.[116]

Accused of propagating "republicanism and social revolution and endangering the diplomatic program of the government," Lelewel nevertheless received a vote of confidence when the Sejm chose to retain the National Government, and he continued to serve in that government until August. Critically needed social and political reform projects were paralyzed by internal quarrels and aborted by diplomatic failures and military defeats in late summer.[117]

On August 17, 1831, General Krukowiecki, one of the instigators of the Warsaw street riots of August 15–16, replaced Czartoryski as President of the National Assembly. Małachowski was given the chief military command.[118] Less than one month later (September 8), the victorious General Paskevich (who replaced Dibich who died of cholera on June 10) entered Warsaw. Sporadic fighting continued for several weeks. The insurrection was finally suppressed in October,

1831. The Congress Kingdom ceased to exist with Nicholas's army in control. Joachim Lelewel joined several thousand émigrés who sought refuge in the liberal capitals of Western Europe.[119]

Lelewel, in the course of 1830–1831, entered the Administrative Council, then the National Government. As President of the *Towarzystwo Patriotyczne* he worked for moderation until the spring of 1831 when he submitted to the radical elements in this patriotic organization, especially regarding the question of peasant emancipation. Before the Sejm declared the November outbreak a national uprising, he traveled to Wierzbno with other members of the Administrative Council in the hopes of resolving rationally the problems which emerged as a result of the actions of the cadets and students in Warsaw. He voiced loyalty to the dictatorship of Chłopicki who in turn expressed allegiance to the tsar-king. When the insurrection was declared a national rising and the king, Tsar Nicholas I of Russia, dethroned, he supported the actions of the National Assembly and worked diligently for the success of the Polish cause.

In the course of the revolution and war with the Russian Empire which followed, Lelewel's political and social ideas crystallized and radicalized, especially his belief in the republican form of government and in the need to improve the conditions of the peasants for the "national good." These views were best expressed in his *Trzy konstytucje polskie* and in the political tracts he wrote and speeches he made in the course of 1830–1831.

In his study of three Polish constitutions, Joachim Lelewel analyzed the constitutions of the *Rzeczpospolita,* the small, autonomous Grand Duchy created by Napoleon, and the Polish Kingdom created by the Congress of Vienna by considering the social as well as the political implications of these three documents. He did not consider the constitutions as isolated documents but in the spirit of their times. He believed that Poland's decline was due to numerous external factors. He also stressed the internal situation which was not due to weaknesses inherent in the constitutions but to the transgressions of the traditional ruling class of Polish society — the szlachta — and to the abuses of power by the magnates who represented the uppermost strata of the szlachta.

Lelewel's knowledge of Poland's past weaknesses and the conclusions he reached as a result of his analysis not only reflected his political and social consciousness but also the clarification of his thought and his deepening patriotism. Once a national revolution was declared, he wanted to see the resurrection of the Polish state. He called for the unification of the Congress Kingdom and the Polish provinces of the Russian Empire and the extension of constitutional privileges to those provinces — which Alexander I had promised in his speech to the Sejm in 1818. Only in exile did Lelewel advocate the recreation of a Polish state with the boundaries of 1772. In 1830–1831, not wanting to antagonize Berlin or Vienna, he accepted the idea of more limited boundaries, even though for him, the partitions of Poland could not be justified under any circumstances.[120]

In his political tracts and speeches of this period of instability and turmoil, Lelewel pointed out how the constitution of 1815 had been abused by the Tsars Alexander I and Nicholas I, and promises to extend constitutional privileges to Lithuania, Volhynia, Podolia, and Ruthenia remained unfulfilled.[121] Thus he supported the Sejm declaration of the dethronement of Nicholas as king and its recognition of the insurrection which erupted in Warsaw as a national rising. When he gave his speech before the Extraordinary Sejm in Warsaw on 10 June 1831, he stated rather emotionally: "Do not ask me whether I am a royalist or a republican. It is sufficient at this time that I am a Pole, and I am concerned with Polish affairs."[122] Nevertheless, his republicanism inhered in all his political tracts and speeches and in his *Trzy konstytucje polskie.*

In calling himself a Pole above all, he apparently cited himself as an example for everyone, irrespective of social and political position, to follow in order to guarantee the success of the National Assembly in its task of reforming the government.[123] But was this not utopian on his part? His definition of the Polish nation was a radical departure from the concept held by the more conservative szlachta (even members of the Kalisz group) and, in particular, the magnates who saw themselves as the political leaders of the nation. The traditional ruling classes wanted political independence, a monarchy, and the preservation of the existing social order. Unlike Lelewel who favored social reform and a democratic republic, they paid little attention to either political rights for or the social improvement of the people. Political independence from the Russian Empire was a common goal after the dethronement of the Romanov king of Congress Poland. Change in the social and political status of the most politically astute segment of Polish society was another matter. The political and social views Lelewel, the intellectual, expressed antagonized many and contributed to the lack of unity among those who were handed the reins of government as a result of the events which began on November 29, 1830.[124]

On 11 June 1831 the Sejm to which Lelewel dedicated his *Trzy konstytucie polskie* vetoed reform. By September the rebels' defeat by the Russian military was assured, and on 18 October 1831 Tsar Nicholas I of Russia, dethroned monarch of Congress Poland, abrogated by decree the Constitution of 1815 and incorporated the Congress Kingdom into the Russian Empire. In the fall of 1831 most members of the National Government found themselves in exile. By the end of October, 1831, Joachim Lelewel found his way to Paris by way of Prussia. Lelewel's advocacy of republican political and democratic social principles intensified after his exile in 1831. He found little time for scholarship during his first years in emigration because he devoted all his efforts to the imperative political tasks facing him and his fellow exiles.

5   Lelewel the Émigré

Rebel v. Despotism: France, 1831–1833

Joachim Lelewel's national ideas and his active participation in the politics of rebellion against the Romanov king and tsar determined his immediate future.[1] In the fall of 1831, as Imperial Russian forces moved to secure Warsaw, Lelewel, condemned a traitor by royal decree, joined the thousands of political exiles who sought refuge in the liberal capitals of western Europe. This "Great Emigration" included Poland's intellectual elite, and it represented the center of Polish political life for two decades following the defeat of the Polish insurgents in 1831.[2] During the first three years following 1831, Lelewel dominated Polish political life in exile by his devoted leadership on behalf of the Polish national cause, and more significantly, by the power and influence of his national ideas.

The French liberal press heralded Lelewel's imminent arrival in Paris.[3] Respectable idealists and moderate republicans, prominent members of the French Chamber of Deputies, men such as Lafayette, Odilon-Barrot, Mauguin, and others, knew of Joachim Lelewel's reputation as a scholar and extended their welcome to him. Moreover, these French leaders, recent participants in the July Revolution in their own country, shared fundamental political and ideological beliefs with the Polish scholar-patriot now in their midst.[4] Many had participated in the *Comité central en Faveur des Polonais,* organized in the immediate aftermath of the November uprising to help the distressed Poles.[5]

When he arrived in Paris, Lelewel met with sympathetic Frenchmen, and he promptly joined the apolitical Provisional Committee of the Emigration (*Komitet Tymczasowy Emigracji*), headed by the liberal, last President of the Polish National Government, Bonawentura Niemojowski. This Provisional Committee disbanded in a matter of a few weeks when a considerable number of its members, including Joachim Lelewel, organized what they considered a permanent and politically active organization with influential French political connections.[6]

The new, Paris-centered Polish émigré organization, the Polish National Committee (*Komitet Narodowy Polski*) was sponsored by General M. de Lafayette. Sympathetic to the Polish uprising of November 1830, Lafayette presided over the French counterpart of the Polish National Committee, the *Comité polonaise.*[7] *Le National,* the influential moderate republican French newspaper edited by Armand Carrel, became an important vehicle in which the Polish exiles, Lelewel and others of all political persuasions, expressed themselves.

Organizational meetings of the Polish National Committee were held in early December, 1831.[8] Officers and a Standing Committee were selected. Joachim Lelewel was chosen president and served in that capacity until the French government ordered the Polish National Committee to disband one year later.[9]

The purpose of the Polish National Committee was defined and adopted at the same time. The Committee assumed the responsibility of looking after the material welfare and the national interests of those Poles recently forced to leave their homeland. It proposed, also, to speak on behalf of the Polish refugees to those governments which granted them asylum and to the various committees sympathetic to the refugees.[10]

The Committee's primary concern was to provide for the material welfare of civilian and military émigrés.[11] Concern for the Poles' national interests involved attempts to gain broad support among the Polish émigrés for the Polish National Committee, and to scrutinize, criticize, and protest when necessary, those official policies of the French government which directly concerned the Polish refugees.[12] Most significantly, however, the Committee proposed to constantly focus public attention on the Polish question.

Encouraged by Joachim Lelewel's commitment, leadership, and guidance, the Polish National Committee promptly adopted a patriotic national program. The organization called for the establishment of a free and independent Poland with pre-1772 boundaries; a Poland with a republican form of government (comparable in many ways to the Polish-Lithuanian Commonwealth); a Poland with a democratic society where the nation (*naród*) consisted of all the people, all social classes; a multi-national Poland where all ethnic groups (Poles, Lithuanians, Ukrainians, and Jews) would live in harmonious federation.

Based in a fundamental adherence to the principles of the rights of man (*sprawa ludzkości*), the political program adopted by the Polish National Committee emphasized opposition to despotism in general and to tsarist despotism in particular.

Once these general principles were adopted by the Polish National Committee, Joachim Lelewel incorporated them into a series of petitions, appeals, declarations, letters, and speeches. Each was addressed to a particular audience. Forceful, progressive ideas, properly and eloquently expressed, became Joachim Lelewel's (and the Polish National Committee's) most powerful weapon, not only on behalf of the national interests of the Poles, but also on behalf of the national interests of all the progressive forces of mankind. Aimed specifically against anachronistic and barbaric despotism, especially its tsarist form, Lelewel's weapon was bound to succeed, in the name of the progressive perfection of mankind.

On Christmas Day, 1831, the Polish National Committee in Paris made its political debut when it issued a proclamation: "To the Polish Warriors."[13] In this document, written by Joachim Lelewel, the Polish National Committee recognized the sad plight of wanderers without fatherland and freedom and attempted to instill hope and confidence that they, the unfortunates, would ultimately persevere. In the proclamation, despotism and tsarism are blamed for the current misfortunes of the Poles who have a proud heritage. The proclamation concludes with patriotically inspiring, but politically explosive, words: "Poland, Poland of the Jagiellonians, freedom and independence, or eternal death! This is our struggle."[14] The document is not only anti-tsarist, it also publicly and openly calls for an independent Poland, not the Congress Poland of 1815 but a sixteenth century Poland, one with pre-1772 boundaries. The proclamation's final words proposed a solemn vow to continue the struggle against tsardom to the death or until the objective of a free and independent Jagiellonian Poland is achieved.

This proclamation was followed by petitions to progressive representative institutions of government in France and Great Britain. Lelewel, again on behalf of the Polish National Committee, wrote the petition which was presented to the French Chamber of Deputies by Mauguin, a prominent member of the opposition.[15] The petition to the French Chamber of Deputies reflected the Committee's concerns with the economic hardships which the Polish refugees experienced and with the French government's restrictions of the personal freedoms of the Polish exiles. For example, the Polish military was pro-

hibited from settling in Paris and was assigned to specific depots in
Avignon and Chateauroux. Civilians were required to settle in Bes-
cançon. Only eminent leaders were allowed to settle in Paris.[16] The
Chamber of Deputies was asked to alleviate these restrictions. More
politically explosive, however, was the third request made in the petition. The Polish National Committee requested permission from the
French government to establish separate Polish legions on French
soil. In return the Committee, recognizing France as the leader of
progressive Europe since 1789, vowed to follow the French Tricolor
anywhere in the cause of freedom and the rights of man.[17]

Almost simultaneously with the "Declaration to Polish Warriors"
and the petition to the French Chamber of Deputies, Joachim Lelewel
and the Polish National Committee began to prepare a petition to the
British House of Commons. Lelewel and members of the Committee
diligently gathered the signatures of approximately 1,000 Committee
members.[18] The petition opened with an appeal to the principles of
the rights of man which Europe, in the last sixty years, permitted
despots to violate. It blamed despots for the partitions of Poland, for
the dispersion of Poland's people, and for the destruction of the independence and sovereignty of the Polish nation, a nation which had
existed for almost ten centuries. It asked, in the name of the rights of
man, if the partitions of Poland by despots were to be considered
permanent. It put forth the case for historical Poland as a Christian
state which protected European civilization from Tartars, Turks, and
despotic Muscovy while living in peace with the rest of civilized
Europe.[19] It then traced the tragic history of the Poles since the partition of 1795 and reflected on the status of the Polish nation in this
current era of its misfortunes. It concluded by appealing to Great
Britain, the representative of model civilization, a state which recognized the principles of the rights of man. The appeal called specifically
for help for the Poles in their struggle against Russian despotism — a
common enemy shared by the British and the Poles.[20]

However noble the petition, this effort by Lelewel on behalf of the
Committee and all Polish émigrés ended in failure. The petition,
when finally presented before the British Parliament, elicited very
little support. Cutlar-Fergusson, D. O'Connell, and several others
spoke on behalf of the Poles, but no action resulted.[21] Throughout
the spring and summer of 1832, tsarist officials in the Polish realm
proceeded with a policy of cruel and intensive russification. The
Court of Saint James apparently considered the Russian action legiti-

mate and voiced no objections. The House of Commons, although sympathetic, was involved in its own, more serious affairs, i.e., the Irish Question and the Reform Bill of 1832.[22]

Appeals, declarations, and proclamations to Italians, Hungarians, Jews, Germans, and all other peoples denied their sovereignty and independence and living under foreign domination, soon appeared under the aegis of the Polish National Committee.[23] Firmly committed to the principle of the rights of man, Lelewel composed these proclamations for the Committee in the romantic spirit of an international brotherhood of people.[24]

In these, he expressed the goals of the struggle of the Polish nation —freedom and independence from despotic, arbitrary rule. He argued that although the Poles' primary struggle was against tsarist autocracy, they, the Poles, considered despotism everywhere their enemy. The Poles now asked their "brothers" to join them in their struggle for freedom and the liberation of historical Poland. Lelewel prophesied that the failure of the struggle of one nation, i.e., of the Poles, for freedom was a warning to other nations, to other peoples, that their struggles, too, would fail.

In addition to writing the appeals, declarations, and proclamations, Lelewel attended various public patriotic functions. Frequently he was an honored speaker. In March, 1832, he spoke before an audience of French republicans and refugees from now Russian held lands. This group met to commemorate the first anniversary of the uprising in Lithuania and Ruthenia (western provinces of Imperial Russia since 1815; historically an integral part of the Polish-Lithuanian Commonwealth).[25] First Lelewel spoke of the common interests of those present. These interests included the achievement of independence for all peoples. Expressing optimism about the future, he referred to the feats of the French army traveling through Lithuania enroute to Moscow during the dynamic Napoleonic era; to the ties among the Poles, Lithuanians, and Ruthenians; and to the firm unity of the Polish and Lithuanian nations as manifested in the Polish-Lithuanian Commonwealth. Finally, he referred to the ancient glory of Lithuania — a glory based on her defense of freedom and independence. This, he said, had been revived in the recent admirable struggle against tsardom.[26]

Lelewel then vividly described the origins of Lithuania and the historical role of her inhabitants. He called the latter the saviors of Ruthenia because they were responsible for protecting the Ruthenians from the Teutonic Knights. The Lithuanians were also protectors of the rights and freedoms of Novgorod, Smoleńsk, and Płock when these had been threatened by despotic Muscovy.[27]

Turning to the present, he stated that the nations of ancient Poland, i.e., the Poles, Lithuanians, and Ruthenians, subjugated since the partition of Poland of 1795, were again preparing to regain independence from despots.[28] He carefully distinguished the Russian autocracy from the Russian people, and he reminded his audience that the enemy was Russian autocracy. The achievement of independence and sovereignty, a goal shared by the French, the Poles, and the Lithuanians, was possible only on the basis of adherence to the principles of the rights of man and the equality of all peoples.[29]

Additional proclamations appeared. In "To the People of Israel," Lelewel recognized the existence of one family of man to which all peoples, Jews, Italians, Germans, and Poles belonged.[30] He identified the historic aspirations of the Jews for a homeland and compared these aspirations with those of the Poles. Both Jews and Poles shared several common experiences, notably oppression by despotic governments or rulers. Looking to history for examples, Lelewel reminded the Jews that in ancient times their people had suffered under the kings of Assyria, Egypt, and Babylon. The Poles, more recently, suffered under the despotic rulers of Russia, Prussia, and Austria. Both Jews and Poles shared a common, binding fate. Both were forced to wander in foreign lands. Sharing this common bond, they must now share another. Lelewel now urged the people of Israel to join the Poles for their common liberation and for the achievement of freedom for all peoples.[31]

He repeated the themes of struggle for freedom and the rights of man (*sprawa ludzkości*) against despotism and privilege, for freedom and equality before the law, and for national independence in proclamations addressed to the Italians, to the Hungarians, and to the Hungarian Diet.[32] The Italians, the Magyars, and the representative institutions of the Magyars were oppressed by Austrian despots. They shared this oppression by despots with the Poles. A common bond, therefore, existed among them, Lelewel insisted. He called on them to join the Poles in their struggle. Again he emphasized in these proclamations, as he did in all the others he wrote during the early 1830s: that the Polish cause was so closely related to the cause of all oppressed peoples that the defeat of the Poles' aspirations implied the inevitable defeat of all peoples in their struggle for liberation from despotic oppression.[33]

Lelewel condemned despotism everywhere, past and present, and he especially deplored tsarist despotism. In the spring and early summer of 1832, Lelewel waged a bitter and intense political campaign against despotism on behalf of the Polish National Committee. In early April, 1832, the official Imperial Russian announcement of the demise of the Polish realm appeared in the French press.[34] The Polish realm, i.e., the Congress Kingdom of 1815, was henceforth an integral part of the Russian Empire, subject to Imperial government and laws. The French government responded rather cautiously to this apparent violation of the Vienna settlement of 1815. France indicated that she did not intend to challenge the Imperial Russian action, in the name of peace and European stability. Simultaneously, the French government promised to continue to provide humane and hospitable political asylum for foreign refugees, Poles included, reserving the right to proscribe these refugees for the maintenance of order and stability.[35] Members of the government opposition in the Chamber of Deputies spoke against the official government position but could do nothing to change the situation. The Russian tsar, Nicholas I, proceeded with his policies of russification in the Polish realm while the Polish exiles stood helplessly by.

Within two weeks after the publication in France of the Imperial Russian *Ukaz* and the Organic Statute, Lelewel and the Polish National Committee issued a lengthy condemnation of the Russian tsar's actions in the Polish realm.[36] Boldly, Lelewel charged Nicholas I with the violation of the Treaty of Vienna (of 1815) which guaranteed the Poles special liberties and institutions, as well as Poland's political independence. With the promulgation of the Organic Statute, the tsar not only flagrantly violated the Vienna settlement but also Poland's oldest traditions and laws (specific reference was made to the abrogation of civil law — to the Lithuanian Statute). Calling Nicholas a despotic tyrant, Lelewel now accused the Russian tsar of usurping the promises of his predecessor Alexander I and condemned him for his barbaric use of terror and violence against his victims in the Polish homeland.[37] Apparently, Lelewel's public criticism brought no significant response. The French government opposition (men such as Lafayette, Mauguin, and Odilon-Barrot) continued their tacit support of the Polish cause, and the French government continued its cautious relationship with the Imperial Russian government. For the latter, the maintenance of domestic tranquility and the peace of Europe remained paramount, rather than the achievement of the political objectives of refugees in France.

A relatively minor incident which occurred in Paris in the first week of June (i.e., the week of 6 June 1832) made Joachim Lelewel suspect by the French government.[38] At the time, Lelewel was one of several foreign émigrés who participated in a patriotic demonstration at the funeral of General Lamarque. A leading member of the republican opposition in France's Chamber of Deputies at the time of his death, Lamarque was also a popular national hero. He had participated with Napoleon in the Italian campaign and had fought alongside Napoleon at Waterloo. He had also championed the cause of the Poles, Italians, and others. The funeral ceremony, initially planned as a patriotic and popular final tribute to a national hero, was transformed suddenly into an imposing and violent protest against the French government of Louis Philippe and the policies of the *juste milieu*. Lelewel was implicated because he gave one of the eulogies and because of his close, personal relationship with the leaders of the French republican opposition. The government apparently feared a repetition of the July Revolution of 1830. Speaking out in the French press against tsarist policies in the Polish realm acknowledged as legitimate by the French government was considered a right guaranteed by French laws. Active participation in what became a violent anti-government demonstration in Paris resulted in Lelewel's being watched rather closely by French authorities.

Within one week after the funeral demonstration, Lelewel experienced more than just the discomforts of surveillance. He faced the wrath of both the Russian Ambassador in France, Pozzo di Borgo, and the French government. On 12 June 1832, on behalf of the Polish National Committee, Lelewel issued a proclamation "To Our Russian Brothers." This appeal, written by Joachim Lelewel and Adam Mickiewicz, the Polish poet, appeared in numerous newspapers throughout France.[39] Several thousand copies were circulated among Russian army officers stationed in the former Congress Kingdom.[40]

Lelewel consistently condemned despotism everywhere, past and present. In this proclamation, he distinguished between the despotic tsarist rulers of the Russian Empire and the Russian people. The latter belonged to the family of man. They suffered under despotism as did the Poles and others. Condemning tsarist despotism, Lelewel reminded the Russians of the common Slavic heritage they shared with the Poles, especially the belief in Slav freedom (*wolność sławiańska*).[41] The Russian and Polish people shared another common bond, one sealed firmly by the blood of martyrs in the cause of this freedom. Reminding the Russians of their abortive revolution of December,

1825, and the sacrifices of Pestel, Muravev, Bestuzhev, and others, he called for a joint struggle of Russians and Poles against despotic tsardom.[42] The appeal concluded with a reference to the slogan of the Polish uprising of 29 November 1830, a slogan which Lelewel had composed: "For Our Freedom and Yours" (*za naszą i waszą wolność*).[43] Rebelling jointly, the Poles and their Russian brothers would overthrow tsarist despotism and re-establish those primitive Slav virtues of freedom and independence which Russians and Poles alike had enjoyed in the past.

The appeals and proclamations, addressed to all progressive forces in Europe — to republicans and liberals in France and Great Britain and to all peoples subjugated by tsarist autocracy or other forms of despotism — represented the national and political aspirations of Joachim Lelewel. Firmly committed to the principles of the rights of man, he opposed despotism in all forms. But he especially opposed the tsarist form, for tsarist despotism was the major cause of past and recent misfortunes of the Poles. Firmly committed to the achievement of a liberated and free, historic Poland, he wanted to see the establishment of republican institutions and the creation of a democratic society there, once despotism was overthrown. Believing in the power of ideas, he set out, from the vantage point of early nineteenth century Paris to gain support for his cause, which was the cause of all peoples. However, his most recent activities against the tsar and the potential influence of his inflammatory ideas aroused the concern of the Imperial Russian government.

The Russian Ambassador in France, Pozzo di Borgo, intervened diplomatically and requested that the French government expel Lelewel and those members of the Polish National Committee who signed the appeal "To Our Russian Brothers."[44] The Russian Ambassador expressed his government's grave concern that this document was an incitement by Polish émigrés to rebellion. Indeed, Lelewel's appeal to the Russians called for an overt struggle by Poles and Russians to liberate Slavdom from despotic tsarist and German (i.e., Austrian and Prussian) oppression. In addition, the Imperial Russian government objected strenuously to the solemn tribute paid to the participants of the Russian uprising of December, 1825.[45]

Official French government interests coincided with those Imperial Russian concerns expressed by the Russian Ambassador. As a result, the government of Louis Philippe ordered the Polish National Committee to disband and its officers to leave Paris. The French Minister of Foreign Affairs, de Broglie, personally warned Lelewel that the

Polish émigré leaders were not to associate with those French republicans who opposed the government.[46] The French Minister of Internal Affairs enumerated the conditions for the dispersion of the Paris Poles. The latter were required to inform the French authorities precisely where they planned to go. They were forbidden to settle in certain areas of France, specifically in the western departments, in large towns, border towns, port cities, in the Vendee, and not within a comfortably safe distance of Paris (fifty *lieues*). No two members of the Polish National Committee were permitted to resettle in any one given place.[47]

Lelewel performed one last service to the Polish national cause before he left Paris in late December, 1832. Four days after the Polish National Committee was ordered to disband (28 December 1832) and shortly before Lelewel left for La Grange, Lafayette's estate, he helped to organize a secret, conspiratorial revolutionary group, the Vengeance of the People (*Zemsta Ludu*).[48] With the French *Charbonnerie,* the Vengeance of the People prepared for a new rising in the Polish lands in the spring of 1833. The new Polish rising was to be coordinated with outbreaks which were planned for Germany and other parts of Europe in 1833.[49] With the creation of the Vengeance of the People, Lelewel accepted a policy of joint conspiratorial activity with oppressed peoples throughout Europe. In the proclamations he had written for the Polish National Committee, a common theme persists, i.e., firm opposition to despotism in all forms. Only if the tsarist and other despots were overthrown would an independent, progressive Poland be established. Now, in a united effort, all European despots — Austrian, Prussian, and Russian — would be overthrown. Lelewel submitted willingly to the demands of the general revolution planned for 1833 because revolution was the means by which his goals would be achieved.

Lelewel's immediate objective was to plan an expedition of émigrés to the homeland to establish contact with Polish conspiratorial groups there. Leaders of the proposed expedition included Józef Zaliwski, one of the instigators of the November uprising in 1830 in the Congress Kingdom.[50] The revolution was to be organized in Galicia. Using Galicia as their base, the conspirators planned to proceed to Russian held Polish lands where the actual revolt would first occur. Walerian Pietkiewicz and Wincenty Tyszkiewicz, both actively associated with Lelewel in the Polish National Committee in Paris, traveled to Kraków and Galicia as representatives of the Vengeance of the People to prepare for Zaliwski's arrival.[51] Armed with revolutionary rhetoric and propaganda, they established preliminary contacts with two conspiratorial groups there — the Association of Twenty-One (*Związek dwudziestu jeden*) and the Nameless Association (*Związek bezimienny*). Additional contacts were to be made in the homeland by Zaliwski and his group.[52] Zaliwski's plans also included a diversionary tactic which would involve Imperial Russian forces so that they could not be used against those outbreaks planned to erupt simultaneously in central and western Europe, e.g., in Frankfurt and in Switzerland. Although the European revolution received priority over a distinctly Polish uprising, Lelewel, faithful to his belief in a united effort by all oppressed peoples to overthrow despotism, conceded to these plans.[53]

The Polish exiles embarked on their precarious mission and failed. The French government promptly discovered and exposed the conspirators' plans. In the spring of 1833, arrests by Austrian officials in Galicia and by tsarist authorities in the former Congress Kingdom followed.[54] Lelewel was arrested and detained briefly in La Grange on orders from the French Minister of Internal Affairs, but he was freed promptly when Lafayette intervened on his behalf.[55] Implicated in the extra-legal expeditions of the Polish refugees to their homeland, by late summer, Lelewel also was accused of contributing to the unrest in Frankfurt and Switzerland. As a result, he was ordered to leave France.[56]

Travelling on foot, he arrived in Brussels, Belgium, on 23 September 1833. Brussels was to be his home for the next twenty-eight years and the center of his political and scholarly activities. In Brussels, he continued to voice opposition to despotism, especially its tsarist form. He continually asserted his belief in the principles of the rights of man and the brotherhood of peoples. He also expressed his patriotic affection for Poland's history, especially for the period of the Polish-Lithuanian Commonwealth when republican institutions flourished. And he prophesied that the Poland of the future would be a republic with a democratic society. Away from the political center of Paris after 1833, Lelewel's active participation in politics diminished. He gradually resumed his interests in scholarship and produced some of his best studies in history and numismatics in Brussels.

What lasting, significant contributions did Joachim Lelewel make in the years 1831–1833 when he reached the pinnacle of his political influence? If a satisfactory answer is to be found, this question must be considered from the point of view of the early decades of the nineteenth century. In many respects, the early 1830s was a period of political innocence. Idealists, influenced by the French Revolutions of 1789 and 1830, aspired to the destruction of the old anachronistic European order — to the end of despotism — and to the dawn of a new millennium based on the principles of the rights of man. Joachim Lelewel was one of many such idealists. Devoted to the principles of the rights of man, he found the existence of despotism the greatest obstacle to the establishment of the millennium. To eliminate this obstacle was a major preoccupation of Lelewel in the years 1831 to 1833. His personal experiences in the tsarist dominated western provinces of the Russian Empire and in the Congress Kingdom with its Romanov king led, at least partially, to his focusing his efforts against despotism at its worst, i.e., despotism in its tsarist form. In exile in France, he organized two political groups to combat despotism. Both groups were shortlived. One, the Vengeance of the People, failed miserably. The other, the legitimate Polish National Committee, met with very limited success.

Lelewel's most successful weapon, in the final analysis, was the written word. The ideas he expressed in the declarations, proclamations, and appeals which appeared between 1831 and 1833 on behalf of the Polish National Committee entered into the mainstream of Polish political life. Lelewel not only raised the national consciousness of the Poles in exile and in the homeland. He also constantly reminded them and the other peoples to whom he addressed the various documents he wrote, that despotism was an oppressive and anachronistic institution, and he equated the Polish cause with the progressive forces in Europe. The re-establishment of the Polish state was possible, but Russian tsarism must be destroyed first.

Lelewel the Émigré

The Romantic Nationalist: Belgium, 1833–1861

In 1833, when Lelewel arrived in Brussels, Belgium had existed as an independent state for three years. In the past one hundred years, this small country had been dominated by Spain, Austria, and France. Since 1815, as a result of the Vienna settlement, Belgium had been united with Holland. The successful Belgian revolution occurred in the early fall of 1830, shortly after the July Revolution in France and one month prior to the abortive insurrection in Congress Poland. Fearing a general European revolution, the King of Holland requested the help of Russian Tsar Nicholas I and his allies to put down the Belgian unrest. In response, Nicholas called for the mobilization of Rusian forces and encouraged Prussia's and Austria's support. The Polish forces under Nicholas's brother the Grand Duke Constantine, Governor General of the Congress Kingdom, were to be the vanguard of the military intervention in Belgium. Meanwhile England and France came to the support of the Belgian separatists. The mobilization of Polish military forces by Constantine, on orders from Nicholas, to be used against Belgium, hastened the outbreak of the revolution in the capital of the Congress Kingdom. On November 29, 1830, the uprising occurred in Poland. This delayed the movement of forces by Russia against Belgium for almost a year. This also helped assure Belgium's victory. Independent Belgium became an important haven for those émigrés who fled from their Polish homeland in the wake of the failure of their uprising and war against Russia.[1]

In the two years that followed the revolutionary year 1830, Belgium received her independence with the support of Britain and France and with the help of the November uprising in the Congress Kingdom of Poland. However, the political situation was not yet stabilized when Lelewel arrived there in 1833. Belgian independence had been achieved, but no peace treaty with the government of Holland had yet been signed because of Holland's reluctance to recognize Belgium's claims to the provinces of Limburg and Luxemburg. Leopold of Saxe-Coburg was chosen King of Belgium and had to contend with this unresolved issue as well as with the status quo powers and the diverse revolutionary elements which gathered in his state.

Polish émigré officers were accepted to serve in the newly created Belgian army. For example, Jan Skrzynecki, Commander of the Polish military forces from 26 February to 11 August 1831, helped to organize the new Belgian army and headed it for a decade (1833–1844). Considerable sympathy for the Polish cause was expressed by the Burmeister of Brussels and by members of the Belgian Parliament, notably by Alexander Gendebein, a prominent leader of the government opposition. Although émigrés and political radicals were permitted entry into Belgium, the Belgian police watched them closely. Lelewel was no exception. His reputation as a republican and revolutionary preceded him, and by the time he arrived in Brussels, the *Sûreté Publique* (Ministry of Justice) had compiled a substantial dossier on him and watched him carefully.[2]

Arriving in Brussels on 23 September 1833, Lelewel settled "by coincidence" in a modest dwelling over a cabaret at *rue de Chene* 26 because a sign attracted his attention. Appropriately, the sign read: "*Estaminet de Varsovie.*"[3] With intense determination, he established contacts with those Polish émigré circles already in existence as well as with European revolutionaries.[4] Soon after his arrival, he met with those émigrés who had recently returned from their clandestine expeditions to the homeland. They informed him of the apathy toward an insurrection which they found there.[5] Two of the emissaries who had recently returned, Konarski and Borzewski, suggested to Lelewel that any uprising which was being planned should be postponed for a few years.[6] The pessimistic reports of those who returned, added to the news that Zaliwski had been imprisoned in Austria and the insurrection in Frankfurt (1833) in which Polish émigrés had participated had failed, substantiated the conclusions Lelewel reached at La Grange concerning his relationship with the Carbonari.[7] He also reevaluated his ideas of an insurrection in the homeland.

In a lengthy letter to Józef Zaleski, written shortly before the abortive Savoy expedition (1834) in which Polish émigrés also participated, Lelewel expressed his disillusionment with the haphazard policies and sporadic and fruitless actions of the Paris-centered Carbonari.[8] He stated that one should not depend on a general revolution for the resurrection of the Polish state but rely more on the cooperation of the population living in the partitioned Polish territories with the Polish revolutionaries in emigration. He rejected reliance on the help of others when he wrote: "The Polish nation cannot resurrect itself except at home and by its own forces . . . not by relying on help."[9] Lelewel did not, however, reject revolutionary action as the means by which to achieve his goal — the reestablishment of the Polish state. Only the focal point of his emphasis shifted, from reliance on and direction by sympathetic Frenchmen to a greater dependence on the Poles themselves.

> The liberation of Poland can come only from within the homeland — moves in Austria, Prussia, and Russia must be organized and united; the emigration cannot be depended upon to bear the entire burden.[10]

Another revolutionary exile, the romantic Joseph Mazzini, expressed similar ideas in the early 1830s concerning the regeneration of Italy. He, too, resented the Carbonarist tradition that France must lead in the European revolution, and he desired to break away from the Carbonari movement. He eloquently proposed that every nation had an historic mission to fulfill and convincingly argued that revolutions, to be successful, must have the support of all the people. Mazzini firmly believed that twenty million Italians, properly motivated and led, could defeat Austria without foreign aid.[11] The idealistic Mazzini envisaged a regenerated Italy taking its rightful place in a fraternal union of independent, democratic republics in a grand European federation.

In the spring of 1834, the mystical and messianic Mazzini organized a new international society which would function for the realization of his noble ideals. On April 15 of that year, six Italians, five Germans, and five Poles met in Bern, Switzerland and signed the Act of Brotherhood and created Young Europe. Shortly afterward, Young Poland, a filial branch of Young Europe, emerged in Switzerland. Branches were quickly formed in France by Joachim Lelewel's colleagues Walenty Zwierkowski and Walerian Pietkiewicz and by Karol Różycki and Bohdan Zaleski.[12] The most important of these branches was located in Tours, and the headquarters of the Central Committee of Young Poland was located there.[13]

Because of Lelewel's recent disillusionment with the Carbonari and his expressed beliefs that the Polish nation could resurrect itself only by the utilization of its own potential, enhanced and strengthened by broad social reforms, Lelewel joined Young Poland at the behest of his colleagues Zwierkowski and Pietkiewicz. In May, 1834, he organized a branch of Young Poland in Brussels.[14]

After he joined Young Poland, Lelewel placed less stress on the possibility of a general European revolution and more on the development of an effective national revolutionary movement. This involved not only developing a more effective cooperation among the Polish left in exile but also in establishing closer relations with Polish revolutionaries in the homeland. Consequently, another expedition to the homeland was planned. Lelewel's advice was sought on both these matters.[15]

The Polish radicals in emigration in the early thirties consisted of two major organizations — the *Towarzystwo Demokratyczne Polskie* (The Polish Democratic Society) and Young Poland. Many members of both were also Carbonari.[16] As the influence of the Carbonari on the Poles declined, several leaders of the Polish left believed that the political and ideological differences which separated the two major radical groups could be compromised and a more united, and effective, action on behalf of the Polish cause would result.

The incentive for the unification of the *Towarzystwo Demokratyczne,* Young Poland, and the Polish *węglarze* (Carbonari) came from Walenty Zwierkowski, Lelewel's alter-ego, in the fall of 1833.[17] Zwierkowski and Walerian Pietkiewicz wanted the newly established Young Poland to serve as the nucleus of a unified left emigration. Individuals would have joint membership, i.e., belong to both the *Towarzystwo Demokratyczne* and Young Poland. In order to prepare Polish society to achieve independence, the sphere of activity of the *Towarzystwo Demokratyczne* was to be limited to the emigration; Young Poland's efforts would be expended in conspiratorial activity in the Polish lands. In response to requests for advice in these matters, Lelewel expressed his opposition to the plans put forth by Zwierkowski, Pietkiewicz, and others. He criticized the Carbonari for its cosmopolitanism and expressed his distrust of the *Towarzystwo* which had broken away from his Paris organization less than two years earlier.[18]

Lelewel heartlessly criticized the Democratic Society in his correspondence with Zierkowski and Pietkiewicz. In his letters of November, 1833, and June, 1834, he inveighed against the cosmopolitanism and "Jesuitism" of this émigré organization.[19] In letters to

Konstanty Zaleski and Walerian Pietkiewicz, he again warned them of the cosmopolitanism of the *Towarzystwo Demokratyczne* while praising the "nationalism" of Young Poland.[20] In a letter to Pietkiewicz in Tours, Lelewel again found fault with the "cosmopolitanism and exclusiveness" of the Democratic Society and warned his colleagues that emphasis must be placed continually on the unique aspects of the Polish question.[21] He repeated his position to Walenty Zwierkowski in Paris in a letter of 25 November 1834 and added: "Remember you are Poles whose first responsibility is to your nationality (*narodowość*) and your fatherland (*ojczyzna*), then finally, to cosmopolitanism. . . ."[22]

Two days later he wrote to Walenty Zierkowski again. He now accused the *Towarzystwo Demokratyczne Polskie* of egoism, i.e., self-interest, a term he applied disparagingly to the Polish aristocracy in his historical writings. In this letter he called the *Towarzystwo Demokratyczne Polskie* "our szlachta republic in miniature,"[23] implying that the members abused that organization which had been founded on republican principles just as the szlachta had abused the institutions of the *Rzeczpospolita* in the seventeenth and eighteenth centuries. Again he emphasized the need for reform of the *Towarzystwo Demokratyczne Polskie* before it could be joined with Young Poland for the "joint activities in the homeland."[24]

Lelewel's expressions of opposition to and alienation from the *Towarzystwo Demokratyczne Polskie* paralleled his growing faith in the principles of Young Poland and Young Europe. Even after he learned from Walerian Pietkiewicz that the Democratic Society changed its emphasis from support of "solidarity of all revolutionary elements of all nations" to national revolution "through the nation to humanity and world citizenship. . . ,"[25] Lelewel continued to express his belief that, in reality, the *Towarzystwo Demokratyczne Polskie* would not change its attitudes. The *Towarzystwo Demokratyczne* and Young Poland remained separate entities, due in no small measure to the advice and influence of Joachim Lelewel.

Disillusioned with Carbonarism and distrustful of the *Towarzystwo Demokratyczne Polskie,* Lelewel weighed the prospects for the success of the national cause and concluded that unification of the two leading radical émigré organizations — the *Towarzystwo Demokratyczne Polskie* and Young Poland — each with its own sphere of activity delineated, could not be expected to achieve independence for twenty million people in the homeland.[26]

However, the tactics of conspiratorial activity by emissaries of the

Polish left in exile — unified or not — but in voluntary federation with a larger organization, i.e., Young Europe, still had possibilities despite Zaliwski's failures. In weighing the individual merits of the two left Polish émigré organizations, Lelewel chose to support Young Poland because it was more receptive to the national cause — to national liberation — and because the idea of a European revolution in coordination with a national revolt for the liberation of his homeland appealed to him. Lelewel accepted the practical objective of Young Europe, "the federal organization of European democracy under one sole direction, so that any nation rising in insurrection should at once find the others ready to assist it. . . ."[27] He felt that the humanitarian ideals of Young Europe were "beautiful and sacred thoughts."[28] Federation implied that Poland would work for her own independence with the moral support of other oppressed peoples of Europe. The humanitarian federalism of Young Europe was extremely compatible with Lelewel's national ideas. The practical goal remained: the political independence of his homeland. The achievement of this objective did not necessarily require a unified Polish emigration. The negotiations between Young Poland and the *Towarzystwo Demokratyczne Polskie* ended without practical results. Lelewel remained on friendly terms with individual members of the latter organization after the failure of the attempt to unify the Polish left in emigration.[29] Ultimately, in 1846, long after Young Poland ceased to exist, Lelewel joined the *Towarzystwo Demokratyczne Polskie.*[30]

In the latter part of February, 1835, Lelewel and his followers once again organized a conspiratorial group. It was to serve as the extra-legal arm of Young Poland. The *Związek Dzieći Ludu Polskiego* (The Association of the Children of the Polish People) established its headquarters in Brussels and planned a new expedition to the Polish homeland for the purpose of establishing contacts with the revolutionaries who already functioned there.[31] Szymon Konarski, a participant in Zaliwski's *partyzantka* and in the Savoy expedition and publisher of the radical émigré biweekly *Północ* (*Midnight*), was chosen to lead the new excursion to the homeland.[32] Armed with a false passport and a political program which called for national emancipation and various other social programs, Konarski embarked on his journey to Kraków in July, 1835.[33] From Kraków he planned to continue his odyssey across Galicia to Russian Poland.[34]

In the Polish lands, Konarski encountered numerous obstacles. Geographic isolation from the émigrés, the hostility of the szlachta in the homeland as well as the antagonism of the Ruthenian, Byelorussian, and Lithuanian peasants, and the competition of emissaries of the rival émigré groups whom he met in the Polish lands all contributed to the failure of Konarski's expedition.[35] Arrested in Wilno in May, 1838, Szymon Konarski appeared before a Commission of Inquiry headed by Trubetskoy. Tried by a military court (28 November 1838 to 25 February 1839), he was found guilty of subversion and was executed by a firing squad on 27 February 1839 in Wilno.[36]

Konarski's objectives remained unfulfilled. He had failed to unify all the independent democratic and republican elements in the homeland into one, "all Polish" organization. He also failed to gain the support of the masses — most were ethnically alien to the Poles — in the partitioned lands for the revolution which Young Poland, the *Związek Dzieći Ludu Polskiego,* and above all, Lelewel, believed would usher in an independent *Rzeczpospolita.* Konarski's execution by a firing squad, however, had one farreaching consequence. It gave Lelewel and the Polish émigrés a martyr for the holy cause of nationalism.

In the years that Konarski was in the homeland, Lelewel's participation in the political activities of the emigration declined significantly. However, he continued to express his political and social beliefs regarding the Polish question. He delivered speeches and wrote short histories of Poland and pamphlets in which he popularized the Polish cause. In this manner, he continued to exert a considerable influence on the Polish émigrés.

In November, 1836, he spoke at a meeting of Poles in Brussels who gathered to commemorate the sixth anniversary of the November uprising.[37] The theme of his talk revolved around the slogan of the 1830 uprising: "*Niepodległość, Całość, Wolność, Braterstwo, i Równość*" ("Independence, Unity, Freedom, Brotherhood, and Equality").

The Polish exiles (wanderers, Lelewel called them), Lelewel reminded his audience, represented a portrait of national misfortune and must continually keep in mind their proud heritage. They must never forget that their fatherland was an independent republic (*rzeczpospolita*) based on the principles of unity, freedom, brotherhood, and equality. He expressed his belief that independence could again become a reality if the Poles utilized their own potential.[38] He spoke of unity (*całość*), another important characteristic of the *Rzeczpospolita.* By "unity" he meant that all peoples — Ukrainians, Kashubs, Ruthenians, Lithuanians, and all the other inhabitants of the old *Rzeczpospolita* — were Poles and formed an integral part of the whole (*całość*) of the homeland.[39]

Freedom (*wolność*) was the soul of ancient Poland, but the principle was lost as the *Rzeczpospolita* developed and the szlachta gained dominance over the other inhabitants. Nevertheless, the principles of freedom and brotherhood must guide the Polish state of the future.[40] And "since the Polish nation never denied the principle of brotherhood to its neighbors, it could rest assured that with the progress of time and the liberation of the people (*lud*), it will again find the principle of brotherhood."[41]

Referring to the ideal of equality (*równość*), Lelewel spoke of an equality to be found in the sovereignty of the people, in democracy.

Concluding his remarks, he again reminded his émigré audience of their responsibilities to their past and to the future of the Polish nation and state, and he urged them to devote themselves wholeheartedly to the Polish cause.[42]

Between mid-1835 and the beginning of 1836, Lelewel wrote a brief history entitled *Polska odradzająca się, czyli dzieje Polski od roku 1795 potocznie opowiedziane* (*Poland in the Throes of Rebirth: A History of Poland since 1795 told in a Colloquial Manner*). The purpose of this study was to enhance national consciousness among Polish youth. The study covered the period of Poland's history from the third partition (1795) to the November uprising (1830–1831).[43] An autobiographical-popular study also dedicated to Poland's youth, it encompassed what Lelewel called the fifth period of Polish history. The author included this fifth period of "*Polska odradzająca się*" ("Poland in the Throes of Rebirth") as an integral part of *Dzieje Polski potocznym sposobem opowiedziane* in those editions published after 1836.[44]

Lelewel characterized this most recent epoch of Poland's history in the following manner:

> The present period . . . rolls along before our eyes; it is incomplete in its span of time, and my narrative of these events which are a part of my life is also incomplete — as are other contemporaries' narratives of this period. Fate had it that in the latest developments I find myself among people in national movements and prominent in guiding the development of the national question. Among these I count many differing in their opinions, personally ill disposed toward me. . . . This is a peculiar situation; one which was not a factor in my narratives of older histories. . . .[45]

Under these difficult circumstances, Lelewel consciously or sub-

consciously gave *Polska odradzająca się* an autobiographical character. The first one-third of this study dealt with the situation in the
three partitioned areas, with the Polish legions of the Napoleonic era,
the Grand Duchy of Warsaw, and the Congress Kingdom. The latter
two-thirds of the book dealt with the November uprising and its immediate aftermath in which the author actively participated.

Lelewel attempted to give a multifaceted picture of the uprising by
discussing its political, social, and military aspects. He developed the
major thesis that just as the Polish state fell in the eighteenth century,
the November uprising ended in defeat because it was dominated by
the magnates, aristocrats and diplomats, searching for foreign assistance. These dominant forces neither knew how nor wanted to take
advantage of strengths inherent in the nation. Lelewel stressed this
point repeatedly in his *Polska odradzająca się*. Napoleon also failed
because he neglected to consider the strengths and aspirations of the
Polish and other nations.[46]

The national aspirations of which Lelewel spoke inhered in the
Polish nation at the time of the November uprising to a greater extent
than during the Kościuszko uprising in 1794, but Lelewel observed
that no attempts were made in 1830 to improve the lot of the people so
that they struggled for their own benefit.[47] Polemicizing, he criticized
the political and social errors of the revolutionary National Government and the leaders of the uprising, and he praised the efforts of the
radical *Towarzystwo Patriotyczne*. He devoted several chapters to
elaborating on the need to enfranchise the peasants and to eliminate
the *pańszczyzna* (*corvée*): "Liberation from the yoke . . . equal and
full participation in citizens' tasks,"[48] he stressed. The latter statement reflected his growing concern with the need for social revolution
to accompany the political revolution he considered necessary to
overthrow tsardom and to establish the Polish state again.

Autobiographical because of the circumstances under which it was
written, *Polska odradzająca się* was primarily written for children.
As such it was didactic, optimistic, and deeply patriotic.

In his introduction Lelewel instructed the children to whom he
dedicated *Polska odradzająca się* not to equate the loss of political
independence with the death of the Polish nation; that in the forty
odd years of its bondage, the Polish nation not only did not die, but
also, on the contrary, was in the throes of rebirth. Although the process was slow, he advised that one should not lose hope and even certainty that Poland would again regain her independence — that
vigorous national virtues lived in the hearts of the Polish people,

especially in the youth. He urged the latter to keep the national traditions alive.[49]

In *Polska odradzająca się,* Lelewel frequently forgot that he was a scholar writing for children. Instead, he wrote an apologetic, a contemporary political document emotionally colored by the feelings and political outlook of an articulate émigré actively engaged in lively political activity in exile.[50] Two obvious examples may be cited: his comments on the Polish peasants mentioned above and his faith in the Poles' reliance on their own potentials for achieving the re-establishment of the Polish state.

> The rural, agricultural estate constitutes approximately one-half of ancient Poland's population. Where then must one look for strength, for the national uprising, but in *it*? What constitutes the nation if not it? Under these circumstances is it to be permitted that these people (*lud*) be constantly under the domination of the tsar or princes and never enjoy its own liberties and independence? Comprehend this, children, that these your fellow creatures, these your brothers, exploited for so many centuries, must be ensured the reform of their injustices... through their liberation from their yoke, through the elimination of the *pańszczyzna,* by providing them with the right to ownership of the land, by broadening their education, and by their total participation as citizens....[51]

This extremely subjective statement concerning the peasant question may be understood best if placed in the perspective of the 1830s, the period of Lelewel's most active participation in the political life of the emigration. In the decade of the thirties the social question, i.e., the issue of social reform, gained momentum among Polish émigré groups. Lelewel vehemently opposed the Czartoryski camp's reliance on traditional, diplomatic means for the creation of an independent Poland from the very beginnings of his exile. In the late thirties, the feud became critical as Lelewel publicly called for the Poles to rely on their own strength. This involved united action of the szlachta with the peasants, the most populous strata of traditional Poland's population. A prerequisite for this united action for Lelewel was the emancipation of the peasants in the Polish lands. This was the program Konarski took with him on his expedition to the homeland, while Lelewel concentrated his efforts convincing the émigrés of the need for social change for the peasants in the Polish lands.

Lelewel expressed another political belief directly related to his position regarding the peasant question in *Polska odradzająca się*. Joachim Lelewel, in the first years of emigration, expressed a faith in the help of others (his association with the Carbonari), and he had advocated united action, ostensibly first under French leadership, and then, after 1833, in federation with and participation in the Young Europe movement. However, while accepting the principles of Young Europe, he chose to concentrate on the activities of Young Poland, a filial branch of Young Europe, and emphatically stated that, in his opinion, the redemption of Poland could become a reality only by the development of her own potential and not by dependence on the help of others. He repeated this faith in the Poles in *Polska odradzająca się*.

> Those who wanted to rebuild the fatherland, instead of looking for and awakening their own potential, roamed as legionnaires, serving foreign governments and military leaders. Do not consider those evil who, after the unfortunate struggle, chose to wander, shunning Siberia and prisons; but grieve for those who, 'as brothers' left the fatherland and formed legions of wandering regiments which were decimated and eradicated in Algeria and Spain . . . woe to those people who seek foreign help; such shall never be free; they will always remain under the threat of dependence and subjugation.[52]

This forceful statement by Lelewel as well as his commentary on the peasants must be considered from the point of view of the milieu in which it was written. This was the period of Konarski's expedition to Poland. Lelewel's and his political associates' attention were focused on the homeland and the need to unite revolutionary forces there and in exile. *Polska odradzająca się*, patriotic, didactic, optimistic, played a significant role in stimulating the national feelings of its readers, young and old.

Ignacy Chrzanowski, Lelewel's sympathetic biographer, concurs with the historian Tadeusz Korzon, probably Lelewel's most articulate critic, that *Polska odradzająca się* had as its goal a heartrending emotional appeal.[53] In this respect, Lelewel's study belongs not to the list of his scholarly works, but to his numerous polemics which brought upon him resounding resentment and criticism from the Czartoryski camp and support of the left elements in exile. *Polska odradzająca się*, not so popular or objective as *Dzieje Polski potocz-*

nym sposobem opowiedziane, the text he wrote for children before the November uprising of 1830, nevertheless appeared in numerous editions. And the optimism Lelewel expressed in its pages not only influenced the development of national consciousness but also brought hope to the romantic nationalists of the nineteenth and twentieth centuries.[54]

The most succinct expression of Joachim Lelewel's national ideas appeared in 1836 in the French *Journal de Rouen* and in the Polish émigré journal *Naród Polski* published in Versailles.[55] The title of his article was "The Legitimacy and Rights of the Polish Nation." In this article, Lelewel stated that the legitimacy of the Polish nation was based on two major criteria — language and the political consciousness of Polish society. Political consciousness, he believed, was the most important unique characteristic of Polish society. Whereas other European societies acquired their attributes as a result of their interests in trade, industry, art, or commerce, the Poles developed theirs in the areas of politics and citizenship.[56] This political consciousness which differentiated the Polish nation from other nations, according to Lelewel, manifested itself in the periods of the Grand Duchy of Warsaw and the Congress Kingdom. However, it developed most fully in the period of the *Rzeczpospolita.* This Polish republic was founded on the principles of brotherhood and equality. The *Rzeczpospolita* acknowledged the sovereignty of the people and the principle of elective monarchy. This political consciousness was the basis of the legitimacy of the Polish nation and state. The Poles rightfully and justifiably sought the redemption of their homeland and the re-creation of an independent republic.[57]

Upon describing the major bases for the legitimate claims and rights of the Polish nation, Lelewel turned his attention to those who argued that Poland's "republicanism" caused her downfall; that only a small portion of one social class, i.e., the szlachta, participated in the politics of the *Rzeczpospolita.*[58] Responding to these criticisms, Lelewel stated that it was true that the people (*lud*) in the *Rzeczpospolita* was subjugated by a minority. He emphasized, however, that serfdom did not develop by law but by blatant abuses and that the Great Sejm (the Four-Year Sejm, 1788–1792) attempted to remedy this unfavorable situation. As a result of the reforms of the Great Sejm, the szlachta was obligated to free the people. This obligation, according to Lelewel, was another criterion for the Poles' claims for a nation state. He believed that Poland could not redeem her independence and integrity or resurrect her institutions until all the people were free.[59]

The author then traced attempts by the Poles to achieve this goal of emancipation in the period of the Grand Duchy. The constitution of the Grand Duchy indicated that all citizens were equal before the law. Lelewel interpreted this to mean that although the constitution retained the name szlachta and the principle of szlachta legitimacy, it nevertheless equated the szlachta with the nonszlachta and peasant citizens.[60]

In the Congress Kingdom, a number of peasants exercised political rights of citizenship. In the western provinces of the Russian Empire requests to free the people were made to Alexander I, and in the period of the last uprising, in Zmudż and in the Ukraine, numerous citizens granted full freedom to the peasants.[61] The present émigrés sought to include all the people in the political activities of the new Polish state. Lelewel cited these developments as evidence that the Polish nation was in agreement with the movement and progress of mankind. Young, renascent Poland must be established on the firm foundation of independence, unity, sovereignty of the people, and republican institutions.[62] Whereas many peoples needed to eliminate their old claims to legitimacy and to search for new principles, the Polish nation needed only to seek and to develop further its established traditions — the traditions which a knowledge of Poland's history revealed.

In the years that followed the publication of the three political documents discussed above, Lelewel continued to advocate the national ideas he enunciated so succinctly in them. But as the years progressed, he frequently expressed them in mystical, religious metaphors. The most obvious example of this was his address to an audience gathered to commemorate the martyrdom of Szymon Konarski (d. 1839) approximately six months after the latter's execution by Russian military authorities in Wilno.[63] In this commemorative address, Lelewel compared the oppressed Polish nation which offered up Konarski as its sacrifice with humanity which had offered Christ for its redemption.[64] He then instructed his audience to emulate Konarski's righteousness and dedication to the national cause and humanity and to strive to achieve Konarski's objectives.[65]

Lelewel continued to use religious metaphors in the few public addresses he delivered in the years immediately following Konarski's execution. In contrast to his political activity in the early years of his exile, between 1839 and 1842, Lelewel participated only at the annual meetings of Poles in Brussels to commemorate the anniversaries of the November uprising.[66]

His withdrawal from active participation in émigré politics, however, was only temporary. Elected President of the *Komitet Narodowy Polski* of the *Zjednoczenie Emigracji Polskiej* (The Polish National Committee of the United Polish Emigration), he wrote a series of appeals and proclamations to the Poles and to the peoples of Europe.[67] These petitions and declarations reflected the national ideas he had expressed during the previous decade. They also constituted Lelewel's major contribution during the nine year period of his activity in the *Zjednoczenie*. He continued to work on behalf of the Polish cause and to popularize democratic ideas among the émigrés and other revolutionary exiles.

One of these was the flamboyant, brilliant, and charismatic Mikhail Bakunin, the Russian anarchist. He visited Lelewel in Brussels in the summer of 1844, and they established a cordial relationship.[68] Bakunin's national feelings, at this time, were in conflict with his democratic principles, and he hoped to resolve this problem in an intelligent manner with a fellow democrat. He saw Lelewel often that summer. They discussed the "Polish revolution, the intentions of the Poles, their plans in case of victory, and their hopes for the future."[69] Bakunin was fascinated with Lelewel's concept of *gminowładztwo* (primitive democracy).[70] At times, they argued about the Little Russians and the White Russians. Lelewel viewed these people of Poland's former eastern territories as Ruthenian people of the Polish nation. Bakunin, in turn, argued that these people should have hated the Poles as oppressors.[71] Despite these differences of opinion, both men favored the establishment of closer relations among all Slavs — Poles, Russians, and others — and agreed to cooperate to help bring this about.

Together they prepared a Russian translation of Lelewel's "Appeal to the Russians and Slavs" (1832) in which Lelewel had called on the Russian people to make common cause with other nations against tsarist tyranny.[72] This appeal would serve to enhance the spirit of cooperation envisioned by the two revolutionaries, but it remained unpublished among Bakunin's papers.[73]

Between 1846 and 1849, Bakunin publicly supported the cause of Poland's independence and proposed to work with the Poles to achieve a democratic Russian revolution and to liberate all Slavs from foreign domination.[74] In 1847, at a large gathering in Paris to commemorate the Polish uprising of 1831, Bakunin spoke in favor of a revolutionary conciliation between the Poles and Russians. Shortly after this speech, i.e., on 19 December 1847, Bakunin returned to Brussels where he resumed his association with Lelewel.[75]

In Brussels, both men prepared for the anniversary celebration in memory of the Decembrist revolt and the martyrdom of Szymon Konarski. Lelewel called the meeting, and Bakunin delivered his second speech in favor of the reconciliation of Polish and Russian democrats. He also spoke of the great future of the Slavs who were destined to renew the decaying Western world, and he predicted an imminent European revolution.[76]

Meanwhile Lelewel continued to focus his attention on the Polish national cause. In the proclamations and appeals which he wrote in the name of the *Zjednoczenie* in the early forties, he advocated the creation of a sovereign Poland with prepartition boundaries. This goal was to be achieved by revolution and by reliance on the Poles' own national strength. This strength would be enhanced by the abolition of certain inequities such as the *pańszczyzna* (*corvée*) imposed on the peasants in the Polish lands and by the establishment of a new social order based on *gminowładztwo,* the primitive form of Slav democracy which Lelewel described in his national histories and alluded to in his earlier political writings. The new Polish state, according to Lelewel, would be based on the principles of the sovereignty of the people, equality, and freedom.[77] He also spoke of Slav brotherhood and reaffirmed the idea that each nation and each people has obligations toward humanity.[78]

In the proclamations and appeals he wrote between 1843 and 1846, he increasingly emphasized the relations of the Polish nation with other Slav nations. In "*Komitet Narodowy Polski do Slowian*" ("The Polish National Committee to the Slavs"), published 25 March 1844, he emphasized a belief in the family of all European peoples and called for the further development of brotherhood among Slavs — Poles, Serbs, Czechs, and others. In an appeal to the people of Britain, also published in 1844, Lelewel stressed the brotherhood of Russian and Polish people.[79] He also referred to the relations of the Warsaw *Towarzystwo Patriotyczne* with Muraviev's Northern Society and Pestel's Southern Society, and to the common enemy of both Russians and Poles — the tyrannical tsar.[80]

A subtle shift occurred in Lelewel's thinking. In the decade of the thirties, and especially in the years 1833 to 1838, his orientation was western European. In contrast, in the 1840s, he consistently urged a unified Polish emigration, under the aegis of the *Zjednoczenie,* to establish closer relations with the Slavs of eastern Europe.

Lelewel added still another new dimension to his national ideas in those proclamations which he wrote in the early forties when he stressed the messianic role of the Polish nation. In a declaration to Polish émigrés, he stated that the oppressed Slav nations looked to the Poles for leadership.[81] In the proclamations to the Slavs, mentioned above, he stated, "The Polish people (*lud*) will lead the Slav people (*lud*) to liberation."[82] He spoke of the martyrdom of the entire Polish nation, referring to its conquest and humiliation as a noble sacrifice for the brotherhood of peoples.[83] He eloquently and emotionally stated that just as Christ who died on the cross was resurrected, so Poland, too, will be resurrected.[84]

In an appeal to the Polish people which appeared in 1845, he again reminded the Poles of their obligations to help other oppressed Slav peoples.[85] Again he emphasized their mission of brotherhood, i.e., their duty to spread "freedom, equality, and brotherhood," and to help Slavs everywhere.[86]

Just prior to the revolutionary outbreaks in Kraków, Poznań, and Galicia in 1846, on behalf of the *Komitet,* Lelewel issued a proclamation "*Do rodaków Ukrainy i innych Ziem Ruskich*" ("To the Natives of the Ukraine and Other Ruthenian Lands") and another to the clergy of the Eastern Orthodox Church.[87] In both proclamations, he stressed the brotherhood of Slavs. In the latter, he reiterated the slogan "*Za naszą i waszą wolność.*" And in July, 1846, in the final address of the *Komitet* to the Polish revolutionary cadres in the homeland,[88] he optimistically proposed that the Poles with their fellow Slav brothers would triumph over despotism and tyranny.[89]

Disappointments and disillusionment followed the failures of 1846 in the homeland.[90] The people of old Poland, i.e., Lithuanians, Ukrainians, and Ruthenians, had refused to follow the self-ordained messianic Poles against the despotic administrations of Austria, Prussia, and Russia, and no resurrected Polish state emerged.

Nevertheless, the exiled Poles' allegiance to the idea of a resurrected Polish state, based on principles enunciated by Joachim Lelewel, continued to thrive. A conquered, humiliated, and oppressed nation continued to dream romantic dreams of resurrection.

After the dissolution of the *Zjednoczenie Emigracji Polskiej* in 1846, the aging Lelewel rarely participated in the politics of the Polish emigration. He limited his activities to only two patriotic speeches before Polish groups in 1847. He spoke at the first anniversary commemoration of the Kraków uprising (February) and the sixteenth, now traditional, anniversary of the November revolution. However, that same year, he joined the *Société Démocratique Internationale* (The Democratic Society for the Union of all Countries).[91] Members included Belgian democrats, German communists, notably Karl Marx and Friedrich Engels, and representatives of various émigré organizations. Neither his relations with Western European revolutionaries nor those with Eastern European Slavs discouraged Lelewel. He continued to pursue his work on behalf of the Polish cause and now chose to associate with a new international organization.

Lelewel's relative isolation from Polish émigré politics in the years 1846–1848 and Marx's and Engels's interest in the Polish question during those same years influenced Lelewel's decision to participate in the *Société Démocratique Internationale*.[92] Although he served with Karl Marx as this organization's Vice President, the ephemeral nature of the *Société* and the differing ideologies of its members precluded any possibilities for action by it.[93]

The subject of Lelewel's relationship with Marx and Engels is worthy of a brief digression from the topic under consideration. According to Bogusław Cygler, author of the most recent study of Lelewel's political activities in exile, Lelewel's association with Marx and Engels was an isolated episode without any far-reaching political consequences.[94] Lelewel met Marx in 1845, according to Jenny Marx's account.[95] Marx was drawn to Lelewel because of his interest in the Polish question,[96] and Lelewel's *Histoire de Pologne*, published in Paris in 1844, provided Marx with a basic introduction to the history of Poland.[97] Obviously, Marx was impressed with the Polish scholar's interpretation.[98] The two scholar-revolutionaries cooperated in the *Société Démocratique Internationale*, but their relations ended abruptly when Marx was forced to leave Belgium (March, 1848). Contacts did not resume between Lelewel and Marx until February, 1860.[99]

Sixty-two years old, in declining health, and isolated from the politics of the Polish emigration, Lelewel observed the kaleidoscopic events of 1848 as a bystander.[100] Hopeful that the Polish question would be resolved satisfactorily at the Frankfurt Assembly, he willingly sent a representative, his colleague Ludwik Lubliner, with two addresses to that deliberative assembly.[101] But an aggressive German nationalism began to emerge, and even the German liberals no longer supported the Polish cause. Only the communists voiced their support.[102] The emergence of an overtly aggressive German nationalism was a blow to Lelewel and to those other Polish émigrés who continued to believe in the romantic notions of the brotherhood of peoples.

Lelewel also sent a representative to the Slav Congress meeting in

Prague in the late spring of 1848. In a letter addressed to that Congress, Lelewel expressed his firm belief in the brotherhood of Slav peoples, and he warned his fellow Slavs of a new enemy — the Pan-Slavism of the tsarist government.[103] His efforts and those of other high-minded intellectuals on behalf of Slav national self-consciousness were fruitless as a result of the upheaval which erupted in Prague just as the Slav Congress adjourned. The humanitarian principles and political ideals that Lelewel and so many other revolutionaries believed in were overpowered by the realities of 1848 and superseded by the new militant realism which enveloped Europe in the last half of the nineteenth century.

After the failure of the "Springtime of Nations," the aged and ailing Joachim Lelewel moved totally away from the politics of the European revolutionary left. Nevertheless, he continued to serve the fatherland. His extensive correspondence with Karol Sienkiewicz, a prominent member of the *Towarzystwo Historyczno-Literackie* (The Historical-Literary Society) in Paris, attests to this.[104]

The correspondence dates from July, 1853, to December, 1859. There are fifty letters, and Sienkiewicz consulted the septuagenarian Lelewel on a number of issues, including Lelewel's autobiography, his family genealogy, his scholarship, his ideas on the uses of history. Lelewel enthusiastically supported Sienkiewicz's work of collecting all available sources dealing with Polish history for the Polish national library in Paris. The earliest letters are rather formal, but it is evident that a genuine camaraderie developed between the two, in spite of the fact that Sienkiewicz was a republican who praised the aristocracy and Lelewel was a republican and a democrat.[105]

In addition, Lelewel once again returned to his scholarly pursuits and began to write his massive five volume geography of the Middle Ages.[106] Completely preoccupied with this study for the next decade, he declined to enter the mainstream of Polish émigré politics.[107]

When the Crimean War erupted, the aged Lelewel refused to support those Polish émigrés who placed their faith in the help of Napoleon III, and he opposed the formation of Polish legions in the Ottoman Empire.[108] Neither Napoleon III nor the Turks rallied to the Polish cause at the appropriate time.[109] Lelewel continued to stress that the Poles should not rely on help from others.

Another opportunity arose and quickly passed for the achievement of the re-establishment of the Polish state in 1863 when revolution erupted in Russian Poland. Lelewel never lived to hear of the outbreak or of its failure or to see the resurrection of his beloved *rzecz-*

pospolita more than half a century later. Gravely ill, Lelewel with the assistance of two colleagues, S. Gałęzowski and E. Januszkiewicz, left Brussels for Paris on 24 May 1861. He died in Paris five days later at the age of seventy-five. He was buried in the cemetery at Montmarte, and in 1929 his remains were transferred to a cemetery in Wilno.[110]

In the preceding pages, this author traced the development of Joachim Lelewel's concepts of Polish nationalism, political republicanism, and social democracy by stressing how his personal experiences in Wilno, Warsaw, Paris, and Brussels influenced their evolution. The critical years of his personal experiences were those which he lived in exile, but his tireless political activities after 1830 on behalf of the Polish cause had no practical or immediate results. However, the national aspirations which he expressed in his writings and voluminous correspondence and at various public commemorations of the November uprising of 1830 and other occasions contributed significantly to the development and preservation of national consciousness among his fellow émigrés. Lelewel's concepts of Polish nationalism, political republicanism, and social democracy found their most concrete and permanent expression in his national histories of Poland.

In the pages that follow, this author proposes to concentrate on specific contributions of Joachim Lelewel to the development of scholarship in Poland in a period of national renaissance which spanned the Age of Enlightenment and the Era of Romanticism. Lelewel's contributions to the development of Polish historiography have been discussed. His national histories are chosen for detailed analysis in the following chapter. It is in his histories of Poland that the nucleus of modern Polish nationalism lies. It is in these histories that Joachim Lelewel developed the cult of the Polish nation.

7   Lelewel's Interpretations of Poland's History

The Early Histories

Joachim Lelewel was one of the most productive and erudite Polish historians of the nineteenth century, the precursor of the new history of the modern era. His contributions to the development of modern historical method in Poland have been discussed. His legacy also includes seminal studies in historiography, compilations of bibliographies, monographs in numismatics, works on diplomacy and government, and genealogies, as well as numerous studies of all phases of history from the ancient and medieval eras to the post-1830 period.

Lelewel also produced a myriad of textbooks, monographs, and pamphlets which dealt specifically with the history of Poland. Considering the primitive state of Polish historical writing in the early nineteenth century,[1] his studies represent a significant contribution to historical scholarship in the traditions of the rationalist historians of the eighteenth century. Paradoxically, his interpretations are a most obvious example of a nineteenth century romanticist's political and didactic uses of history. In his national histories, he aspired to the recovery and ennoblement of a people deprived of its individual, social, political, and national freedoms. Lelewel's histories, deeply rooted in the intellectual renaissance and nascent nationalism of the late eighteenth and early nineteenth centuries, cannot be evaluated in isolation from these phenomena, nor from the crucial circumstances which surrounded the extinction of the Polish state as a sovereign political entity.

By concentrating on Lelewel's national histories, the present author proposes to identify their common characteristics, to examine and to assess the strengths and the weaknesses of his interpretations, and to determine their most enduring values.

Several years before his death, Lelewel wrote a brief autobiography. In it, he admitted to two common goals relative to his histories of Poland. He proposed to study the history of the Polish nation by isolating it from the general processes of history and to emphasize the unique individuality of the Polish nation and the latter's relationship to the development of the Polish state.[2] Above all, he searched for Poland's past greatness, discovered it, and publicized it. Preoccupied with this theme of Poland's past greatness, he continually emphasized that a nation with a historic past such as the Polish nation's had the right to exist as a political entity and that this goal could become a reality once again only through the efforts of the Poles themselves. In Lelewel's national histories of Poland, as in his more specialized monographs, he frequently idealized Poland's past greatness, especially the centuries of szlachta (gentry) democracy. He looked for national explanations for Poland's fall; called for responsible individuals and social classes to save Poland; and optimistically and repeatedly emphasized that Poland, given her past greatness, would re-emerge as a sovereign state.

The major studies of Poland's past by which Lelewel influenced historians of all political and social persuasions, political activists, e.g., Karl Marx and Friedrich Engels,[3] and popular audiences included the following. All were written between 1813 and 1855: *Historia Polski do końca panowania Stefana Batorego* (*The History of Poland to the End of the Reign of Stefan Batory*), *Panowanie Stanisława Augusta* (*The Reign of Stanisław August*), *Dziesięć upłynionych wieków historii Polski* (*Ten Past Centuries of Poland's History*), *Dzieje Polski potocznym sposobem opowiedziane* (*A History of Poland Told in a Colloquial Manner*), and *Uwagi nad dziejami Polski i ludu jej* (*Observations on the History of Poland and Its People*). The objectives of these studies differed — some were scholarly; others were written primarily for popular and/or political purposes. What these volumes have in common is that they provided a significant stimulus to the renascent national consciousness of the intellectuals at the centers of Polish culture before 1830–31, i.e., Wilno and Warsaw, and influenced the development of republican political thought and democratic social ideas among many generations of Poles everywhere, but especially those émigrés who found themselves scattered throughout western Europe after the failure of 1831.

In his early youth, Joachim Lelewel expressed a desire to write a national history of Poland.[4] At the age of twenty-eight he achieved this goal when he completed his lengthy *Historia Polski do końca panowania Stefana Batorego.*[5] In this not very original first effort, Lelewel presented a sketch of political events and stressed Poland's relations with other European states. A modest first effort, this national history was significant for at least two reasons.

First, Lelewel divided or periodized the history of Poland differently than did most of his contemporaries. Rather than divide the history of Poland according to ruling dynasties, e.g., Piast, Anjou, Jagiellonian, and the elected monarchs, he preferred to divide Polish history into specific eras, or epochs, each determined by climactic transformations of the state. He characterized the earliest period, which encompassed the history of Poland from c. 890 to the death of Bolesław Krzywousty (1140), as "*Polska podbijająca*" ("Conquering Poland") — an era of autocracy. He called the second period "*Polska podzielona*" ("Divided Poland"). This second period lasted from the death of Bolesław Krzywousty (1140) to the death of Władysław Łokietek in 1333 and was characterized by the rule of the magnates, i.e., the elitist upper aristocracy. The third period, "*Polska kwitnąca pod gminowładztwem szlacheckiem*" ("Prospering Poland under Szlachta Democracy"), spanned a period of two hundred and fifty-five years — from the reign of Casimir III the Great (1333–1370) to the election of Zygmunt III in 1588. During this era of Poland's history, szlachta (gentry) democracy evolved. At the time he wrote this history, Lelewel considered the third period still incomplete and briefly outlined a projected fourth period (1587–1795). He finally added the fourth period to his manuscript in 1848. This final era he called "*Polska upadająca*" ("Poland in Decline"). He characterized this most recent period of Poland's history as an era of debasement by the magnates, an era of szlachta anarchy. In his later studies, he refined this periodization, but basically its structure remained unchanged. In a biography of Joachim Lelewel, published in 1946, the late Professor Chrzanowski wrote: "To this day the validity of Lelewel's periodization has not been challenged successfully."[6]

Secondly, in this his first effort at Polish national history, as in his later studies, Lelewel applied the theories he developed in the *Historyka*. While isolating Poland's history from the processes of general history, he attempted to portray Poland, not in isolation but in relation to the universal progress of mankind. For his major task, he proposed "to identify and diagnose the differences . . . between the affairs and concerns of Poland and the affairs of other peoples, so as to find Poland's unique national character (*żywioł*) which differentiated her peoples from foreigners."[7]

Preoccupied with this idea throughout his entire life, Lelewel continually searched for the *narodowy żywioł*, i.e., the national character, or *duch narodowy* (the national spirit) in Poland's past. He searched for these nebulous forces in her laws, politics, social institutions, traditions, and in general, in her entire cultural heritage. He found the Slav virtues of *wolność* (freedom) and *obywatelstwo* (citizenship) most fully developed among the Poles.[8] These indigenous virtues were the unique attributes of the Poles' national character. In addition, he proposed to demonstrate that Poland's strength and power expanded in a direct relationship to her faith in her own national spirit and in her efforts to thwart adverse foreign influences. Accordingly, Poland weakened whenever she betrayed or deserted her national spirit; whenever she allowed internal excesses to develop; whenever she followed a foreign "nationality"; or whenever she heeded the advice of her own "evil teachers," especially the Jesuits, or her own alienated and "foreignized" aristocracy.

Lelewel expressed this last point of view as early as 1817 in a brief review of Niemciewicz's *Śpiewy historyczne*.[9] In this review and commentary, and in other minor writings, one finds an idealized and exaggerated portrait of "*Polska kwitnąca*" ("Prospering Poland"), i.e., Jagiellonian Poland when and where szlachta democracy dominated. During this period of Poland's history the noblest characteristics of the Poles' national spirit matured. In this era which preceded the period of Poland's decline and fall, the development of *wolność* (freedom) and *obywatelstwo* (citizenship) rendered all restraints unnecessary. An awareness of political and social justice manifested itself in the Polish lands, and the oppressed and persecuted found comfort there. Religious tolerance guaranteed refuge to men of all opinions and beliefs almost without limit.[10] Because of these qualities and not as a result of conquests, Poland developed into a great state.

> The nation, united with Lithuania, exerted a daily influence on the Kingdom of Prussia, took Livonia under its protection, influenced the Danube, the Don, and the Narva; and the nations from the Elbe, Lapland, and the Adriatic and the Rhine asked for kings because Poland found in the Lithuanian family of Jagiello authorities who knew how to steer the ship in an enlightened, prosperous state. The Polish nation without a doubt

was distinctive, prosperous, and politically active, but only in an effectively benign manner. The other European countries were shaken by anarchy and drenched in blood to the detriment of the liberty of all their peoples. Poland alone was the envy of all.[11]

Unfortunately, those brightest of times when the Slav virtues developed most fully among the Poles and contributed significantly to the growth of Poland's power, also marked the beginnings of Poland's decline. The elective throne, after the extinction of the Jagiellonian dynasty in 1572, resulted in the election of kings who were unable to utilize the talents of the nation efficiently. This contributed to the decline in position of all social and political classes and to growth of internal instability. These changed internal conditions were aggravated by new, external threats, e.g., the Livonian wars and the Cossack wars. Lelewel detected the beginnings of Poland's decline during the reign of Stefan Batory (1575–1586) who violently opposed *gminowładztwo szlacheckie* (szlachta democracy) which had evolved so fully in Jagiellonian Poland. In the sixteenth and seventeenth centuries Poland experienced serious setbacks. Still, the virtues and nobleness of the Poles sustained them. The virtuous characteristics of the Polish nation helped turn the tide and at least temporarily lifted the nation from its decline.[12] By the late eighteenth century, Poland experienced a unique national renaissance.

Lelewel repeated similar themes in *Historia Polski do końca panowania Stefana Batorego.* The love of *wolność* and *obywatelstwo,* awareness of political and social justice, and tolerance were the attributes which manifested themselves in Casimir III the Great. This fourteenth century ruler stressed peace, granted privileges to the Jews, and was a friend to the peasants.[13] During Casimir's reign, peace, order, and justice flourished because of his awareness of the "national spirit" of the people. And Poland did not fear her neighbors during the thirty-seven year reign of Casimir the Great.[14]

Tolerance toward religious dissenters during Casimir's reign was sharply contrasted with the infamous Spanish inquisition by Lelewel. He described the equality of the social estates,[15] and he again mentioned the ideals of *wolność* and *obywatelstwo* deeply engrained in the Polish szlachta and manifested in the Poles' struggles against the Muscovites and Swedes in the seventeenth century.[16] Repeatedly he emphasized the point that these national characteristics, enhanced by Casimir and his illustrious predecessor Władysław Łokietek, contributed to the progressive development of the Polish state during the period of szlachta democracy. His praise for the republican virtues of the szlachta and those authoritarian rulers, e.g., Casimir, who encouraged the development of the Poles' national spirit for the benefit of all, permeated Lelewel's review of Niemcewicz's poetic history and Lelewel's history of Poland to the end of the reign of Stefan Batory.

As in the review of *Śpiewy historyczne,* in *Historia Polski do końca panowania Stefana Batorego,* Lelewel again indicated that the seeds of Poland's decline were to be found in the period of Poland's most glorious epoch, and he especially noted specific foreign elements as influential contributory factors. For example, the szlachta, the idea of *wolność* and *obywatelstwo* deeply engrained in their national character, were granted privileges by a foreign king, Louis of Hungary (the Košice Charter, 1374).[17] Consequently, in the years that followed, the dominance of the szlachta estate emerged. One segment of this gentry estate, the magnates, eventually sought and acquired special privileges. They ultimately abused their power.[18] The tolerant Church in Poland, influenced by foreign elements, notably the Jesuits, became detrimental; the oppression of the *kmieć* (peasant) began gradually and gained momentum; and the townsmen neglected their political responsibilities.[19] The outcome of these developments resulted in the introduction of feudalism.[20] Despite this pessimistic portrait of decline, Lelewel proposed to instill hope and certainty in the hearts of his readers by assuring them that a nation which possessed the virtuous attributes of which he spoke undoubtedly faced a promising future.

Lelewel discussed briefly the problem of Poland rising from its decline in the eighteenth century in his review of Niemcewicz's *Śpiewy historyczne,* in his history of Poland to the end of the reign of Stefan Batory, and more fully, in *Panowanie króla polskiego Stanisława Augusta Poniatowskiego* (*The Reign of the Polish King Stanisław August*).[21]

This study of the reign of Stanisław August (1764–1795) first appeared anonymously in *Pamiętnik Warszawski* (*The Warsaw Journal*) in 1818 and consisted of forty pages. The following year it was published again, this time as an appendix to Teodor Waga's popular school textbook *Historia książąt i królów polskich* (*The History of Poland's Princes and Kings*), slightly expanded (sixty-six pages). A significantly longer version (168 pages) appeared at the time of the uprising in 1831, and eight editions including one in French and another in German, appeared after Lelewel's exile and death. The final edition appeared in 1888 and was based on the text which appeared as volume VI of *Polska dzieje i rzeczy jej.*[22]

Lelewel based the 1818 and 1819 versions on his lectures and on his recollections of the comments of his father and his uncles "who knew the Poniatowskis." He recalled, "I was a child, yet the events and stories which were repeated made a lasting impression on me."[23] In the enlarged third edition, unencumbered by censorship, Lelewel referred to various studies which dealt with the question of the fall of the *Rzeczpospolita*[24] and cited numerous source materials useful in the study of the period. He referred to published diaries of a large number of sessions of the Sejm and to other accounts preserved in manuscript form; to numerous leaflets, printed and in manuscript, scattered in various places; to letters, acts, periodicals, detailed memoirs, and other materials.[25] *Panowanie Stanisława Augusta* may also be considered a memoir, i.e., an historical source particularly useful for the domestic history of the thirty year reign of Stanisław August, rather than either a scholarly work or a political polemic.[26]

The major theme of *Panowanie Stanisława Augusta* was that Polish society experienced a gradual renaissance during the reign of Stanisław August, with a partial restriction on former ancient privileges and promises to extend certain rights to the lower classes, and that if Poland declined, it was because of foreign violence and the arrogant egoism or self-interest of the aristocracy.

The Polish nation "revealed to the world that approaching its fall, after a lengthy decline, it had regained the strength which was a prerequisite for a national revival."[27] For in the last struggle for Poland's independence, i.e., the Kościuszko uprising of 1794, not only the szlachta, as in the Confederation of Bar, but also the townsmen, countryfolk, and the army came to the defense of the fatherland.[28] The nation demonstrated that "in its very decline it found the beginnings of its belated renaissance."[29]

Unfortunately for Poland:

> Unfriendly neighbors appeared, exceedingly treacherous and very numerous; and scheming and malevolent countrymen accomplished acts of treason with increasing fierceness and insolence.[30]

Returning his attention to domestic developments, he severely criticized the egoism, or self-interest, of the aristocracy (magnates) and spoke highly of the alliance between Poland's last elected king, Stanisław August, and the Polish nation. He praised the Polish szlachta (gentry) for allowing the townsmen to participate in the political life of the contemporary republic. This broadening of its political base helped to revive the *Rzeczpospolita*.[31]

Lelewel also referred to the hardships inflicted on the Polish peasants — which the 3 May 1791 Constitution only promised to alleviate. He marvelled at the strength the *Rzeczpospolita* could acquire if privileges were granted to her strongest and most industrious class — the peasants.[32] The promises to alleviate the plight of the peasants which were stated in the 3 May 1791 Constitution were not fulfilled, and Poland fell "in the midst of her renaissance."[33] These words appeared as precursors to Lelewel's later views concerning the causes for Poland's fall — not only political but also social causes. They also indicated his early concern with the peasant question. His interest in this problem grew, and in exile his ideas about peasant reform and the need of the participation of the peasant masses in the revolutionary struggle against tsardom and other forms of despotism were accepted by various democratic émigré organizations.

Panowanie Stanisława Augusta was not meant as a political polemic, but Lelewel's political beliefs permeated this study. His opposition to the self-interests of the aristocracy, evident in all his national histories, was also present in his study of the reign of Stanisław August. His republican convictions and his arguments in favor of expanding the social base of political participation were obvious in his interpretation of the political causes of Poland's decline and fall during the reign of Stanisław August. His reign began as "an attempt at reform and change of the *Rzeczpospolita* and ended as a war for independence and the final partition by three powerful neighbors."[34]

In the opening pages of *Panowanie Stanisława Augusta,* Lelewel expressed his opposition to the type of absolute monarchy which had developed in pre-revolutionary France. He claimed that it was alien to the concept of monarchy which had evolved in the *Rzeczpospolita.*[35] He argued that certain Polish aristocrats, educated in Luneville and Nancy in the mid-eighteenth century, favored the establishment of an hereditary monarchy in the *Rzeczpospolita* based on the French model. By establishing such a hereditary monarchy, these Polish aristocrats proposed to solidify their own privileges. Lelewel warned his readers that such actions harmed Poland's traditional republican foundations.[36]

Lelewel accepted, in principle, the idea of an elective monarchy, although he criticized the foreign influences exerted in the election of Stanisław August, the last king of the *Rzeczpospolita.* His sympathies for this elected monarch permeated his entire study.[37] In discussing the strengths and weaknesses of this tragic figure in Polish history, Lelewel stressed that Stanisław August knew the needs and feelings of the nation and desired what was best for the Polish nation. However, this king was "as unfortunate as is each Pole" who was deceived by the powerful forces surrounding his fatherland in this period of its national renaissance. Forced into exile, Stanisław August died in St. Petersburg on 12 February 1798, at the age of sixty-six.

Lelewel's interpretations of Poland's past and his reasons for her decline evolved and became more sophisticated from year to year. An appropriate illustration of this was his brief study, *Paralela Hiszpanii z Polską,* written as a series of lectures, but not published until 1831.[38] As in *Panowanie Stanisława Augusta,* there was also no excessive idealization of Poland's past in this comparative study of the histories of Spain and Poland, but Lelewel again focused on the "republican" virtues of the Polish nation. He indicated that the development of Spain's politics of absolutism was the logical consequence of the unification of the crowns of Castile, Aragon, Granada, and Navarre. In contrast, he asserted that Poland's political development reflected the role of her kings who ruled with the szlachta estate, i.e., with the nation, and not as absolute monarchs.[39] The Polish nation, in contrast to the Spanish, expanded the borders of its state not by conquest but by peaceful extension of its rights and privileges to the gentry in Lithuania, Prussia, and Mazovia. The Polish nation's greatness was based on "tendencies of *wolność* and *obywatelstwo.*"[40] Lelewel concluded that the ultimate cause of Poland's fall was the power of her neighbors. However, he also placed more emphasis than he had previously on internal factors which contributed to Poland's downfall. In reference to these, he focused intensively on the faults of the nation in the seventeenth and eighteenth centuries:

> In Poland, all internal evils and distresses resulted from the interests of the rulers and the errors of the szlachta. Each individual considered himself independent; he impatiently resisted any limitations on his personal freedom. The szlachta estate knew that it was all. From this source emerged the imposition of taxes and duties advantageous for the estate; creating hardships for others; leading to the arbitrary subjugation of other estates and sometimes resulting in severe judgments against them. . . . The errors of the szlachta estate humbled the land and the people. Dreadful anarchy and dissolution exposed the *Rzeczpospolita* to doom.[41]

He emphasized, however, that internal causes of decline can exist without effect for a long time. They can bring suffering, revolution, and the overthrow of order in a country, but not the country's downfall. External factors aggravate the internal factors and hasten the ruin of a country and a nation by creating an environment for revolution, for the overthrow of order in the land. The foreign influences aggravating the Polish situation included Poland's powerful neighbors and the Jesuits. The Poles forfeited the religious tolerance they enjoyed by permitting the Jesuits to interfere in the religious affairs of the *Rzeczpospolita*.[42]

The intolerance precipitated by Jesuit actions and "political and moral degradation and abuse brought discredit upon the people and the laws, and impaired the virtues and numbed the spirit of citizenship."[43] Limited in what he could say about the three neighboring powers, Lelewel concentrated on the adverse influences of the Church.

In expressing his opinions, Lelewel considered it his responsibility to justify his interpretation to his readers: "Excuse me if conciseness led me to this conclusion. . . . I am thoroughly convinced that either verbosity and redundance or straightforward and emphatic expression would lead me to the same truths."[44]

Neither in writing his short studies nor in writing his more lengthy monographs did Joachim Lelewel forget about his youthful dream of writing a comprehensive history of Poland. The matter of his growing patriotism and political consciousness played a significant role in this. Early in his scholarly career, he recognized the great need for a popular history, for school texts, and for scholarly studies and proceeded to fulfill these needs.

In 1819 he revised Waga's work[45] and reviewed the first national history for the people, i.e., Izabela Czartoryska's study *Pielgrzym w Dobromilu* (*Pilgrim in Dobromil*). In his review,[48] Lelewel expressed concern for the need for a history for the people (*lud*), saying that the history of the fatherland was ". . . an eternal spring, refreshing the nationality (*narodowość*), strong enough to stimulate the most szlachta-like feelings, acknowledging in the people . . . in the agrarian estate . . . the vigorous effects resulting from instilling in their hearts the ancient, simplistic virtues and freedoms . . . in spite of the dissipation, offenses, and errors of the Polish nation, it exists among the European nations and glitters in its own uniqueness. . . ."[47]

A great need also existed for a national history for school children in the Polish lands in the early decades of the nineteenth century. The few existing scholarly works, e.g., Naruszewicz's multivolume *Historia Narodu Polskiego* and the work of the Protestant J. G. Lengnich, *Historia Polona a Lecho ad Augusti II Mortem* written in 1740, were not suitable.[48] Chronicles and the texts published by the Jesuits in the late eighteenth century were not the types of materials needed to inspire youth with national consciousness and a spirit of citizenship once the intellectual and cultural national renaissance of the late eighteenth century began. There were but a few appropriate histories. The most popular for students was the Piarist Teodor Waga's *Krótkie zebrania historii i geografii polskiej* which first appeared in 1767 and again in 1770 (twenty editions in one hundred years) and which Lelewel revised in 1819.[49] Another popular work was Jerzy Samuel Bandtkie's *Krótkie wyobrażenie dziejów Królestwa Polskiego* (1810). Lelewel, writing in 1822, recognized the heavy reliance on Waga and Bandtkie although he believed both authors' works inadequate to satisfy the need for elementary histories for Poland's youth.[50] In answering the question, "What kinds of books are needed?", Lelewel stated that what was always needed was "a clear, straightforward, easy, smooth, and concise publication, neither too easy nor too difficult for young people to handle."[51] He praised Czartoryska's efforts as a step in the right direction, but suggested only that the most efficient way to alleviate the problem of inadequate texts was to translate known works in general history by foreign authors, e.g., J. Breton, W. Robertson, and others.[52]

In 1829, a decade after the publication of Izabela Czartoryska's *Pielgrzym w Dobromiliu* and Lelewel's revised version of Waga's history, and six years after his comments on the need for elementary textbooks, *Dzieje Polski Joachim Lelewel potocznym sposobem opowiedział do nich dwanaście krajobrazów skreślił* (*The History of Poland Narrated in a Colloquial Manner by Joachim Lelewel with Twelve Maps Sketched by the Author*) appeared. A more complete history than his *Dziesięć upłynionych wieków* published in 1828, *Dzieje Polski potocznym sposobem opowiedziane* was a significant contribution to Polish historical scholarship for several reasons. Lelewel's approach, i.e., his periodization, mentioned in reference to his history of Poland to the end of the reign of Stefan Batory, appeared in a revised version. The work was also a synthesis in which the author presented a political, cultural, social, and economic history of his nation. This, for Lelewel, constituted the totality of Poland's history. In the text of *Dzieje Polski potocznym sposobem opowiedziane,* the author also included an atlas with several maps to which he referred his readers.

The history, intended for young people, was simply written and interesting to read. It included various aspects of Poland's history from the ancient legends about the origins of the Polish nation, such as the fable of the brothers Lech, Czech, and Rus, to the events leading to the third partition of Poland in 1795.

In the opening pages of this history, the author warned his youthful readers not to accept fables as historical truth; "I would willingly omit them as I do not like fables, but you my children, may resent me for my omissions, for not pointing out to you their weaknesses and guiding you from mythical roads onto the path of truth. I shall repeat, then, with your permission, that all these are only introductory thoughts. . . . Only from Ziemowit I begin my narration to you, my children, of the history of the Polish nation and her kings."[53] Again he stressed to his young readers that the historian must depend on truth. "Whoever thinks and wants to be a witness to history loves truth and avoids fantasy."[54]

It is not difficult to determine Lelewel's political leanings in this particular history, and his national consciousness is obvious. He emphasized the peaceful development of the Poles and the pristine virtues of the Polish nation as in his earlier works. His major interest and stress in *Dzieje Polski potocznym sposobem opowiedziane* was to teach his young readers about *narodowość* and *obywatelstwo* — the nationality and spirit of citizenship of the Polish nation which encompassed not only the szlachta but all estates, including the peasants.[55]

He also proposed to instill in his readers a sense of moral responsibility so that they would consciously retain and develop these virtues. "Recognize, my children, that nothing except tradition and language can preserve nationality and citizenship."[56] Throughout the text Lelewel referred to the significance of aspects such as the Polish language and customs for a renascent Polish state and to the period of the Polish *Rzeczpospolita* when these virtues developed freely and fully.[57]

His didactic tendencies and his stress on the national, republican, and democratic traditions of the Polish nation, although idealized, nevertheless did not distract greatly from the objectivity of the author's judgment. For example, in his search for the reasons for Poland's fall, he found that a combination of internal and external factors led to the final partition.

Lelewel told his readers to be instructed by Poland's history — to become aware of reasons for her period of weakness and strength so that causes of weakness could be avoided in the future and sources of strength developed to their fullest potential.[58] He asked his readers to excuse him for relating to them "so many horrible affairs" — about the egoism and foulness of the aristocracy, of the destruction of the national spirit and for the sake of fashionable, foreign influences, of the increasing degradation and oppression of the *kmieć* (peasant) estate, and of the abuses of the traditional republican virtues which led to anarchy.[59] But while criticizing the szlachta for oppressing the peasants, Lelewel also praised them for their republican virtues, for example, their belief in free elections. Criticizing the 3 May 1791 Constitution for its monarchic and dynastic tendencies, he praised certain monarchs, notably Bolesław Chrobry, Władysław Łokietek, and the latter's son Casimir the Great. These wise and virtuous rulers, in Lelewel's opinion, recognized the "national spirit" and encouraged its development.[60]

In the last chapter, he instructed his readers to "read about the history of old Poland to find in it the many errors and shortcomings committed by our predecessors and also to find much good."[61] He added, "One of the effects of these shortcomings is the necessity for us to do penance. . . ."[62] He believed that it was important, during this present and prolonged period of weakness, to keep alive Polish national consciousness, the spirit of citizenship, and the language, customs, and traditions. These would be the foundations upon which a new state, larger than the truncated Congress Kingdom, would some day emerge.[63]

⌘ Poland's History: Studies in Exile

After the failures of 1830–31 and the organic incorporation of the Congress Kingdom into the Russian Empire, Lelewel actively participated in émigré politics and neglected his scholarly activities. However, in the latter part of the decade of the thirties, he again turned to scholarship. In addition to significant contributions to the study of numismatics, archeology, and geography,[64] Lelewel again turned to his national histories.[65] He firmly believed that his histories of Poland could serve a very practical purpose. He wanted to enlighten the Polish exiles, to contribute to the development of the émigrés' critical political thinking, and above all, to instill in them a conscious and deep love of their fatherland.[66] In addition to influencing the Polish émigrés, Lelewel's national histories, translated into numerous languages, kept alive the Polish question among the Russians, French, Germans, and the English.

Lelewel's inclination to idealize Poland's past was evident in the various national histories discussed above. However, this inclination to idealize Poland's past was most obvious in his writings which appeared after his emigration to Paris and Brussels. After 1831, Lelewel wrote not only for his fellow countrymen and exiles but also for a foreign audience. He stressed the didactic purposes of his histories more in the studies which he wrote while in exile. He had proposed to influence his audiences by instilling in them a consciousness of Poland, her role in universal history, and the necessity for her resurrection as a political entity. With the publication of his two volume *Histoire de Pologne* (1844), he looked forward to achieving his goal.

This two volume history, published in French, included Lelewel's most sophisticated national history — a study he had written eight years earlier.[67] A German edition appeared in 1845,[68] and a decade later, his Polish translation from the French original, *Uwagi nad dziejami Polski i ludu jej* (*Observations on the History of Poland and Her People*) appeared, being "the results of Lelewel's researches and thoughts of many years."[69] These thoughts reflected a skillful blend of scholarship and patriotism. Here more than in his earlier national histories and monographs, the romantic's doctrinaire nationality and his commitment to republicanism and to the democratization of society took precedence over the sober and critical historian's objectivity. In this study, the scholar and the Pole consciously advocated the stimulation of the Polish national spirit and its unique elements not only among the szlachta but also among all strata of the population. The result of Lelewel's efforts aroused both praise and criticism of historians and political activists interested in the cultural, social, and political aspects of the Polish question.[70]

The *Uwagi* stood as a separate entity and also served as a complement to *Dzieje Polski potocznym sposobem opowiedziane*.[71] In both these studies, Lelewel de-emphasized external events such as wars or diplomacy and relations between monarchs or dynasties. Instead, he concentrated on internal affairs, and especially on the Polish nation and people and their crucial role (for Lelewel) in history. Lelewel capitalized on a favorite recurrent theme. Once again he stressed the idealized virtues of the Slav peoples, i.e., *wolność, równość, obywatelstwo* (freedom, equality, citizenship), as they were most obviously manifested to Joachim Lelewel in the Polish national spirit — especially in one stratum of the Polish population, the szlachta (gentry).

There are many similarities and differences between the two studies. The major differences occur in purpose and in periodization. The purpose of *Uwagi* differed from that of *Dzieje Polski potocznym sposobem opowiedziane* in that the former was not a colloquial narrative for popular consumption, easily understood by children, but a book for a mature audience, Polish and foreign, and not dedicated to young readers. For example, the author omitted the fables and didactic commentaries of an "old, experienced uncle" speaking to his nephews and young readers. These appeared profusely in *Dzieje Polski potocznym sposobem opowiedziane.*[72]

In *Uwagi,* the first social history of Poland, Lelewel interpreted Poland's history as a dynamic process of organic development. He portrayed this development as an evolution by stages and a maturation of class conflicts, and he made allusions that the Polish state will eventually emerge victorious as a result of the peoples' will to reassert their primal virtues.[73]

Influenced by Rousseau and the German historicists, e.g., Herder and Niebuhr, and by his own belief in the republican ideals of freedom, equality, and brotherhood, and convinced of the need to extend these privileges to all classes in society, Lelewel idealized the pristine conditions he believed existed among the Slavs. He stressed the negative influences of Western civilization and organized Christianity on the Slavs and especially on the Poles, and the latter's ability to persevere despite these adverse influences. The Slavs, and particularly the Poles, were sometimes overwhelmed by the influences of foreign peoples, he asserted. But they always repelled those alien forces which threatened their independence or their freedom.[74]

This basic drive of the Slavs to freedom attracted to it all segments of society, most notably the Polish people (*lud*) — the latter only in their pre-Christian period. "Before the introduction of Christianity, all peoples were free . . . the agrarian estate shared equality with the warrior." With the introduction of Christianity came feudalism and the development of the stratification of the Slav population and the beginnings of social struggles.[75]

Lelewel divided the Polish people into two classes or estates of citizens — the szlachta (gentry) and the *kmieć* (peasants). He assumed that the division occurred at some time in the pre-Christian past.[76] For a time, the *kmieć* shared equally with the szlachta the same privileges of citizenship (*obywatelstwo*) but eventually lost these privileges when feudalism was introduced. Inequality was hastened by the leaders of the people (*naczelnicy*) who came under the influence of Western civilization and Christianity.[77] The resultant class conflict for freedom (*wolność*) and equality (*równość*), Lelewel depicted as a struggle which resulted in the oppression of the *kmieć* by the szlachta. This conflict was superseded by a struggle between the victorious szlachta and the magnates and finally by a struggle of the szlachta and the magnates against the crown. For Lelewel, this was the content of Poland's history, and this is how he depicted it in *Uwagi nad dziejami Polski i ludu jej.*

The periodization differed somewhat from that in *Dzieje Polski potocznym sposobem opowiedziane* (and from Lelewel's earlier studies) in scope and emphasis. The periodization in *Uwagi* was based on social criteria. The four periods were: I *Samowładztwo* (*Absolutisme*; Autocracy); II *Możnowładztwo* (*Aristocratie*; Rule of the Magnates); III *Gminowładztwo Szlachty* (*Democratie Nobiliaire*; Szlachta Democracy); and IV *Gminowładztwo Szlacheckie w Zawichrzeniu* (*Perturbation de la Democratie Nobiliaire*; Szlachta Democracy in Turmoil).[78] In the children's history, the periods included I *Polska Podbijająca: Panujacy Królowie Piastowie Samowładni* (Conquering Poland: The Ruling Autocratic Piasts); II *Lechia jest w podziałach: panujący Książęta Piastowie z Możnowładztwen* (Lechia is Divided: The Piast Princes Rule with the Magnates); III *Polska Kwitnąca: Narody jednoczą się z Polską: Panują Jagiellonowie: Gminowładztwo Szlacheckie* (Poland Flourishes; Nations Unite with Poland: The Jagiellonians Rule: Szlachta Democracy); IV *Polska Upadajaca: Panujacy Królowie Obierani; Wazowie, Piastowie, Sasi: Gminowładztwo Szlacheckie Arystokracja Zawichrzone* (Poland Declines: Ruling Monarchs are Elected; Vasa, Piast, Saxon: Szlachta Democracy in Turmoil because of the Aristocracy).[79]

The chronological limits of the first period, i.e., of Autocracy (*Samowładztwo*) are the same in both *Dzieje Polski potocznym sposobem opowiedziane* and *Uwagi*. Both encompass the beginnings of the Polish state in 860 to the death of Bolesław III Krzywousty in 1138. However, the second period in *Uwagi,* i.e., the period of Magnate Rule (*Możnowładztwo*), ends not as in the earlier studies with the death of Władysław Łokietek (1333) but with the Koszyce Charter of 17 September 1374 (also called the Košice Charter and the Kassa Charter). In addition, the third period of *Uwagi*, i.e., Szlachta Democracy (*Gminowładztwo Szlachty*), ends not with the election of Zygmunt III (1587) as it does in the children's history, but with the Battle of Guzów (1607), the struggle in which the magnates with the help of Austria and the Society of Jesus emerged as victors. As a result, the fourth period in *Uwagi,* i.e., Szlachta Democracy in Turmoil (*Gminowładztwo Szlacheckie w Zawichrzeniu*) is shorter by twenty years. In spite of these variations, scholars such as Ignacy Chrzanowski and contemporary Marxist historians, notably Marian Henryk Serejski, concur that Lelewel's periodization remains valid to the present time.[80]

Lelewel's idea that the history of Poland, like the history of every nation, reflected the struggle of the various social classes for authority, participation in government, for well being, and for laws and privileges, also remained valid for contemporary scholars of social history. In writing a social history of Poland, Lelewel pioneered a new approach to the study of his nation's past.

> Hube, Helcel, Maciejowski see the skill, astuteness, and genius of the crowned rulers, but I see in the course of development, in the transformation of national life, that the important factor is the social relations of the common people (*lud*), in its ideals....[81]

Lelewel interpreted these social relations as a struggle between two social groups. One desired equality and regarded its achievement as possible and justifiable, while the other favored inequality. The latter group believed that inequality was based on natural facts and was necessary for the existence of a state and a society which was influenced by self-interest (egoism) and patriotic motives. The group that desired inequality of a country's inhabitants also believed in the general inequality of peoples. This group perceived its goals within the realm of possibility in society and government.[82]

A patriotic, nostalgic émigré, Lelewel the scholar now consciously used history to plead the Polish cause, to awaken national consciousness among the Poles, and to instill in the minds of his readers his own democratic-republican social and political views. These themes permeated *Uwagi.* Lelewel's faith in freedom (*wolność*), equality (*równość*), and brotherhood (*braterstwo*), led to his belief that one day these virtues would again manifest themselves in a Polish state because they had existed in prehistoric Poland and inhered in the national character of the Poles. In *Uwagi,* Lelewel interpreted every social grievance, i.e., the deprivation of any segment of the population of freedom, equality, or brotherhood, as a serious offense against the fatherland.

In the first period of Poland's history, autocracy developed and engulfed all democratic, communal elements because of the need to weld all the scattered and atomized peoples into one individual national unity.[83] Bolesław Chrobry (Bolesław the Great, the Brave, 992–1025?) accomplished this goal. He created a powerful state.[84] Then the *Lechs*, i.e., the szlachta, gradually established their dominance over the *kmieć gmin*. Simultaneously, the szlachta weakened the absolutism which they no longer needed once they had asserted their authority. The powerful (*można*) szlachta then separated itself from the humbled *gmin* and thus created the foundations for future aristocratic rule (*możnowładztwo*).[85]

In the second period of Poland's history, the period of aristocratic (magnate) rule, vengeance took hold on the szlachta. The aristocracy, not wishing to expand the political corpus, isolated itself from the szlachta at the Council in Łęczyca in 1180. They acquired special privileges and dispensations. The aristocracy then divided the land without legal restraints. As a result, adversity ruled the land.[86] But a spirit of citizenship (*duch obywatelski*) awakened in the nation. It countered these developments and weakened the magnates' power. Władysław Łokietek's political activities, "governed by the national spirit (*duch narodowy*), subdued the excesses of the magnates; the Sejm Chęcinski and the Sejm Wiślicki, and others provided the nation with the opportunity to participate in the political life of the state. . . ."[87] The "Golden Age" of Poland appeared on the horizon.

In the era of Szlachta Democracy (*Gminowładztwo Szlacheckie*), Lelewel's third period, Poland stood at the pinnacle of her power. On the other hand, freedom, equality, and brotherhood appeared as attributes of all the szlachta, and no individual rulers dominated. All were nurtured by one communal thought — the thought of citizenship (*obywatelstwo*). Lelewel's ideals became a reality as the national spirit permeated the land.

For a time, given the Koszyce (Kassa) Charter privileges, the magnates continued to exert power — longer in Lithuania than in the crown lands.[88] Slowly the aristocracy fused with the knight class (*stan rycerski*). The latter grew stronger, but the lawmakers in the Sejm established laws for all and united all parts of the *Rzeczpospolita*.[89] The Sejms at Radom and Piotrków evolved to the highest level of sophistication and asserted their benevolent dominance over all inhabitants, and the magnates with their privileges were held in check.[90]

Lelewel then identified weaknesses inherent in this third period of Poland's history. These augured the decline of the Polish state. Lithuania's preparations for union; calls for reform in the *Rzeczpospolita*; the Union of Lublin; the sovereignty of the omnipotent people (*prawo-*

dawstwo wszechwładnego ludu) without a head of state; the elective monarchy; the abuse of the *liberum veto*; conferations; wars; the victory near Byczyna in 1588 which assured the Polish throne to the Vasas — all indicated the growing weakness and decline of the Polish state.[91]

What preserved the country from total collapse in this her third epoch of history? Lelewel found the answer in the attributes of the Polish szlachta, in their spirit of citizenship (*obywatelstwo*). His national consciousness and faith in republican and democratic principles was most profound when he spoke of szlachta democracy (*gminowładztwo szlacheckie*).

> All the szlachta express themselves in a brotherly manner. . . .
> What saved the country from disintegration in its decline? . . .
> Nothing except brotherhood! . . . Brotherhood impressed deeply
> in the national thoughts and feelings, guided by the spirit of
> citizenship. . . . In the creation of the Polish *Rzeczpospolita* . . .
> freedom, equality, brotherhood, independence . . . these alone
> provided the stimulus for the greatness of this estate (*stan*).[92]

Kings, chancellors, and others, willingly surrendered their personal demands and obediently supported this spirit of citizenship.[93] The *Rzeczpospolita* continued to exist.

Lelewel convincingly informed his readers that only the *lud szlachecki* of the Polish nation conceived of the idea of freedom and developed the *Rzeczpospolita*. There were republican towns and inhabitants in the ancient and medieval eras, ". . . Republican federations of towns, cantons, free associations of small republics, but Poland alone developed a sizable national republic (*rzeczpospolita*); she raised and established the foundations to which old Europe hastened so as to grow young again and to improve the standard of living of its inhabitants.[94] Lelewel emphasized that "not war or conquest, violence or force, raised or stabilized this great *Rzeczpospolita*."[95] The *Rzeczpospolita* was not an aggressor, he asserted. The history of Poland in the period of her greatness was not a history of the problems of war, nor of awesome events, not of sagas, nor of men who dominated events. Poland's greatness developed differently from these — it was founded on sociability and on progress brought about by brotherhood, by the gallantry of the Sejms, and by the establishment of justice for a significant number of people.[96]

Such almost mystical adoration of the Slav virtues as they were developed by Poland's szlachta during the period of *Gminowładztwo Szlacheckie* appeared in Lelewel's earlier histories, but he expressed them most eloquently and profoundly in *Uwagi,* written in 1836, a year of intense political activity for Lelewel. He not only spoke out against the aristocratic camp,[97] but also expressed extremely radical opinions in favor of peasant reforms and emancipation.[98] Given these circumstances, the question arises: Why did Lelewel praise only one segment of Poland's population — the szlachta — in *Uwagi*?

For Lelewel, in at least one historical era, one stratum of the population realized his ideals of freedom, equality, and brotherhood. These ideals found concrete expression in the *Rzeczpospolita* of the szlachta. In the third decade of the nineteenth century, these virtuous ideals, imbued in the minds of the Polish szlachta and extended to all strata of the population, could provide the strength of will for the creation of a future Polish republic — a republic in which all segments of society participated and where social democracy prevailed.

Lelewel not only focused on the praiseworthy characteristics of the Polish gentry in the era of grandeur which he described so vividly. He also identified and analyzed those political and social errors committed by them which led to the weakening of the state. The most significant political errors of the szlachta, according to Lelewel, concerned the lands of Śląsk and Prussia. Unique opportunities arose for the *Rzeczpospolita* to acquire these two important lands and to extend the powers and prestige of the *Rzeczpospolita.* In both cases, the Polish szlachta remained indifferent, and the territories were lost. Lelewel argued that this error of the arrogant, apathetic szlachta (republicans) was never to be forgiven.[99] He also criticized the szlachta for serious social errors. He blamed them for restricting their privileges and not extending them to the townsmen and peasants.[100] Lelewel reproached the szlachta for forbidding the townsmen to own landed property and for holding artisans and merchants in contempt.[101]

In addition, the *kmieć* (peasants) lost all rights of citizenship. They became "slaves of the masters (*panowie*) and fell into destitution."[102] Lelewel devoted many pages to the plight of the *kmieć.* He described their progressive impoverishment, their lack of education, and their general destitution in this the third period of Poland's history.[103] For this degradation of the *kmieć,* he censured both the szlachta and the aristocracy who "betrayed and deserted the national spirit, who yielded to the contagion of foreign influences, who sought titles and privileges to the detriment of society."[104] Even the "great tribune of the szlachta," Jan Zamoyski, was guilty of these transgressions. As a result, between 1586 and 1605, szlachta democracy found itself in turmoil.[105]

Lelewel summarized the third period of Poland's history in the following manner: Because of the development and maturation of szlachta democracy which emerged because of a spirit of nationality, Poland stood at the pinnacle of her power. She lost this dominant position gradually because the szlachta abandoned their sense of nationality by oppressing the townspeople and the peasants. The magnates contributed to the loss by fighting against the szlachta democracy in alliance with the crown.

The fourth period of Poland's history as an independent political entity began under the circumstances described above and lasted until the partition of 1795. For Lelewel, this, Poland's period of decline, was a period of struggle in which foreign principles overpowered the national spirit (*duch narodowy*) of the Poles. In this era which spanned one hundred-eighty-eight years, the national spirit, the basis of Poland's greatness, was lulled to sleep. When it stirred near the end of the eighteenth century, it was too late, and foreign forces prevailed.

Lelewel began his discourse on Poland's fourth period of history by describing certain characteristics of the Slavs, i.e., their sense of nationality, freedom, brotherhood, and camaraderie.[106] The Poles adopted these Slav attributes and developed them to a relatively high level of sophistication in the lands in which they settled.[107] These virtues, as developed among the Poles, not only differentiated the Poles from other Slavs, but also provided the nucleus of the unique national spirit (*duch narodowy*) of the Poles.[108] This national spirit, in turn, determined Poland's greatness. Coincidentally, foreign influences permeated the land and contributed to Poland's decline.

Completing his brief introductory remarks, Lelewel discussed in great detail Poland's futile struggle against foreign influences in religion and politics. The origins of Poland's decline coincided with the appearance of the Jesuits in Poland in the late sixteenth century. The policy of religious tolerance assured the Jesuits freedom of action when they first arrived. However, their evangelizing, insistence on the use of Latin in schools, and their intolerance of dissidents weakened the national spirit of the szlachta.[109] Continuing his discourse, he again cited the Jesuit influences in schools and their strong opposition to republicanism as factors which contributed to the further weakening of the national spirit. By the reign of Zygmunt III (Vasa,

1587–1632), religious intolerance was widespread.[110] By the mid-seventeenth century, the Counter-Reformation triumphed in Poland. Rampant intolerance weakened considerably her national spirit.

The interference of the Jesuits in Poland's religious affairs coincided with the interference of foreign powers in Poland's domestic affairs. The election of foreign kings, after the extinction of the Jagiellonian dynasty in 1572; and the influences of foreign political ideas, especially "royalism" and the idea of social hierarchies on Poland's aristocracy also contributed to the weakening of the national spirit and to the ultimate destruction of the *Rzeczpospolita*. By 1648, the *Rzeczpospolita* showed signs of considerable strain.[111] Nevertheless, in the midst of her defeats, confusions, and anarchy, lifegiving forces stirred.[112] In the quarter of a century which followed, a national revival developed with the election of Michał Wiśniowiecki (1669–1673) and his successor Jan III Sobieski (1674–1696). This national revival, however, was shortlived. Wiśniowiecki's four year reign was marked by continued foreign interference and by Hapsburg and Turkish encroachments on Polish territory. Sobieski faced the Cossacks, Swedes, and other foreign intruders. By the turn of the century, the nation weakened once again. Foreign influences also adversely affected society and contributed especially to the worsening of the fate of the lower classes, the common people (*lud*).[113]

Lelewel devoted numerous pages to social conditions and relations in the Polish lands in the seventeenth and eighteenth centuries. He discussed the increasing atrophy of the sense of brotherhood, and reflected on its relationship to the growing oppression of the people (*lud*).[114] The szlachta not only separated from the lower, non-szlachta classes and unmercifully pushed the latter aside, but they also enchained the lower classes in bondage. The szlachta justified its social politics by searching for loopholes and resorting to absurdities to refute and discredit the exploited people. The szlachta:

> ... Repeat that the people (*lud*) is peaceful and patiently bears its yoke; thus it must be satisfied. They repeat that it is necessary to deprive the people of their goods and chattel so that they would not grow rich, become arrogant and proud, and to keep them in a subdued state so that they do not rebel; public safety and security requires this. It is absolutely necessary for the state.[115]

The pleas of well-meaning reformers to find ways to ease the fate of the oppressed people fell on deaf ears. The plight of the peasants was not alleviated even as a result of the oath of Jan Casimir (1648-1668) in Lwów in 1656. At that time, he vowed that when his native land was freed, the peasant population would be liberated from serfdom. On the contrary, peasants' hardships were enhanced by the imposition of increased obligations (*pańszczyzna*).[116] More than a century later, in 1780, reformers again expressed concern for the relief of the peasants, but even Zamoyski's proposals of that year were cast aside, and the idea expressed that any relief given to the peasants could awaken revolt gained wide acceptance.[117]

Lelewel examined in considerable detail the oppression of the people in the seventeenth and eighteenth centuries in Lithuania and in the Ukraine, and the violation of the principles of brotherhood and political equality by the szlachta which led to the Cossack unrest and the eventual loss of the Ukraine.[118] The oppression of the Cossacks and the general degradation of the agrarian class occurred throughout the Ukraine and was followed by Chmielnicki's uprising against the Poles in 1648.[119] Lelewel did not hold Chmielnicki responsible for the Cossack wars which immersed the *Rzeczpospolita* in the depths of a "deluge of catastrophe," but he accused the Polish warrior caste (*stan rycerski*). The latter, according to Lelewel, abused the republican principles upon which the Polish state was based by their reluctance to grant full rights of citizenship (*obywatelstwo*) to the Cossacks.[120]

Lelewel did not hold the Polish warrior caste totally responsible for the violence which erupted. He also accused the Jesuits of contributing to the unrest. The activities of the Society of Jesus in Poland and Lithuania fostered the development of religious intolerance, especially among the Polish szlachta. This religious intolerance, he argued, was also incompatible with the principles of political freedom and freedom of conscience — the principles of the *Rzeczpospolita*. This interference by the Jesuits contributed to the ultimate loss of the Ukraine.[121] More significant, it contributed to the weakening of the *Rzeczpospolita*.

Despite the religious, political, and social offenses of the szlachta, Lelewel proposed that the differences between Poland and the Ukrainians could have been resolved most favorably for all concerned by the Union of Hadziacz. In 1657, the year of Chmielnicki's death, a union of Poland and Ruthenia was negotiated at Hadziacz between the Poles and the new Hetman Ivan Vygovsky (Wyhowski). It called for the creation of a Ruthenian grand duchy consisting of the principalities of Kiev, Bracław, and Chernigov. The newly created Grand Duchy of Rus' (Ruthenia) would be similar to the Grand Duchy of Lithuania and would be granted analogous privileges and responsibilities. This agreement assured the transformation of the Polish *Rzeczpospolita* into a federation of Poland, Lithuania, and the Ukraine. The three nations were to be united under a common, freely elected king and stand by each other in war. Lelewel observed that this abortive Union of Hadziacz (ratified by the Polish Diet in 1659) could have completed the Union of Lublin of 1569. Most significantly for Lelewel, the republican virtues of the *Rzeczpospolita* could develop most fully for the benefit of all — Poles, Lithuanians, and Ukrainians.[122]

Lelewel censured neither the szlachta nor their *gminowładztwo,* for despite their social, religious, and political faults:

> Szlachta democracy (*gminowładztwo szlacheckie*) did not decline of its own accord but was disrupted by those elements which infected the purity of the national spirit and were contaminated by foreign elements and especially by those who heeded the Roman clergy and foreign kings, and by the aristocracy.[123]

Throughout the text of *Uwagi nad dziejami Polski i ludu jej,* the author reiterated his major thesis, i.e., that a vigorous and great Poland was erected on the loyalty of its inhabitants to the national spirit (*duch obywatelski*) and declined because of foreign influences which spread rapidly because of the Roman Catholic Church, as represented by the Jesuits; the reigns of foreign kings; and the self-interests (egoism) of a de-nationalized aristocracy.[124]

Lelewel held the kings and magnates responsible for the szlachta's excesses regarding the *liberum veto.* He agreed with Rousseau that the *veto* was not fundamentally evil because it assured general freedom.[125]

He argued convincingly that the influence of the foreign spirit (*duch cudzoziemski*) on the szlachta resulted in that estate's most frequent transgression, i.e., their oppression of the people (*lud*). While criticizing the szlachta for subjugating the people, Lelewel reminded his readers that in other lands the oppression of the people was worse than in Poland. He suggested that "the Lithuanian and

Ruthenian peoples beyond the Dnieper in Czernichów under the tsarist yoke recalled those times of the ancient *Rzeczpospolita* when conditions were superior. . . ."[126]

In general, in his criticism, Lelewel did not condemn the institutions of independent Poland. His words:

> It cannot be said that Poland succumbed because everything in her was corrupted, but because the degree of corruption was sufficient so she could not compete vigorously against the three partitioning powers, her pernicious neighbors.[127]

In contrast to the French edition which included the period of the third partition of Poland, the Polish edition of 1855 ended with Lelewel's commentary on Poland in anarchy in the seventeenth century. For the historically significant years just prior to Poland's fall, he referred his readers, in the Polish edition, to his comments on Niemciewicz's *Śpiewy historyczne,* written in 1817.[128] In doing so, he indicated that his interpretation of the history of Poland in the late eighteenth century had not changed since that year.

Lelewel's foremost contribution to historical scholarship in Poland was the *Historyka,* his theory and method of history which provided future generations of Poles with a systematic guide to the study of history in the manner of Ranke and other pioneers in the art and science of history.

As Poland's first modern national historian, Lelewel sought to present a comprehensive portrait of Poland's past, and he evolved a periodization of Poland's history which remains valid in the twentieth century. He was the first in Poland to include the cultural, religious, political, intellectual, and social aspects of Poland's past in his studies. He built on the works of Adam S. Naruszewicz (1733–1796) and Teodor Waga (1739–1801); added new materials; argued against compartmentalization and for the utilization of various disciplines related to history; and he used a new approach to arrive at unique interpretations of his nation's past. The first comprehensive history of Poland resulted.

Dealing with complex and frequently controversial problems concerning Poland's past, Lelewel sometimes arrived at conclusions invalidated by later scholars. The most obvious weakness in his national histories was his *a priori* theory of *gminowładztwo* — the communal democracy of the people (*lud*) in Poland's prehistoric past. Another weakness was that his histories reflected the political views of the author. His republicanism and democratic social feelings permeated the national histories.

In his interpretations of Poland's history, Lelewel stressed the negative influence of Western civilization and was especially harsh on the influences of the Church. His criticism of the Church is understandable as an Enlightenment scholar's critique of a major force of obscurantism — of opposition to progressive change. But Joachim Lelewel, influenced by and trained in the Enlightenment tradition, belongs more to the Romantic Era than to the Age of Reason. He did not see the eighteenth century as the best of all possible worlds, found weaknesses in politics and society, and emphasized continually an optimistic faith in the progressive development of nations and mankind. His interest in the peasant question and his support of the extension of rights and privileges to all strata of the population is the most obvious manifestation of this belief.

In interpreting Poland's history, he stressed the unique characteristics of the Poles, their national consciousness, spirit of citizenship, inherent feelings of brotherhood, and their *gminowładztwo* which dated back to the pre-feudal period. Lelewel found these noble characteristics a source of Poland's past greatness. Much like Herder, Michelet, Thierry, and Robertson, Joachim Lelewel saw the potential of the people (*sił ludności*) and called on the szlachta, Poland's traditional nation, to instill a national consciousness in the *lud* so that the szlachta and the people together would bring about the creation of a new Polish state based on the ancient, and to Lelewel, republican and democratic ideals.

Joachim Lelewel's knowledge of the past and his faith in the future provided a stimulus to the development of national consciousness among intellectuals at the centers of Polish culture, i.e., Wilno and Warsaw, before 1830 and influenced the development of republican and democratic political and social thought among his countrymen everywhere.

8 General Observations and Conclusions

Lelewel: Before His Exile

Poland's first national historian was Joachim Lelewel. In his highly personal interpretation of his nation's past, he stressed its republicanism and what he considered to be social equality. He attempted to instill these ideals in his audiences and his reading public by his words and actions. He was a republican who firmly believed that Poland's traditional republican institutions should be retained and restored. He also believed that the people were the basis of the fatherland and therefore were entitled to certain fundamental rights. Lelewel's political activities and experiences influenced his thought greatly. In his attempts to contribute effectively to the cause of Poland's independence, Joachim Lelewel reflected on the romantic, national ideas of his age. These, however, did not coincide with the national consciousness of a majority of the nobles and gentry in Poland at the time. Neither did his ideals coincide with the exigencies of power politics in the restless early decades of the nineteenth century.

Between 1821 and 1824, Lelewel's stimulating lectures inspired his students at Wilno and made them increasingly aware of their history, of the unique characteristics of the Polish nation, and of the need for fundamental social change. The weaknesses of the Poles had to be overcome through the efforts of the Poles before their state could again become a viable political entity. This was Lelewel's principal message.

Lelewel became the idol of students such as Adam Mickiewicz and Leonard Chodźko who regarded the historian as the very embodiment of those national virtues which he attempted to instill in them. Lelewel's lectures highlighting the glories of Poland's past may not have been known to tsarist government agents in the western provinces and might have escaped their attention had it not been for a change in the policies of Alexander I toward the western provinces and notably toward the Poles. The change was further aggravated by the policies of Tsar Nicholas I. Any expression of Polish ideas, no matter how insignificant, was considered dangerous. The early 1820s had "witnessed the maturation of conspiratorial groups with a strong national coloration in the western provinces of the Russian Empire."[1] This coincided with Novosiltsev's determination to "uproot impudent Polish nationalism in the western provinces and to completely exorcise Polonization and Jacobinization from the [Wilno] Educational District."[2] As part of the reaction engineered by Metternich, the heavy hand of tsardom was settling down on everything in the Polish lands that savored of national aspirations toward independence, and it was only logical that Wilno, a center of these aspirations, would not be overlooked. It was precisely at the University of Wilno that the first fruits of Romantic nationalism — in history, in literature, and in living — had made themselves felt, not in the least owing to Joachim Lelewel.

In 1824, Lelewel and his three colleagues were dismissed from the University, and several students and former students, including Adam Mickiewicz, were arrested, tried, and exiled. Lelewel retired into private life for a brief period but continued his research and writing. In 1828, he actively entered politics. As a deputy to the Sejm in Warsaw, representing the Żelechów district, he soon gained a reputation as a liberal because of his republican views. His ideas affected members of those political and university circles in the Polish lands which provided the leadership for the 1830 insurrection in the Congress Kingdom. The concerns of the tsarist Russian government which led to the investigation and the termination of Lelewel's appointment at the University of Wilno were not wholly unfounded.

It is an established fact that Lelewel participated in the revolutionary movement in the Polish lands prior to 1830. It is also an established fact that Lelewel did not favor the timing of the November, 1830, insurrection, and he bitterly opposed losing his place in the Sejm to become a member of the revolutionary National Government in 1831. As a result of the outbreak of the glorious, yet disastrous, insurrection in 1830, Lelewel was called from the bedside of his dying father to act as an advisor to the insurgents. He did not decline the call although the demands of the insurrection were distasteful to him.

Lelewel's position was that of Minister of Education in the National Government. In all councils of state, he took a firm stand on two issues: that Lithuania and Ruthenia (Rus) should at all costs be included in the common struggle with the tyranny of tsardom, and that the emancipation of the peasants should be publicly proclaimed as part of the rising. In other words, not only did he want national revolution but also social revolution. Lelewel's reluctance to participate in the National Government indicated that his primary concern was the pursuit of academic interests and not a political career. However, his sense of citizenship led him to accept the position in the government which was offered to him. His advocacy of the need for social revolution was a reflection of his awareness of the potential of the people (*lud*) as a force for progressive change. This potential could be tapped by the insurgent leaders as a decisive source of support for the revolutionary cause.

After 1831, Lelewel participated in the revolutionary movements in Europe. He actively worked with the Carbonari, and he helped to organize the Young Poland movement. On native soil, Young Poland did not assume any importance until Szymon Konarski returned to the homeland in 1836 and attempted to organize a revolutionary movement there. After Konarski's martyrdom in Wilno in 1839, the Young Poland movement lost its impetus and was largely ineffective. Lelewel's attitude toward the Young Europe movement changed as early as January, 1834, although he had participated in planning Konarski's expedition at the time. He had disapproved of looking to other governments for help in resolving the Polish question. Now he saw that looking to other peoples, i.e., participation in Young Europe, was also ineffectual. He wrote:

> Woe to that people which raises itself by the help of others! Such a nation will never be free. Experience has shown that counting on diplomacy to help destroys every move. Such material is poor stuff to build with. From it can arise at best a Duchy of Warsaw, or a 'Kingdom' . . . clay structures which rain and sleet will suffice to wash away.[3]

After 1834, he concentrated his efforts on encouraging the Poles to rely only on themselves and to keep alive the republican and democratic ideals of the *Rzeczpospolita*.

Joachim Lelewel's prolific contributions to the development of historiography in Poland before his exile are of great fundamental value. History was being introduced as a new discipline in the schools of Poland by the turn of the century. Sources had to be gathered, materials catalogued, methods of study devised. The chronological, narrative approach was no longer adequate in the Polish lands or elsewhere. Lelewel realized this and began his work, accepting the basic premise that history involved the economic, cultural, and social aspects as well as the political. He devoted most of his life to scholarship. His studies of the origins of the social order in northern and eastern Europe, his collecting of folk tales and sagas of Scandinavians and Slavs, his interest in geography and numismatics have been alluded to briefly. His researches into the early history of his own land, his emphasis on particular periods of Poland's history, his interpretation of history, and his theory of history all resulted in lasting contributions to the development of modern historical scholarship in Poland. Lelewel's histories of Poland were a significant stimulus to the renascent national consciousness of the intellectuals at the centers of Polish culture before 1830. After the failure of the insurrection and war with imperial Russia, a period of russification began in the Polish lands, and the most articulate of Poland's intellectuals found themselves in exile in western Europe. Among the exiles was Lelewel. As an émigré, Lelewel continued to criticize the foreign domination of his fatherland by despots and to instill national ideas — of freedom, equality, brotherhood, and citizenship — in the minds of his audiences and his reading public.

In speaking of Joachim Lelewel's social and political consciousness, it is difficult to separate his ideas of nationalism from the romanticism of his age. Lelewel posed a revealing question: "What is the purpose of the historian?" His response followed: "An historian must study peoples, their sufferings and wrongs."[4] It is evident from the perusal of his selected writings that Joachim Lelewel the historian was very much aware of the "sufferings" of the Polish nation not only at the hands of foreign powers but also at the hands of a minority who had abused the privileges entrusted to them at various times throughout Poland's history. He believed that the Polish nation had the natural right to national self-government and that to achieve political independence all social classes and ethnic groups had to unite in common cause. Also, he firmly believed that the new Polish state had to be a republic. As had been stated previously, Lelewel did not differ from his contemporaries in Europe to any great degree. He identified the virtues of his nation and wrote the history of his nation. He studied Poland's institutions and proposed political and social solutions for her national problems. In doing this, Lelewel the historian, at times, became Lelewel the publicist.

However, the latter should by no means be overemphasized so that

Lelewel's lasting contributions to historical scholarship are ignored. His *Historyka* provided future historians with a guide to the study of history. Lelewel's own approach to the study of history was far superior to the approaches of his predecessors who relied on the traditional narrative-chronological exposition rather than on analysis and synthesis. Joachim Lelewel aptly stated that "scholarship was the preoccupation of my life; it is my second father. If ever I gave any service to my country, it is in no other way except in the field of learning."[5]

⊛ Lelewel: Post 1830–1831

The year 1831 was a significant turning point for Joachim Lelewel. He recalled later in life:

> In September . . . I parted with my mother for the last time (d. 1837), with my brothers and sisters and my entire family, with my library, with my scholarly concerns, with engravings, and with my notes and the materials which I had accumulated for a number of years, . . . finally with my fatherland.[6]

The Paris to which he fled was the center of the international revolutionary movement, and "ready to receive the Poles with their military experience as valuable allies."[7] In December, 1831, Lelewel set up his own Polish National Committee in order to declare solidarity with the struggling nations and peoples of Europe. Whereas Czartoryski's Hotel Lambert group relied on traditional, diplomatic methods for the re-establishment of the Polish state, Lelewel's group issued manifestoes, appealing to every likely source of support. Manifestoes addressed to the British House of Commons, the French Chamber of Deputies, Hungarians, Russians, and others were drawn up.[8]

Lelewel's address to the Russian people resulted in the diplomatic intervention of the Russian ambassador who induced the French government to dissolve the National Committee and expel Lelewel from Paris, then from France.[9] In the fall of 1832, he found asylum in the capital of the newly created state of Belgium, and he remained there until shortly before his death in 1861.

The Polish National Committee which Lelewel organized was as ineffective as Prince Adam Czartoryski's Hotel Lambert group and the Polish Democratic Society.[10] Lelewel continued to participate in and to influence politics after 1831, but he also returned to his multifarious scholarly activities — to geography, numismatics, and history.

His endeavors in historical-geography and numismatics resulted in contributions which remain significant to this day. In exile, Joachim Lelewel continued his studies of the geography of antiquity, and in 1836 his famous work was published. His interest in Celtic numismatics resulted in the two volume *Etudes numismatiques et archéoliques* (*Studies in Numismatics and Archeology*). Volume one, *Type gaulois, ou celtique* (*French and Celtic Types*) appeared in 1841. In the field of numismatics, he gained recognition as a pioneer and master, and he was elected, posthumously, as a member of the International Congress of Numismaticians in 1891.[11]

He also continued his work in history. He wrote a history of contemporary Poland for children and young people entitled *Polska odradzająca się* (*Poland in the Throes of Rebirth*). In his work, he dealt with what he called the fifth period of Polish history, a period, according to Lelewel, which was not yet concluded because Poland had not yet been restored as a sovereign entity. He revised four volumes of *Poland in the Middle Ages* in the years 1846 to 1851, and he added *Narody na ziemiach sławiańskich przed powstaniem Polski* (*Nations in the Slav Lands Before the Rise of Poland*) in 1853.[12]

The intensity of his activity is evident from the fact that he also prepared a multivolume edition of his collected works for publication (*Poland: Her History and Affairs*). Included in this collection was his *Uwagi nad dziejami Polski i ludu jej* (*Remarks on the History of Poland and Her People*). This work was written in French in 1836 and translated into Polish by its author for publication a decade later. These national histories are noteworthy because of his interpretations and because of their political implications.

Lelewel, the historian, wrote that "in order to bring to fruition the history of the fatherland — critically and synthetically, I followed procedures similar to those I used in the field of ancient history. And I soon was aware of the political implications and objectives for which the history of the fatherland could be used. The nation which loses its existence and looks for its rebirth by remembrance of the past gains strength."[13]

He went on to state that the remembrance of a nation's past, whether it is beneficial or harmful to the nation, is a significant consideration for him and for historians in general. A consciousness of the nation's past strength could be utilized for good or evil purposes.[14] When Lelewel studied Poland's past, he felt that he was fortunate that he uncovered Poland's honorable and positive aspects and that he could make them known to many people through his books.[15]

Joachim Lelewel's interpretation of Poland's national history was, in many respects, influenced by his political experiences. His early national consciousness was manifest in his works and actions prior to the insurrection. In his histories of Poland and in his lectures, he emphasized the crucial need for Poles to maintain their language, customs, and traditions, and he tried to instill in his audience pride in their past — especially in the unique republican institutions which had existed in pre-partition Poland, in the *Rzeczpospolita*. He was a typical representative of the militant republicanism which began manifesting itself on the European continent in the early nineteenth century. A member of the intelligentsia, he participated in secret societies, and looked with equanimity on the prospect of revolutionary upheaval to advance the universal cause of liberty, equality, and brotherhood.

In exile, Lelewel's interest in Poland's future became more significant for him than the universal principles of Mazzini's Young Europe. After his exile, Lelewel continued to study the ancient greatness and republicanism of the Slavs.[16] In *Three Polish Constitutions,* he had sought reasons for Poland's weakness and demise in her political institutions and had decided that the egoism, or self-interests, of those in power was the chief cause. He concluded that there were no inherent weaknesses in Poland's traditionally republican institutions. Writing in 1836, he reaffirmed this view, again citing, among the reasons for Poland's demise, the egoism of those in power who wanted to profit from the weakening of the common people. He emphasized that the loyalty of the people (*lud*) was a necessary prerequisite for the resurrection of the Polish state as a sovereign entity.

Owing to his political activism and democratic social sentiments, Lelewel believed that a historian who studied the history of a state and nation and who lost sight of the part played by the people was superficial. He should not consider their numbers but should recognize the communal relationships of the people, for "this is a quiet but potential power on which, in each period of time, depends the fortune of the nation and the state."[17] That he recognized and countenanced the communal relationships of all the people is evident when one considers Lelewel's role in the extra-legal activities of Young Europe. But in this particular content, he was referring specifically to the social relations of Poland's indigenous population. In exile, Lelewel's interest was concentrated on Poland's future more than on the future of all peoples in Europe.

In *Uwagi nad dziejami Polski i ludu jej,* Lelewel noted that the golden age of the Polish nation was the pre-Christian era in which the estate of the workers on the land was equal to that of its defenders, i.e., the peasants were equal to the gentry.[18] Lelewel's belief in the role of the people seems feasible when one considers his political activities and their relevance to the conclusions he reached in his works. He was well aware of the failure of the leaders of the revolt of 1830–1831 to gain support of the masses. He had prophesied that the insurrection would be a national and social revolt. He was incorrect. In exile, he was aware of the factionalism of the Great Emigration. He disagreed with Adam Czartoryski's conservative monarchism and emphasis on traditional diplomatic methods for the re-establishment of the Polish state. He also disagreed with the Democratic Society which represented the opposite extreme of the political spectrum and tended toward socialism. Lelewel took the middle course among the émigrés. As a result, both the monarchists and the extreme left criticized him.[19]

The political activities of the exiles as well as a historian's knowledge of Poland's past led Joachim Lelewel to conclude that Poland would arise only by her own efforts. Writing in 1844, he predicted failure for those people who waited for help from others, and he argued that such people would never be free, that such people "will always be under the threat of subjugation, servitude, and subordination."[20] For Poland to arise by her own efforts, it was necessary to have the support of the people. What was needed even before that was an effective leadership group. Lelewel readily found the potential leaders who were needed for the successful resurrection of the Polish state. For him, they were the young, politically conscious students and intellectuals, in the Polish lands and abroad, who would read his histories, discuss his theories, and his proposed solutions for the national problems, and act at the most opportune moment. That he sought to influence his young readers is exemplified in the fact that he dedicated many of his works to the youth of Poland. An open letter to the children of Poland, dated 25 January 1836, supports these observations:

> As I prepare to finish my *History of Poland from the Fall of the Rzeczpospolita,* my thoughts turn to the children, to the youth, the great hope of Poland in the throes of renascence. I do not know how, but this work [the history he is writing] will reach them and will become implanted in their hearts, in young hearts and in your souls my dearest children of desolate Poland.[21]

This emotional appeal, however, should not detract from the content of his histories. His purpose was to make the youth conscious of Poland's glorious past, real or imagined, and of their role and the role of all strata of society in Poland's future. He especially wanted to make the young cognizant of their right to determine the government of the sovereign state to which they would belong — a sovereign state similar to that which had existed in the past. He thought, moreover, that considering the progress of mankind in Europe, the slowly recuperating Polish nation would find her own ideas and her own assured existence only in republicanism.[22] The traditional nation would provide the best possible rulers and administrators for Poland. However, social reforms were also needed, and social democracy (which according to Lelewel had existed in Poland's pre-Christian past) had to be achieved.

After 1831, Lelewel produced some of his most outstanding work in historical-geography and numismatics. Numerous works in history — collections of new or previously published studies — were also published. These facts substantiate the point that Lelewel's political activities were not his primary concern. Above all, he was a scholar.

In his approach to history, Joachim Lelewel adhered to the general principles of European Romanticism, i.e., freedom of the individual, society, and nation, and to the liberalism resulting from them. These principles are reflected specifically in his interpretation of the history of Poland. The ideas he expressed in his works buttressed the patriotic national movement of the Poles who were subjugated to the three foreign autocracies. His endeavors also had a more far-reaching effect. Principles of modern Polish historiography were established largely through the efforts of Joachim Lelewel.

Notes

❀ Preface

1. Matthew A. Fitzsimmons *et al.* (eds.), *The Development of Historiography* (Harrisburg: The Stackpole Co., 1954), p. 196.

❀ 1: Introduction

1. Helena Więckowska, "Lelewel w opinii historyków polskich," *Kwartalnik Historyczny*, LXVIII (1961), pp. 899–912. See also Bernard Ziffer, *Poland: History and Historians: Three Bibliographical Essays* (New York: Mid-European Studies Center, 1952), p. 22.

2. Marceli Handelsman, "Joachim Lelewel: Próba charakterystyki twórczości," *Przegląd Historyczny*, XXXIV (1937–1938), p. 335.

3. Helena Więckowska, "Komentarz," in Joachim Lelewel, *Materiały autobiograficzne: Dzieła* (Warszawa: Państwowe Wydawnictwo Naukowe, 1957), I, p. 368.

4. Ignacy Chrzanowski, "Lelewel," in *Great Men and Women of Poland*, edited by Stephen P. Mizwa (New York: The Macmillan Co., 1941), p. 184.

5. *Ibid.*, pp. 185–187.

6. *Ibid.*, p. 187.

7. Ignacy Chrzanowski, *Joachim Lelewel: człowiek i pisarz*, do druku przygotował i przedmową poprzedził Stanisław Pigoń (Kraków: Spółdzielnia Wydawnicza "Czytelnik," 1946).

8. Joachim Lelewel, *Listy emigracyjne Joachima Lelewela*, wydała i wstępem poprzedziła Helena Więckowska (Kraków: Nakładem Polskiej Akademii Umiejętności, 1948–1956), 5 vols. and index.

9. Helena Hleb-Koszańska i Maria Kotwiczówna, *Bibliografia utworów Joachima Lelewela* (Wrocław: Wydawnictwo Zakładu Narodowego Im. Ossolińskich, 1952).

10. Marian Henryk Serejski, *Koncepcja historii powszechnej Joachima Lelewela*. Wydanie 1 (Warszawa: Państwowe Wydawnictwo Naukowe, 1958).

11. Witold Nowodworski, *"Bibliograficznych ksiąg dwoje" Joachima Lelewela* (Wrocław: Zakład Narodowy Im. Ossolińskich, 1959).

140 / *Romantic Nationalism and Liberalism*

12. Franciszek Bronowski, "Recenzja Abrahama M. Basewicza, *Joachim Lelewel, polskij rewolucioner, demokrat, uczenyj,*" *Kwartalnik Historyczny,* LX (1963), p. 489.

13. Aniela Kowalska, *Mochnacki i Lelewel: Współtwórcy życia umysłowego Warszawy i kraju, 1825–1830* (Warszawa: Państowy Instytut Wydawniczy, 1971), and Boris Popkov, *Pol'skii uchen'ii i revoliutsioner Ioakhim Lelevel'* (Moscow: Izdatel'stvo 'Nauka', 1974).

14. Frank Mocha, "The Karamzin-Lelewel Controversy," *The Slavic Review,* 31 (1972), pp. 592–610. Kenneth F. Lewalski, "Lelewel's Third Exile: Alternatives for Relocation," *The Polish Review,* XXIII (1978), pp. 31–39.

§ 2: Family Background and Formative Years

1. Joachim Lelewel, "Letter to Karol Sienkiewicz in Paris," 17 April 1859, *Korespondencyja z Karolem Sienkiewiczem* (Poznań: Nakładem Księgarni J. K. Żupańskiego, 1872), pp. 78–84. See also Joachim Lelewel, *Przygody w poszukiwaniach rzeczy narodowych polskich: Dzieła,* opracowała Helena Więckowska (Kraków: Krakowska Drukarnia Naukowa, 1957), I, pp. 40–41.

2. Joachim Lelewel, "Letter to Karol Sienkiewicz in Paris," 17 April 1859, *Korespondencyja z Karolem Sienkiewiczem,* p. 79.

3. Irena Lelewel Friemannowa in Prot Lelewel, *Pamiętniki i diariusz domu naszego,* przygotowała do druku i opatrzyła przypisami Irena Lelewel Friemannowa (Wrocław: Zakład Narodowy Im. Ossolińskich, 1966), p. 89.

4. Prot Lelewel, *Pamiętniki i diariusz,* pp. 18–19. Prior to 1775, one spelling was not used consistently. In the *Rzeczpospolita,* citizenship as a member of the Polish szlachta was accorded by an act of the Sejm to gentry of foreign birth. The szlachta, often referred to as the nobility, formed about one tenth of the population of Poland. This group alone enjoyed full political rights. Its members included great landowners (magnates) as well as smallholders and landless squires who frequently served in the households of the wealthy.

5. Prot Lelewel, *Pamiętniki i diariusz,* p. 21. Joachim Lelewel, "Letter to Karol Sienkiewicz in Paris," 17 April 1859, *Korespondencyja z Karolem Sienkiewiczem,* pp. 79–80.

6. Joachim Lelewel, *Ibid.,* p. 83.

7. Prot Lelewel, *Pamiętniki i diariusz,* p. 21.

8. Joachim Lelewel, *Przygody: Dzieła,* I, pp. 40–41.

9. Prot Lelewel, *Pamiętniki i diariusz,* p. 25.

10. *Ibid.,* p. 26. Pius Kiciński (1752–1828) was known as an enlightened speaker. His speeches appeared in *Mowy miane na sejmie 1788 i 1792* (Warszawa, 1799) and in *Głos na sesji sejmowej wrzesnia 1790* (in *Wyborże mów Małackiego*). Cited by Irena Lelewel Friemannowa (ed.), *Pamiętniki i diariusz* by Prot Lelewel, p. 93.

11. Witold Nowodworski, *"Bibliograficznych ksiąg dwoje" Joachima Lelewela* (Wrocław: Zakład Narodowy Im. Ossolińskich Wydawnictwo, 1959), p. 31.

12. Joachim Lelewel, "Letter to Karol Sienkiewicz," *Korespondencja z Karolem Sienkiewiczem,* p. 75. Cited by Józef Dutkiewicz (ed.) in his comments to Joachim Lelewel, *Panowania Stanisława Augusta: Dzieła* (Warszawa: Państwowe Wydawnictwo Naukowe, 1961) VIII, pp. 463–466.

13. Four — Julian, Teresa, Józef, and Wincenty — died in childhood; Joachim, Prot, Jan, Marcela, and Maria reached adulthood.

14. Joachim Lelewel, "Letter to T. Januszewicz in Paris," 1 April 1854, *Listy emigracyjne Joachima Lelewela,* wydała i wstępem poprzedziła Helena Więckowska (Kraków: Nakładem Akademii Umiejętności, 1948–1956), Vol. IV, letter no. 1073, p. 194. Hereafter cited as *Listy emigracyjne.*

15. Prot Lelewel, *Pamiętniki i diariusz,* pp. 39–53. The family also suffered hardships during the period of the Grand Duchy. In 1814, the Russians took animals and other supplies from Wola Cygowska. In the period of the Congress Kingdom conditions improved.

16. Lelewel, *Przygody: Dzieła,* I, p. 38. Prot Lelewel, *Pamiętniki i diariusz,* pp. 53–54. Prot's account is more detailed than Joachim's.

17. Joachim Lelewel, *Listy do rodzeństwa pisane* (Poznań: J. K. Żupański, 1878–1879), Vol. I, pp. 11–24.

18. Prot Lelewel, *Pamiętniki i diariusz,* p. 53, pp. 66–68.

19. *Ibid.,* pp. 66–67.

20. Joachim Lelewel, *Bibliograficznych ksiąg dwoje w których rozebrane i pomnożone zostały dwa dzieła Jerzego Samuela Bandtkie* (Wilno: Nakładem i Drukiem Józefa Zawadzkiego, 1826), Vol. II, p. 118.

21. Prot Lelewel, *Pamiętniki i diariusz,* pp. 67–68.

22. Lelewel, *Przygody: Dzieła,* p. 39. Also Lelewel, *Listy do rodzeństwa pisane,* I, p. 22, p. 31.

23. Stefan Kieniewicz and Witold Kula (eds.), *Historia Polski* (Warszawa: Państwowe Wydawnictwo Naukowe, 1959), Vol. II, part ii, p. 170.

24. Jerzy Michalski, *Z dziejów Towarzystwa Przyjaciół Nauk* (Warszawa: Nakładem Towarzystwa Naukowego Warszawskiego z Zasiłku Ministerstwa Szkolnictwa Wyższego, 1953), p. 23.

25. Lelewel, *Przygody: Dzieła,* I, pp. 40–41.

26. *Ibid.,* p. 40.

27. *Ibid.*

28. *Ibid.,* p. 41.

29. Józef Bieliński, *Uniwersytet Wileński, 1579–1831* (Kraków: Druk W. L. Anczyca i Spółki, 1899–1900), III, pp. 531–551.

30. Lelewel, *Przygody: Dzieła,* pp. 41–42. Also Lelewel, *Listy do rodzeństwa pisane,* I, pp. 94–95, p. 104.

31. Below, p. 20ff.

32. Lelewel, *Przygody: Dzieła,* I, p. 42.

33. *Ibid.,* p. 43.

34. *Ibid.* Also Marian H. Serejski, *Joachim Lelewel: Z dziejów postępowej myśli historycznej w Polsce* (Warszawa: Państwowe Wydawnictwo Naukowe, 1953), p. 18.

35. Lelewel, *Przygody: Dzieła,* I, p. 42. Also Bieliński, *Uniwersytet Wileński,* III, p. 559.

36. Artur Śliwiński, *Joachim Lelewel: Zarys biograficzny lata 1786–1831,* wydanie drugie przejrzane i uzupełnione (Warszawa: Wydawnictwo Kasy Im. Mianowskiego, 1932), p. 47.

37. Lelewel, *Przygody: Dzieła,* I, pp. 43–44.

38. *Ibid.,* pp. 45–46. Also Lelewel, *Listy do rodzeństwa pisane,* I, p. 4; II, p. 10.

39. *Ibid.,* p. 46. Also Joachim Lelewel, *Korespondencyja z Tytusem Hr. Działyńskim,* wydał Zygmunt Celichowski (Poznań: Nakładem Biblioteki Kornickiej, czcionkami drukarni Kuryera Poznańskiego, 1884). This correspondence deals with literary and scholarly matters. Included is much valuable information on the publication of manuscripts of Polish-Lithuanian laws. Between 1821 and 1830, Lelewel and Działynski had prepared 26 folios which were published. Publication was not resumed until c. 1840 by Działynski. By this time Lelewel was in exile in western Europe.

40. *Ibid.,* pp. 44–47.

41. *Ibid.,* pp. 46–48.

42. *Ibid.,* p. 49.

43. *Ibid.*

44. *Ibid.,* p. 50. Also Lelewel, *Listy do rodzeństwa pisane,* I, pp. 21–23.

⚙ 3: The University Professor and Productive Scholar

1. The question of Lelewel's appointment is treated extensively by Józef Bieliński, *Uniwersytet Wileński, 1579–1831* (Kraków: Druk W. L. Anczyca i Społki, 1899–1900), III, and by Lelewel's biographers. See e.g., Artur Śliwiński, *Joachim Lelewel: Zarys biograficzny lata 1786–1831* (Warszawa: Wydawnictwo Kasy Im. Mianowskiego, 1932).

2. Nina Assorodobraj in Joachim Lelewel, *Pisma metodologiczne: Dzieła,* opracowała Nina Assorodobraj (Warszawa: Państwowe Wydawnictwo Naukowe, 1964), II, p. 16.

3. Aleksander Gieysztor *et al.* (eds.), *History of Poland* (Warsaw: Polish Scientific Society, 1968), p. 410. Also Maurycy Mochnacki, *Powstanie narodu polskiego w roku 1830–1831,* drugie wydanie (Wrocław: Nakładem Zygmunta Schlettera, 1850), II, p. 47. Also Bieliński, *Uniwersytet Wileński,* III, pp. 538–539, pp. 540–542, p. 548.

4. Lelewel developed and expanded the ideas he first expressed (in print and lectures) at the start of his brief university teaching career over a period of twenty years. These included his student years at the university in Wilno as well as the two periods he spent on the faculty there. It is beyond the scope of

this discussion to deal intensively with the evolution of Lelewel's ideas. The subject is more than adequately treated by Nina Assorodobraj, "Wstęp," in Lelewel, *Dzieła,* II, pp. 7–46.

5. Lelewel adapted the title for his work from either G. J. Vossius, *Ars historica* or J. Schroek, *De commini poetae et historici munere* (Wittenburg, 1726), according to Assorodobraj in Lelewel, *Dzieła,* II, p. 22. The former was a Dutch historian (1577–1649); the latter a German historian (1733–1808).

6. Assorodobraj in Lelewel, *Dzieła,* II, p. 17, pp. 20–22, p. 683.

7. Lelewel, *Dzieła,* II, p. 178.

8. *Ibid.,* p. 179.

9. *Ibid.,* pp. 180–183.

10. Joachim Lelewel, *Podanie niepewne: Wybór pism historycznych* (Wrocław: Wydawnictwo Zakłada Narodowego Im. Ossolińskich, 1950), p. 79. See also Joachim Lelewel, *Dzieje Polski potocznym sposobem opowiedziane i aneksy: Dzieła,* opracowała Janina Bieniarzówna (Warszawa: Państwowe Wydawnictwo Naukowe, 1961), VII, pp. 39–46.

11. Lelewel, *Dzieła,* II, pp. 183–190.

12. *Ibid.,* pp. 186–187.

13. *Ibid.,* pp. 190–191.

14. *Ibid.,* p. 191.

15. *Ibid.*

16. *Ibid.*

17. Below, p. 64ff.

18. Lelewel, *Dzieła,* II, pp. 192–193.

19. *Ibid.,* p. 199, pp. 224–225.

20. *Ibid.,* p. 208.

21. Joachim Lelewel, *Listy do rodzeństwa pisane* (Poznań: J. K. Żupański, 1878–1879), Vol. I, pp. 198–199, p. 225. Lelewel, *Dzieła,* II, pp. 17–22, p. 683.

22. Lelewel, *Dzieła,* II, p. 507.

23. Lelewel, *Dzieła,* II, pp. 534–535.

24. *Ibid.,* p. 533.

25. *Ibid.,* pp. 539–542.

26. *Ibid.,* p. 546.

27. Stanisław Pigoń, *Z dawnego Wilna: szkice obyczajowe i literackie* (Wilno: Wydawnictwo Magistratu M. Wilna, 1929), p. 29.

28. Mochnacki, *Powstanie narodu polskiego,* II, p. 69.

29. Joachim Lelewel, *Przygody w poszukiwaniach rzeczy narodowych polskich: Dzieła,* opracowała Helena Więckowska (Kraków: Krakowska Drukarnia Naukowa, 1957), I, pp. 52–55.

30. Bieliński, *Uniwersytet Wilenski,* II, p. 749. Also Lelewel, *Przygody: Dzieła,* I, p. 55.

31. The University of Warsaw began to function by orders of the tsar and

hereditary king of the Congress Kingdom of Poland in January, 1817, and was closed after the abortive Polish uprising of November, 1830, by orders of the tsar.

32. Bieliński, *Uniwersytet Wileński*, II, p. 749.

33. Joachim Lelewel, *Bibliograficznych ksiąg dwoje* (Wilno: Nakładem i Drukiem Józefa Zawadzkiego, 1823-1826), II, p. 177.

34. *Ibid.*, p. 178.

35. *Ibid.*, pp. 179-180.

36. *Ibid.*, pp. 181-183.

37. *Ibid.*, Vol. I, pp. 11-13.

38. Śliwiński, *Joachim Lelewel: Zarys biograficzny*, p. 100.

39. Witold Nowodworski, *"Bibliograficznych ksiąg dwoje" Joachima Lelewela* (Wrocław: Zakład Narodowy Im. Ossolińskich Wydawnictwo, 1959), analyzes and evaluates the long term significance of Lelewel's two volumes. Irena Treichel, *Pierwszy podręcznik bibliotekarski*, z przedmową Heleny Więckowskiej (Wrocław: Nakład Biblioteki Uniwersytetckiej w Łodzie, 1957), is a valuable shorter study.

40. Lelewel, *Bibliograficznych ksiąg dwoje*, I, pp. 144-147.

41. *Ibid.*, Vol. II, pp. 160-165.

42. *Ibid.*, pp. 237-267.

43. Lelewel, *Dzieła*, VII, pp. 274-277.

44. *Ibid.*, p. 284, p. 298.

45. Lelewel, *Przygody: Dzieła*, I, pp. 59-60.

46. Joachim Lelewel, *Polska odradzająca się: Dzieła*, opracowała Helena Więckowska (Warszawa: Państwowe Wydawnictwo Naukowe, 1961), VIII, p. 67.

47. Marian Kukiel, *Czartoryski and European Unity* (Princeton: Princeton University Press, 1955), p. 142.

48. Jerzy Zdrada, "Joachim Lelewel o początkach cenzury w Królestwie Polskim," *Przegląd Historyczny*, Vol. 59 (1968), pp. 287-293.

49. Stefan Kieniewicz and Witold Kula (eds.), *Historia Polski* (Warszawa: Państwowe Wydawnictwo Naukowe, 1959), II, p. 401.

50. Lelewel, *Przygody: Dzieła*, I, p. 60.

51. Józef Bieliński, *Królewski Uniwersytet Warszawski, 1816-1831* (Warszawa: Skład Główny w Księgarni E. Wende i Ska, 1911), II, p. 753. Also Lelewel, *Przygody: Dzieła*, I, p. 62.

52. Lelewel, *Przygody: Dzieła*, I, p. 62.

53. Kieniewicz and Kula (eds.), *Historia Polski*, II, pp. 392-393. The population of Wilno in 1820 was ca. 30,000 — supplemented by several hundred students and transient szlachta from the surrounding areas.

54. Bieliński, *Uniwersytet Wileński*, II, pp. 540-544. Also Pigoń, *Z dawnego Wilna*, pp. 29-30.

55. Lelewel, *Dzieła*, VIII, p. 581. Also Bieliński, *Uniwersytet Wileński*, II, p. 544. And Mochnacki, *Powstanie narodu polskiego*, II, p. 54.

56. After completion of his studies at the University of Wilno, Adam Mickiewicz was obligated to teach in a secondary school in Kaunas (1819–1821) because of a government scholarship which enabled him to study in Wilno. In 1821–22 he secured a leave and spent the year among his friends in Wilno. Thus he was there to welcome Lelewel. Returning to Kaunas in 1822, he taught there for one additional year (1822–23). Then he managed a second leave for two years, but his plans to go abroad were aborted by his arrest in 1823 and his subsequent exile to St. Petersburg. See Wiktor Weintraub, *The Poetry of Adam Mickiewicz* (Leiden: Mouton and Co., 1954), p. 15. The Society of Philarets and its participants are discussed in detail by Aleksander Kamiński, *Polskie związki młodzieży: 1804-1831* (Warszawa: Państwowe Wydawnictwo Naukowe, 1963), pp. 450–465.

57. Śliwiński, *Joachim Lelewel: Zarys biograficzny*, p. 80.

58. Mochnacki, *Powstanie narodu polskiego*, II, pp. 60–63. Also Kamiński, *Polskie związki młodzieży*, pp. 424–425, pp. 435–449.

59. Mochnacki, *Powstanie narodu polskiego*, p. 63.

60. Charles Breunig, *The Age of Revolution and Reaction, 1789-1850* (New York: W. W. Norton and Co., 1970), p. 183.

61. Henryk Mościcki (ed.), *Promieniści-Filomaci-Filareci*, wydanie trzecie (Warszawa: Nakład Gebethnera i Wolffa, 1934), p. 16, p. 49.

62. *Ibid.*, p. 14.

63. *Ibid.*, p. 15.

64. Stanisława Pietraszkiewiczówna, *Dzieje Filomatów w zarysie* (Kraków: Druk W. L. Anczyca, 1912), p. 1. Also, Mościcki (ed.), *Promieniści-Filomaci-Filareti*, p. 8. The Society of Philomaths was first organized in June, 1806, as the *Towarzystwo Doskonalącej się Młodzi w Naukach i Umiejętnościach*. Then at the beginning of the academic year 1807–08 it adopted the name *Towarzystwo Filomactyczne*. In 1817, the society was reorganized as a secret group. See Kamiński, *Polskie związki młodzieży*, p. 25, pp. 289–373.

65. Mościcki (ed.), *Promieniści-Filomaci-Filareti*, p. 9. Also Weintraub, *The Poetry of Adam Mickiewicz*, pp. 21–22.

66. Weintraub, *The Poetry of Adam Mickiewicz*, p. 14, discusses Zan's "theory of radiance" and its effects on the *Promieniści*. The group proposed "to radiate" (*promieniować*) their influence on others.

67. Pietraszkiewiczówna, *Dzieje Filomatów w zarysie*, p. 84, p. 136.

68. *Ibid.*, p. 90.

69. Mościcki (ed.), *Promieniści-Filomaci-Filareti*, p. 11.

70. *Ibid.*, p. 12.

71. Mochnacki, *Powstanie narodu polskiego*, II, pp. 61–62.

72. Pietraszkiewiczówna, *Dzieje Filomatów w zarysie*, pp. 121–124.

73. Mochnacki, *Powstanie narodu polskiego*, II, p. 45.

74. Pietraszkiewiczówna, *Dzieje Filomatów w zarysie*, p. 18, p. 144.

75. Weintraub, *The Poetry of Adam Mickiewicz*, pp. 14–15.

76. Adam Mickiewicz, "Do Joachima Lelewela zokoliczności rozpoczęcia kursu historii powszechnej w uniwersytecie Wileńskim, 6 stycznia 1822," *Dzieła* (Warszawa: Społdzielnia Wydawnicza "Czytelnik," 1955), I, pp. 93–100.

77. Lelewel, *Dzieła,* II, pp. 141–142.

78. *Ibid.,* p. 193.

79. Joachim Lelewel, *Wykłady kursowe z historii powszechnej w uniwersytecie Wileńskim, 1822–1824: Dzieła,* opracował Marian Henryk Serejski (Warszawa: Państwowe Wydawnictwo Naukowe, 1959), III, pp. 99–119.

80. *Ibid.,* pp. 57–69.

81. Lelewel, *Dzieła,* III, p. 145.

82. *Ibid.,* p. 148.

83. *Ibid.,* pp. 150–151, p. 164.

84. *Ibid.,* pp. 167–168.

85. *Ibid.,* p. 224, p. 230, p. 248.

86. *Ibid.,* p. 224, p. 230, p. 248.

87. *Ibid.,* pp. 273–301.

88. *Ibid.,* pp. 301–345.

89. *Ibid.,* pp. 280–288.

90. *Ibid.,* p. 289.

91. *Ibid.,* pp. 290–291. Francis Dvornik, *The Slavs in European History and Civilization* (New Brunswick: Rutgers University Press, 1962), p. 4ff. speaks of the introduction of the Germanic Church system among the Slavs in the tenth century.

92. Lelewel, *Dzieła,* II, pp. 589–628. Lelewel's interpretation is contrasted with the interpretations of Naruszewicz, Karamzin, and Schlözer.

93. Lelewel, *Dzieła,* III, pp. 338–340.

94. *Ibid.,* pp. 490–491.

95. *Ibid.,* pp. 419–559; pp. 673–674 (editor's comments).

96. Joachim Lelewel, *Historia Polski do końca panowania Stefana Batorego: Dzieła,* opracował Zygmunt Kolankowski (Warszawa: Państwowe Wydawnictwo Naukowe, 1962), VI. Also Lelewel, *Dzieła,* VIII, pp. 215–265, pp. 265–424.

97. Lelewel in his review of Czartoryska's *Pielgrzym w Dobromilu* expresses vehemently his opposition to the German state, i.e., the Holy Roman Empire, but accepts German intellectual influences, e.g., German historical methods. See Lelewel, *Dzieła,* I, p. 52, and *Dzieła,* VII, pp. 273–299.

98. Lelewel, *Dzieła,* III, pp. 376–377.

99. Below, p. 104ff.

100. Lelewel, *Przygody: Dzieła,* I, p. 63. The review appeared in installments in numbers four, eight, and nine, in 1822, 1823, and 1824 of *Severnyĭ Arkhiv.* A journalistic venture of Bulgarin (Bułharyn) and N. Grech, *Severnyĭ Arkhiv* appeared in St. Petersburg, 1822–1840. Sometime in 1822 or early in 1823, it was designated as the official organ of the Imperial Ministry of Education. See Tadeusz Bułharyn, "Letter to Joachim Lelewel, 13 Febru-

ary 1823, *Listy do Joachima Lelewela z 1821–1830 poddał P. Lelewel: Biblioteka Warszawska* (Warszawa: Gebethner i Wolff, 1877), I, pp. 226–227. Hereafter cited as Bułharyn, *Listy do J. Lelewela*. Bulgarin (Bułharyn) and Grech eventually became proponents of the "Official Nationality" policies of Nicholas I through their newspaper *Severnaya Pchela* (*The Northern Bee*) which was published in St. Petersburg, 1825–1855. Nicholas Riasanovsky, *Nicholas I and Official Nationality in Russia, 1825–1855* (Berkeley: University of California Press, 1967), pp. 60–72, p. 275.

101. Lelewel, *Dzieła*, II, pp. 607–611. For an interesting analysis of the political implications of the appearance of Lelewel's review in *Severnyĭ Arkhiv,* see Frank Mocha, "The Karamzin-Lelewel Controversy," *The Slavic Review,* XXXI (September, 1972), pp. 592–610.

102. Bułharyn, "Letter to Joachim Lelewel," 8 December 1823, *Listy do J. Lelewela,* I, p. 224.

103. Lelewel, "Letter to his Father," 17 June 1823, *Listy do rodzeństwa pisane,* I, letter no. 16, p. 389. Also Bułharyn, "Letter to Joachim Lelewel," 2 January 1823, *Listy do J. Lelewela,* I, p. 225.

104. Lelewel's contacts with Russian scholars were only temporarily disrupted. In 1828, Lelewel corresponded with the Slavophile historian and journalist M. N. Pogodin. The brief correspondence with Pogodin began four years after Pogodin's polemic in defense of several statements which Karamzin had made in his *History of the Russian State.* Pogodin met Lelewel for the first time in Brussels in 1842. Pogodin's trip west in 1842 was one of several journies he made between 1839 and 1853 in order to strengthen contacts with Western Slavs. Więckowska, "Komentarze," in Lelewel, *Dzieła,* I, pp. 143–145. Also Hans Kohn, *Pan-Slavism: Its History and Ideology,* 2nd edition, revised (New York: Vintage Books, 1960), p. 141.

105. Lelewel, *Dzieła,* VIII, p. 74.

106. Kukiel, *Czartoryski and European Unity,* p. 138.

107. Lelewel, *Dzieła,* VIII, p. 550. Weintraub, *The Poetry of Adam Mickiewicz,* p. 18.

108. Lelewel, *Dzieła,* VIII, p. 563.

109. *Ibid.,* p. 550.

110. *Ibid.,* pp. 550–551.

111. *Ibid.,* p. 551. For the administrative role of the University of Wilno in the western provinces of the Russian Empire, see Kamiński, *Polskie związki młodzieży,* pp. 283–284.

112. Lelewel, *Dzieła,* VIII, p. 552.

113. *Ibid.,* p. 553.

114. *Ibid.*

115. *Ibid.,* pp. 557–563.

116. *Ibid.,* p. 574. Two months after their arrest, Cezary Plater and three fellow students were among those inducted into the army. See Lelewel, *Dzieła,* VIII, p. 551. Also Lelewel, *Dzieła,* VII, p. 262.

117. Lelewel, *Dzieła,* VIII, pp. 574–577.

118. *Ibid.*
119. *Ibid.,* p. 577.
120. *Ibid.,* p. 579.
121. *Ibid.,* p. 580.
122. *Ibid.*
123. *Ibid.,* p. 577.
124. *Ibid.,* p. 517, p. 577.
125. Lelewel, *Dzieła,* III, p. 21. See also Mościcki (ed.), *Promieniści-Filomaci-Filareci,* p. 65. Pigoń, *Z dawnego Wilna,* p. 54.

§ 4: Lelewel in Warsaw Before and During the
November Uprising

1. See the editor's introduction to Joachim Lelewel, *Korespondencja z Tytuszem hr. Działyńskim,* wydał Dr. Zigmunt Celichowski (Poznań: Nakładem Biblioteki Kornickiej czcionkami Drukarnia Kuryera Poznańskiego, 1884), pp. 1–4. Hereafter cited as Lelewel, *Korespondencja z Działyńskim.* Work on this project continued sporadically between 1821 and 1830 and again after 1840. Eventually, Działyński and W. Kieliński, a bibliographer from Kornik, completed the work, in consultation by correspondence, with the exiled Lelewel.

2. Joachim Lelewel, "Letter to Tytus hr. Działyński," 3 December 1824, *Korespondencja z Działyńskim,* pp. 7–9. The title of the first volume is *Historyczne pomniki języka i uchwał polskich i mazowieckich z wieku XV i XVI.* Tom I: *Księgi ustaw polskich i mazowieckich na język polski w latach 1449, 1450, 1503, 1541 przekładanie po raz pierwszy staraniem Joachimem Lelewelem drukiem ogłoszone.*

3. Lelewel, "Letter to Tytus hr. Działyński," 9 August 1829, *Korespondencja z Działyńskim,* pp. 27–29. Lelewel, "Letter to Tytus hr. Działyński," 20 September 1829, *Korespondencja z Działyńskim,* pp. 33–35. See also Joachim Lelewel, *Przygody w poszukiwaniach rzeczy narodowych polskich: Dzieła,* opracowała Helena Więckowska (Kraków: Krakowska Drukarnia Naukowa, 1957), I, pp. 69–71.

4. Lelewel, *Dzieła,* I, p. 72. Witold Nowodworski, *"Bibliograficznych ksiąg dwoje" Joachima Lelewela* (Wrocław: Zakład Narodowy Im. Ossolińskich Wydawnictwo, 1959), pp. 129–136.

5. Lelewel, *Dzieła,* I, p. 72.

6. Jerzy Michalski, *Z dziejów Towarzystwa Przyjaciół Nauk* (Warszawa: Nakładem Towarzystwa Naukowego Warszawskiego z Zasiłku Ministerstwa Szkolnictwa Wyższego, 1953), p. 149.

7. *Ibid.,* pp. 150–151.

8. *Ibid.,* pp. 183–191.

9. Joachim Lelewel, *Historia: Obraz dziejów polskich: Dzieła,* opracowała Janina Bieniarzówna (Warszawa: Państwowe Wydawnictwo Naukowe, 1961), VII, p. 309.

10. *Ibid.*, p. 310, p. 316. Lelewel theorized that the *lechites* (Lechowie) came from areas such as Mazovia and Pomerania. He believed 'hat they were the most eminent citizens of primal Poland, and he traced the origins of the Polish gentry (szlachta) to them.

11. *Ibid.*, pp. 314–315; pp. 316–317; pp. 318–319.

12. *Ibid.*, pp. 317–319, pp. 322–330.

13. Władysław Łokietek is the only king in Polish history who occupied the throne on three different occasions: 1289–1290; 1296–1300; 1305–1333. He was formally crowned king of all Poland at Kraków in 1320, the year that city was named the capital of all Poland. It remained the capital until 1596 when it was succeeded by Warsaw.

14. Lelewel, *Historia: Obraz dziejów polskich: Dzieła*, VII, p. 344.

15. *Ibid.*, p. 345.

16. *Ibid.*, pp. 362–363.

17. *Ibid.*, pp. 362–363, pp. 368–369.

18. *Ibid.*, pp. 382–384.

19. Prot Lelewel, *Pamiętniki i diariusz domu naszego*, przygotowała do druku i opatrzyła przypisami Irena Lelewel-Friemannowa (Wrocław: Zakład Narodowy Im. Ossolińskich Wydawnictwo, 1966), p. 291. Also, Lelewel, *Dzieła*, I, p. 84.

20. Prot Lelewel, *Pamiętniki i diariusz*, p. 10.

21. *Ibid.*, pp. 279–280. Prot describes his arrest in February, 1826, and mentions Joachim's experiences. The arrests in the Congress Kingdom were related to the suppression of the Decembrist revolt in the Russian Empire in which the Southern Society was actively involved.

22. Lelewel, *Dzieła*, I, pp. 145–147.

23. A. Krausher, *Towarzystwo Warszawskie Przyjaciół Nauk: 1800–1832* (Kraków: G. Gebethner i Spółka, 1902–1906), VII, p. 427. Facsimile of Lelewel's letter of resignation appears. He resigned because of the serious illness of his father who died four days after Lelewel's resignation.

24. Artur Śliwiński, *Joachim Lelewel: Zarys biograficzny lata 1786–1831*, wydanie drugie (Warszawa: Wydawnictwo Kasy Im. Mianowskiego, 1932), p. 175.

25. Marian Kukiel, "Uwagi i przyczynki do genezy rewolucji listopadowej i wojny 1831 r.," *Teki Historyczne*, Vol. IX (1958), p. 41.

26. Władysław Bortnowski, *Walka o cele powstania listopadowego* (Lódz: Zakład Nar. Im. Ossolińskich we Wrocławiu, 1960), p. 2.

27. Stefan Kieniewicz and Witold Kula (eds.), *Historia Polski* (Warszawa: Państwowe Wydawnictwo Naukowe, 1959), II, p. 202.

28. *Ibid.*, p. 201. The seventy-seven were chosen by local Dietines (*Sejmiki*) in which the szlachta interests were represented. The deputies were chosen by *zgromadzenia gminne* which represented the interests of other property owners and/or educated citizens.

29. The four sessions were held March 27–April 27, 1818; September 13–

October 13, 1820; May 13–June 13, 1825; and May 28–June 28, 1830. Lelewel participated in the fourth, final session.

30. Szymon Askenazy, "Poland and the Polish Revolution," *The Cambridge Modern History,* edited by Sir A. Ward *et al.* (New York: The Macmillan Co., 1907), X, pp. 445–474.

31. See, for example, Bortnowski, *Walka o cele powstania listopadowego,* p. 15. Kieniewicz and Kula (eds.), *Historia Polski,* II, pp. 260–261.

32. Askenazy, *The Cambridge Modern History,* X, p. 450.

33. Joachim Lelewel, *Polska odradzająca się: Dzieła,* opracowała Helena Więckowska (Warszawa: Państwowe Wydawnictwo Naukowe, 1961), VIII, pp. 61–67. According to Marian Kukiel, *Czartoryski and European Unity, 1770–1861* (Princeton: Princeton University Press, 1955), p. 119, p. 140, p. 143, Alexander planned this unification as late as 1825. Only in 1827 did his successor Nicholas I decide against it.

34. Lelewel, *Dzieła,* VIII, pp. 71–73. Also Kieniewicz and Kula (eds.), *Historia Polski,* II, p. 266. Also Tadeusz Łepkowski, *Warszawa w powstaniu listopadowym,* wydanie drugie (Warszawa: Wiedza Powszechna, 1965), p. 24.

35. Łepkowski, *Warszawa w powstaniu listopadowym,* pp. 24–25.

36. *Ibid.,* p. 26. Also Kieniewicz and Kula (eds.), *Historia Polski,* II, p. 257, pp. 267–272. Also Lelewel, *Dzieła,* VIII, p. 70.

37. Aleksander Gieysztor *et al., History of Poland,* translated by K. Cekłaska (Warsaw: Polish Scientific Publishers, 1968), p. 442.

38. Lelewel, *Dzieła,* VIII, p. 69, pp. 77–78. See also Askenazy, *The Cambridge Modern History,* X, p. 459.

39. Lelewel, *Dzieła,* VIII, p. 67. See also Łepkowski, *Warszawa w powstaniu listopadowym,* p. 31.

40. Above, p. 40ff. Numerous Polish student groups existed and functioned in the Congress Kingdom, in the western provinces of the Russian Empire, and in western Europe. For example, a branch of *Panta Koina* existed in Berlin for a short time. See Aleksander Kamiński, *Polskie Związki Młodzieży, 1804–1831* (Warszawa: Państwowe Wydawnictwo Naukowe, 1963).

41. Gieysztor *et al., History of Poland,* p. 444.

42. *Ibid.*

43. Prot Lelewel, *Pamiętniki i diariusz,* p. 279. Also Kieniewicz and Kula (eds.), *Historia Polski,* II, pp. 302–307, and Kukiel, *Czartoryski and European Unity,* p. 144.

44. Gieysztor *et al., History of Poland,* p. 445.

45. Prot Lelewel, *Pamiętniki i diariusz,* pp. 287–289. Joachim Lelewel, *Dzieła,* VIII, p. 80.

46. Gieysztor *et al., History of Poland,* pp. 445–446. Also Kukiel, *Czartoryski and European Unity,* p. 147.

47. Kukiel, *ibid.* Also Kieniewicz and Kula (eds.), *Historia Polski,* II, pp. 304–307.

48. Kukiel, *ibid.* Also Lelewel, *Dzieła*, VIII, p. 82.

49. Kieniewicz and Kula (eds.), *Historia Polski*, II, pp. 304–307.

50. *Ibid.*, p. 305.

51. Lelewel, *Dzieła*, VIII, pp. 89–90. Also Gieysztor *et al.*, *History of Poland*, p. 450.

52. Kukiel, "Uwagy i przyczynki do genezy rewolycji listopadowej i wojny 1830 r.," pp. 40–62.

53. Gieysztor *et al.*, *History of Poland*, p. 450.

54. Kukiel, "Uwagi i przyczynki do genezy rewolucji listopadowej i wojny 1831 r.," p. 40.

55. *Ibid.*, pp. 43–46. Also Kukiel, *Czartoryski and European Unity*, p. 166. Also Prot Lelewel, *Pamiętniki i diariusz*, p. 345.

56. Kukiel, *Czartoryski and European Unity*, p. 165.

57. *Ibid.*, p. 166.

58. *Ibid.*, p. 168. Also Kieniewicz and Kula (eds.), *Historia Polski*, II, p. 425.

59. Joachim Lelewel, *Pamiętnik z roku 1830–31*, przedmową i przypisami zaopatrzył Janusz Iwaszkiewicz (Warszawa: Biblioteka Polska, 1924), p. 14, p. 17. There is general agreement among historians on this point. See, e.g., Kieniewicz and Kula (eds.), *Historia Polski*, II, p. 424 and Artur Śliwiński, *Powstanie listopadowe*, wydanie nowe (Londyn: Wydawnictwo Polaków z Zagranicy, 1946), p. 31.

60. Śliwiński, *ibid.*

61. Lelewel, *Pamiętnik z roku 1830–31*, p. 15.

62. Łepkowski, *Warszawa w powstaniu listopadowym*, p. 70. Also Śliwiński, *Powstanie listopadowe*, pp. 33–34.

63. Lelewel, *Dzieła*, VIII, pp. 90–91.

64. *Ibid.*, pp. 91–92.

65. *Ibid.*, p. 92.

66. Kieniewicz and Kula (eds.), *Historia Polski*, II, p. 426. Also Łepkowski, *Warszawa w powstaniu listopadowym*, p. 94.

67. Śliwiński, *Powstanie listopadowe*, pp. 38–39. Lelewel was elected President of the *Towarzystwo Patriotyczne in absentia.*

68. Lelewel, *Dzieła*, I, p. 192.

69. Lelewel, *Dzieła*, VIII, p. 93.

70. Lelewel, *Dzieła*, VII, pp. 152–165.

71. Lelewel, *Dzieła*, I, p. 194.

72. *Ibid.*, p. 199.

73. *Ibid.*

74. *Ibid.*, p. 200.

75. Kukiel, *Czartoryski and European Unity*, p. 173.

76. Lelewel, *Dzieła*, VIII, p. 94.

77. *Ibid.*, p. 62.

78. *Ibid.*

79. Lelewel, *Dzieła*, I, p. 237.

152 / *Romantic Nationalism and Liberalism*

80. *Ibid.*, p. 238.
81. *Ibid.*, p. 239.
82. Colonel Wyleżyński was Chłopicki's emissary. Lubecki and another deputy named Jezierski were also sent on a similar mission to St. Petersburg by the government which had preceded Chłopicki's. See Askenazy, *Cambridge Modern History*, X, p. 467.
83. *Ibid.*
84. Lelewel, *Dzieła*, I, p. 264.
85. Śliwiński, *Powstanie listopadowe*, p. 51.
86. *Ibid.*, p. 52.
87. *Ibid.* Also Gieysztor *et al.*, *History of Poland*, p. 452.
88. Śliwiński, *Powstanie listopadowe*, p. 55.
89. Lelewel, *Dzieła*, I, p. 265.
90. *Ibid.*, p. 268.
91. *Ibid.*, p. 269, p. 272.
92. *Ibid.*, pp. 266–267.
93. *Ibid.*, p. 271. On this day, the *Towarzystwo Patriotyczne* organized a demonstration against Nicholas and in honor of Pestel, Bestuzhev, and the other participants of the December uprising of 1825. At this time, the revolutionary slogan *"Za naszą wolność i waszą"* appeared. It is attributed to Lelewel. The Polish democratic left, after its exile, continued to cite this slogan which indicated the solidarity of peoples against tsarist oppression. See Aleksander Kamiński, *Polskie związki młodzieży*, p. 90.
94. Lelewel, *Dzieła*, I, pp. 269–272.
95. Above, p. 59ff.
96. Lelewel, *Dzieła*, I, p. 281.
97. Joachim Lelewel, *Trzy konstytucje polskie: Dzieła*, opracował Józef Dutkiewicz (Warszawa: Państwowe Wydawnictwo Naukowe, 1961), VIII, p. 485.
98. *Ibid.*, p. 487.
99. *Ibid.*, pp. 488–489.
100. *Ibid.*, p. 483.
101. *Ibid.*
102. *Ibid.*, p. 485.
103. *Ibid.*, p. 490.
104. *Ibid.*, p. 536.
105. *Ibid.*, p. 537.
106. *Ibid.*, p. 492.
107. *Ibid.*, p. 537.
108. *Ibid.*, pp. 537–538.
109. *Ibid.*, p. 539.
110. *Ibid.*, p. 482.
111. Lelewel, *"Nadanie własności ziemskiej włościanom: Dzieła*, VIII, pp. 182–188. This article also appeared in 1843 and 1859 as one of the appendices to Lelewel's *Polska odradzająca się*.

112. Askenazy, *The Cambridge Modern History*, X, p. 471.

113. Joachim Lelewel, *Wybór pism politycznych* (Warszawa: Książka i Wiedza, 1954), pp. 23-24.

114. *Ibid.*, p. 24.

115. Władysław Zajewski, "Sprawa reformy rządu w czerwcu 1831 r.," *Przegląd Historyczny*, Vol. I (1961), pp. 635-637.

116. *Ibid.*, p. 637.

117. Lelewel, *Dzieła*, p. 357, p. 360.

118. These events are dramatized in a five-act play by Stanisław Wyspiański (1869-1907) entitled *Lelewel*. The leading protagonist is Joachim Lelewel. Wyspiański portrays Lelewel as the personification of Polish national virtues, a true patriot. In the drama, Lelewel seeks compromises with Czartoryski, his political antagonist, for the national good. But Lelewel and the other Poles are helpless in the hands of Fate and the ominous force of the Muscovites' cannons. Only one edition of the drama appeared during Wyspiański's lifetime — in 1899. A second edition was published in 1906. Stanisław Wyspiański, *Lelewel: Dzieła zebrane* (Kraków: Wydawnictwo Literackie, 1958), III, pp. 1-89.

119. Lelewel, *Pamiętnik z roku 1830-31*, p. 110.

120. Lelewel, *Dzieła*, VIII, p. 482.

121. Joachim Lelewel, *Mowy i pisma polityczne: Polska dzieje i rzeczy jej* (Poznań: J. K. Żupański, 1855-1864), XX, pp. 53-58, pp. 58-61, pp. 61-64, pp. 64-70.

122. Lelewel, *Dzieła*, VIII, p. 487, p. 489.

123. The question of reform is discussed fully by Władysław Zajewski, "Sprawa reformy rządu w czerwcu 1831 r.," *Przegląd Historyczny*, Vol. I (1961), pp. 635-662.

124. Lelewel, *Dzieła*, I, pp. 220-221.

❀ 5: Lelewel the Émigré

1. Joachim Lelewel, *Pamiętnik z roku 1830-31*, przedmową i przypisami zaopatrzył Janusz Iwaszkiewicz (Warszawa: Biblioteka Polska, 1924). Documents of the Polish capitulation to the Imperial Russian forces appeared in the official government newspaper in France, *Le Moniteur universel*, 3 October 1831, pp. 1737-1739. Nicholas I's *Ukaz*, issued on the occasion of the surrender of Warsaw, appeared in *Le Moniteur universel*, 10 November 1831, p. 2094. The moderate republican newspaper of the government opposition in France, *Le National*, reported the end of the Polish insurrection briefly. See *Le National*, 22 September 1831, p. 1.

2. For his participation in the revolutionary National Government, Joachim Lelewel was branded a traitor and condemned to death *in absentia* by Tsar Nicholas I. See *Le National*, 10 October 1831, pp. 1-2, and 21 October 1831, pp. 3-4. Other Poles were also condemned. However, Nicholas I's *Ukaz* of 2 November 1831 promised amnesty for some categories of Polish

rebels. *Le National,* 27 November 1831, p. 11. While amnesty was promised, the Imperial government's policies in the Polish lands were extremely harsh. *Le National,* 15 December 1831, p. 1.

3. *Le National,* October 2, 10, 18, 21, 1831; November 27, 29, 1831; December 18, 1831. Lelewel joined General Lafayette, President of the *Comité Central en Faveur des Polonais,* and Samuel George Howe, President of the American-Polish Committee, and others in a public banquet in Paris to celebrate the first anniversary of the "Polish revolution of 29 November 1830." See Leon Chodźko (ed.), *Recueil des traites, conventions et actes diplomatiques concernant la Pologne, 1762-1862* (Paris: Amyot, éditeur, 1862), pp. 893-898.

4. *Le National,* 21 October 1831, pp. 1-2. Also Natalja Gąsiorowska (ed.), *W stulecie wiosny ludów* (Warszawa: Państwowy Instytut Wydawniczy, 1948-1951), III, p. 196.

5. Adam Lewak (ed.), *Le Général La Fayette et la cause polonaise: lettres-discours-documents* (Varsovie: Gebethner and Wolff, 1934), pp. i-xxx.

6. Joachim Lelewel, *Całoroczne trudy Komitetu Narodowego Polskiego na dniu 8 grudnia 1831 r. we Francji zawiązanego* (4 vols.; Paryż: Drukarnia A. Pinard, przy ulicy D'Anjou-Dauphine, 1831-1833), I, pp. 23-32. Also *Le National,* 25 November 1831, p. 3 and *Le National,* 1 December 1831, p. 2.

7. The newly organized Polish National Committee (*Komitet Narodowy Polski*) was located on the third floor of a building located at rue Taranne, 12. Lafayette's *Comité Central en Faveur des Polonais* was located in the same building. Various organizations and groups, e.g., Philhellenes, Saint Simonists, French republicans, held meetings in the rooms on the first floor. See Gąsiorowska (ed.), *W stulecie wiosny ludów,* III, p. 208.

8. Lelewel, *Całoroczne trudy,* I, pp. 30-32.

9. *Ibid.,* p. 154. Members of the Standing Committee included Lafayette's aide-de-camp Leon Chodźko, several members of the last Diet (Sejm) of the Congress Kingdom, and members of the Jacobin Patriotic Society (*Towarzystwo Patriotyczne*). Lelewel, *Całoroczne trudy,* I, pp. 32-33.

10. Lelewel, *Całoroczne trudy,* I, pp. 30-32.

11. *Ibid.,* pp. 17-19. Also Lelewel, *Całoroczne trudy,* II, pp. 119-162. Also Lelewel, "Letter to the Editor of the *Morning Herald,*" 25 January 1832, *Listy emigracyjne Joachima Lelewela,* wydała i wstępem poprzedziła Helena Więckowska (5 vols.; Kraków: Nakładem Polskiej Akademii Umiejętności, 1948-1956), I, letter no. 13, pp. 18-19. Hereafter cited as *Listy emigracyjne.*

12. Lelewel, *Całoroczne trudy,* II, pp. 169-171 and pp. 173-174. Especially important for the Polish National Committee was support by the Polish military in exile. Influential military officers such as General Bem refused to cooperate with, or to support, the Polish National Committee in its efforts to represent the interests of all exiled Poles. This, added to the defection of a number of more left-oriented members in March, 1832, ultimately weakened

the Committee, but the immediate impact on the Committee was negligible since the situation was quite fluid throughout 1832. The Committee exerted considerable influence throughout the year until the French government ordered its dissolution. The policies of the French government which the Polish National Committee opposed included the use of Polish military refugees in France, in Algeria, and in Portugal — areas of vital French national interests but not of the Poles'. Significant as these concerns were for the Polish National Committee, they are beyond the scope of this study.

13. Lelewel, *Całoroczne trudy,* I, pp. 3–4 and pp. 33–36. The French version appeared in *Le National,* 6 February 1832, pp. 2–3. The Polish and French texts are essentially the same.

14. Lelewel, *Całoroczne trudy, I, p. 16 and pp. 34–36.*

15. *Ibid.,* pp. 48–51. *Le National,* 14 February 1832, p. 3. The petition with a letter by Lelewel appeared in *Le National,* 22 February 1832, pp. 2–3. The petition was discussed during the session of 21 February 1832 of the Chamber of Deputies. Lafayette, Mauguin, Odilon-Barrot all spoke sympathetically on behalf of the Poles. Before adjourning, the Chamber of Deputies voted 600,000 francs for aid to all refugees in France, including the Poles. A transcript of the session appeared in *Le National,* 22 February 1832. On 8 March 1832, the Polish question was again debated in the French Chamber of Deputies along with the Spanish and Greek questions and their relationship to the July Revolution of 1830 in France. See *Le National,* 9 March 1832, p. 4. The government opposition sympathized with the Poles. In fact, sympathy for the Poles was widespread in France, but the government of Louis Philippe needed to maintain cordial relations with the courts of Russia, Austria, and Prussia and refused to allow the Poles or other foreign refugees in France to get out of hand. All refugees in France were subject to a special law concerning foreigners, effective April, 1832.

16. Lelewel, *Całoroczne trudy,* I, p. 48.

17. *Ibid.,* p. 49.

18. Lelewel, *Całoroczne trudy,* II, pp. 134–136. Also Lelewel, "Letter to the Polish Circle in Avignon," 4 July 1832, *Listy emigracyjne,* I, letter no. 46, pp. 72–73.

19. Lelewel, *Całoroczne trudy,* II, pp. 193–194.

20. *Ibid.,* pp. 196–197.

21. *Ibid.,* pp. 134–136. Also Lelewel, "Letter to Walenty Zwierkowski in Paris," 20 July 1832, *Listy emigracyjne,* I, letter no. 50, p. 77. The petition was published and widely circulated in Great Britain. For example, it appeared in the *Courier* and in the London *Times* on 2 July 1832. See Lelewel, *Całoroczne trudy,* II, p. 140 and pp. 228–229.

22. Two useful works on the subject are George Woodbridge, *The Reform Bill of 1832* (New York: Thomas Y. Crowell Co., 1970) and E. Llewellyn Woodward, *The Age of Reform* (2d ed.; Oxford: Clarendon, 1962).

23. Lelewel, *Całoroczne trudy,* I, p. 37.

24. Lelewel, *Całoroczne trudy,* II, pp. 127–131. Also Joachim Lelewel, *Mowy i pisma polityczne: Polska dzieje i rzeczy jej* (Poznań: Nakładem Księgarni J. K. Żupańskiego, 1864), XX, pp. 75–95.

25. Lelewel, *Mowy i pisma polityczne: Polska dzieje i rzeczy jej,* XX, pp. 118–119.

26. *Ibid.,* pp. 118–119.

27. *Ibid.,* pp. 119–120.

28. *Ibid.,* p. 121.

29. *Ibid.,* p. 122.

30. Lelewel, *Całoroczne trudy,* II, pp. 243–244.

31. *Ibid.,* pp. 248–249.

32. Lelewel, *Całoroczne trudy,* I, p. 37; III, p. 268 and pp. 278–281.

33. Lelewel, *Całoroczne trudy,* III, p. 281.

34. *Le National,* 6 April 1832, p. 2. *Le Moniteur universel,* 25 April 1832, pp. 1123–1124. The texts of Nicholas I's *Ukaz* of 14 (26) February 1832 and the Organic Statute appear.

35. *Le National,* 7 April 1832, p. 3.

36. *Le National,* 23 April 1832, pp. 3–4.

37. *Ibid.,* p. 4.

38. Lelewel, *Całoroczne trudy,* III, pp. 251–267. A vivid but one-sided anti-government account is presented by B. Sarrons, secretary to General Lafayette. See B. Sarrons, *Memoirs of General Lafayette and the French Revolution of 1830* (2 vols.; London: Richard Bentley, New Burlington Street, 1832), II, pp. 387–417. The official government newspaper, *Le Moniteur universel,* 6 June 1832, p. 1291, reports the incident briefly without mentioning names of specific participants. In effect, according to this account, anarchy prevailed briefly in Paris, but the troops of the line and the National Guard put down the unrest. The King arrived at the Tuileries amid acclamations. Thus, confidence in his government was restored. The republican opposition press, *Le National,* 4–5 June 1832, p. 1, described Paris in a state of siege. *Le National,* 9 June 1832, p. 1, reported that a threat of civil war existed. *Le National,* 3 July 1832, p. 3, reported that Joachim Lelewel was to leave Paris without delay.

39. Lelewel, *Całoroczne trudy,* II, pp. 229–233. Also Lelewel, *Mowy i pisma polityczne: Polska dzieje i rzeczy jej,* XX, pp. 135–136. *Le National,* 1 January 1832, pp. 1–2 (in French). The Proclamation is reprinted in Witold Łukaszewicz and Władysław Lewandowski (eds.), *Postępowa publicystyka emigracyjna, 1831–1864; wybór źródł.* Seria II *Materiały zródłowe do dziejów polskich walk narodowy zwolenczych* (Wrocław: Zakład Im. Ossolińskich, 1961), VI, pp. 51–55. Łukaszewicz identifies Adam Mickiewicz as co-author, p. 55.

40. W. Łukaszewicz, "Wpływ masonerii, karbonaryzmu i Józefa Mazziniego na polską myśl rewolucyjna w latach poprzedzających wiosnę ludów," in Gąsiorowska (ed.), *W stulecie wiosny ludów,* III, p. 308.

41. Lelewel, *Całoroczne trudy,* II, p. 229.

42. *Ibid.,* p. 230.

43. *Ibid.,* p. 232.

44. Lelewel, *Całoroczne trudy,* III, pp. 261–267. This is Lelewel's account of his meeting with the French Minister of Foreign Affairs, de Broglie, in reference to "To Our Russian Brothers." *Le National,* 29 December 1832, p. 3, reports that this proclamation was directly responsible for the dissolution of the Polish National Committee, and that Pozzo di Borgo requested that the French government do so. The accounts coincide.

45. Lelewel, *Całoroczne trudy,* II, p. 232.

46. Lelewel, *Całoroczne trudy,* III, p. 265. In return for accommodating the Imperial Russian request, Nicholas I recognized officially the government of Louis Philippe and thus legitimized the July Revolution. See *Le National,* 8 September 1832, p. 1.

47. Lelewel, *Całoroczne trudy,* III, pp. 281–282.

48. The protocol of the organizational meeting of the Vengeance of the People (*Zemsta Ludu*) is published in Łukaszewicz and Lewandowski (eds.), *Postępowa publicystyka emigracyjna,* VI, pp. 63–64.

49. Karol Lewicki (ed.), *Pamiętniki spiskowców i więźniów Galicyjskich w latach 1832–1846* (Wrocław: Zakład Im. Ossolińskich, 1954), contains excerpts from the memoirs of a number of participants. Also see Chodźko (ed.), *Recueil des traites,* p. 952. Also Marian Kukiel, "Lelewel, Mickiewicz and the Underground Movements of the European Revolution (1816–1833)," *The Polish Review,* V (Summer, 1960), p. 75.

50. Gąsiorowska (ed.), *W stulecie wiosny ludów,* III, p. 231. Also Witold Łukaszewicz, *Szymon Konarski (1803–1839)* (Warszawa: Spółdzielnia Wydawnicza "Książka," 1948), pp. 42–45.

51. Seweryn Goszczyński, "Podróz mojego życia: urywki wspomnień i zapiski do pamiętnika (1801–1842)" in Lewicki (ed.), *Pamiętniki spiskowców,* pp. 79–81.

52. *Ibid.,* pp. 82–84.

53. Lewicki (ed.), "Wstęp," in *Pamiętniki spiskowców,* pp. xiv–xvii.

54. Chodźko (ed.), *Recueil des traites,* pp. 957–958.

55. Marie Joseph Lafayette, *Memoires, correspondance et manuscrits du Général Lafayette.* Puliés par sa famille. (6 vols.; Paris: H. Fournier aine, éditeur, 1837), VI, pp. 712–716. Also *Le Moniteur universel,* 1 April 1833, pp. 905–906 and p. 911. Also *Le National,* 12 March 1833, p. 1 and p. 3.

56. Lelewel, "Letter to Walenty Zwierkowski in Paris," 17 July 1833, *Listy emigracyjne,* I, letter no. 121, p. 156. Also Lelewel, "Protestacya w chwili opuszczenia Francyi z rozkazu rządu," in *Mowy i pisma polityczne: Polska dzieje i rzeczy jej,* XX, pp. 175–187. Lelewel's ultimate choice was Belgium, but he considered other options. See Kenneth F. Lewalski, "Lelewel's Third Exile: Alternatives for Relocation," *The Polish Review,* XXIII (1978), pp. 31–39.

❀ 6: Lelewel the Émigré

1. Konstanty Kamiński, "Polacy w Belgii w latach 1832-63," *Przegląd Humanistyczny*, V (1977), pp. 113-127.

2. Joachim Lelewel, "Letter to Walerian Pietkiewicz in Tours," 13 August 1833, *Listy emigracyjne Joachima Lelewela*, wydała i wstępem poprzedziła Helena Więckowska (5 vols.; Kraków: Nakładem Polskiej Akademii Umiejętności, 1948-1956), Vol. I, letter no. 129, p. 167. Hereafter cited as *Listy emigracyjne*. Also Emmanuel Halicz (ed.), "Towarzystwo Demokratyczne w Brukseli, 1847-1848 i działalność w nim Marksa, Engelsa, Lelewela," *Z Pola Walki*, IV (1961), pp. 100-127. These are police documents with a brief commentary by the editor.

3. Joachim Lelewel, *Przygody w poszukiwaniach rzeczy narodowych polskich: Dzieła*, opracowała Helena Więckowska (Kraków: Krakowska Drukarnia Naukowa, 1957), Vol. I, p. 87.

4. Lelewel, "Letter to Walerian Pietkiewicz in Tours," 23 September 1833, *Listy emigracyjne*, Vol. I, letter no. 143, pp. 193-194.

5. Lelewel, "Letter to Walerian Pietkiewicz in Tours," 16 October 1833, *Listy emigracyjne*, Vol. I, letter no. 149, p. 203.

6. Lelewel, "Letter to Lt. Col. A. Gorecki in Avignon," 23 September 1833, *Listy emigracyjne*, Vol. I, letter no. 144, p. 195.

7. Lelewel had spent the spring and summer of 1833 as a guest of Lafayette at the latter's estate at La Grange. Here in relative political isolation Lelewel re-examined his political and social philosophy and decided to modify or change his relations with the Carbonari and the Polish émigré groups. Within two months after he settled in Brussels, i.e., by December, 1833, he severed his ties with the Carbonari and joined the newly formed Young Poland. See, e.g., Lelewel, "Letter to Walerian Pietkiewicz in Tours," 10 November 1833, *Listy emigracyjne*, Vol. I, letter no. 153, p. 213. Lelewel, "Letter to Walenty Zwierkowski in Nancy," 16 November 1833, *Listy emigracyjne*, Vol. I, letter no. 154, p. 215. Lelewel, "Letter to Walerian Pietkiewicz in Tours," 18 November 1833, *Listy emigracyjne*, Vol. I, letter no. 155, p. 216. Lelewel, "Letter to Walenty Zierkowski in Nancy," 18 December 1833, *Listy emigracyjne*, Vol. I, letter no. 162, p. 224. Also see Bogusław Cygler, *Działalność politczno-społeczna Joachima Lelewela na emigracji w latach 1831-1861* (Gdańsk: Gdańskie Towarzystwo Naukowe, 1969), pp. 77-94.

8. Lelewel, "Letter to Józef Zaleski in Sèvres," 27 January 1834, *Listy emigracyjne*, Vol. I, letter no. 172, p. 241. In his other correspondence dating from this period, the feeling of disillusionment is very evident. See, e.g., Lelewel, "Letter to Walerian Pietkiewicz in Tours," 27 January 1834, *Listy emigracyjne*, Vol. I, letter no. 173, pp. 244-245. Lelewel, "Letter to Leon Chodźko in London," 28 January 1834, *Listy emigracyjne*, Vol. I, letter no. 174, p. 246. Lelewel, "Letter to General M. R. Lafayette in La Grange," 29 January 1834, *Listy emigracyjne*, Vol. I, letter no. 175, pp. 247-248.

9. Lelewel, "Letter to Józef Zaleski in Sèvres," 27 January 1834, *Listy emigracyjne,* Vol. I, letter no. 172, p. 241.

10. *Ibid.,* p. 242.

11. William L. Langer, *Political and Social Upheaval: 1832–1852* (New York: Harper and Row Publishers, 1969), pp. 114–118.

12. Helena Więckowska, "Wstęp," in Lelewel, *Listy emigracyjne,* Vol. I, p. xix.

13. *Ibid.*

14. Lelewel was concerned about the cosmopolitanism of this organization as he had been about the Carbonari and joined reluctantly. Lelewel, "Letter to Walerian Pietkiewicz in Tours," 20 October 1834, *Listy emigracyjne,* Vol. I, letter no. 211, p. 291. Also Lelewel, "Letter to Walerian Pietkiewicz in Tours," 9 November 1834, *Listy emigracyjne,* Vol. I, letter no. 216, p. 296.

15. Walenty Zwierkowski, "Letter to Joachim Lelewel," 14 November 1834, quoted in Marja Stecka, "Układy T-wa Demokratycznego z Młodą Polską," *Przegląd Historyczny,* XXII (1919–1920), p. 169.

16. Walenty Zwierkowski, e.g., belonged to both the Carbonari and Young Poland and joined the *Towarzystwo Demokratyczne* in May, 1835. See Marian Tyrowicz, *Towarzystwo Demokratyczne Polskie: 1832–1863* (Warszawa: Książka i Wiedza, 1964), p. 820.

17. Stecka, "Układy T-wa Demokratycznego z Młodą Polską," p. 163.

18. Lelewel, "Letter to W. Zwierkowski in Nancy," 16 November 1833, *Listy emigracyjne,* Vol. I, letter no. 154, p. 213. Lelewel, "Letter to W. Pietkiewicz in Tours," 18 November 1833, *Listy emigracyjne,* Vol. I, letter no. 155, p. 215.

19. Lelewel, "Letter to Walerian Pietkiewicz in Tours," 5 June 1834, *Listy emigracyjne,* Vol. I, letter no. 197, p. 273.

20. Lelewel, "Letter to Konstanty Zaleski," 6 November 1834, *Listy emigracyjne,* Vol. I, letter no. 214, p. 294. Lelewel, "Letter to Walerian Pietkiewicz and Walenty Zwierkowski in Tours," 9 November 1834, *Listy emigracyjne,* Vol. I, letter no. 216, pp. 296–299.

21. Lelewel, "Letter to Walerian Pietkiewicz in Tours," 21 November 1834, *Listy emigracyjne,* Vol. I, letter no. 219, p. 302.

22. Lelewel, "Letter to Walenty Zwierkowski in Paris," 25 November 1834, *Listy emigracyjne,* Vol. I, letter no. 222, p. 306.

23. Lelewel, "Letter to Walenty Zwierkowski in Paris," 27 November 1834, *Listy emigracyjne,* Vol. I, letter no. 224, p. 347.

24. *Ibid.*

25. Stecka, "Układy T-wa Demokratycznego z Młodą Polską," pp. 165–166.

26. Lelewel, "Letter to Walenty Zwierkowski in Versailles," 18 January 1835, *Listy emigracyjne,* Vol. I, letter no. 233, pp. 315–316.

27. E.E.Y. Hales, *Mazzini and the Secret Societies: The Making of a Myth* (London: Eyre and Spotteswoode, 1956), p. 139.

28. Lelewel, "Letter to Walerian Pietkiewicz in Tours," 21 November 1834, *Listy emigracyjne,* Vol. I, letter no. 219, p. 301.

29. Lelewel, "Letter to Walenty Zwierkowski in Versailles," 15 January 1835, *Listy emigracyjne,* Vol. I, letter no. 232, p. 315.

30. The *Towarzystwo Demokratyczne Polskie* was most active between 1836 and 1849. It played an essential role in preparing for the revolt in Galicia in 1846. However, as a result of its failure, the organization, in the manner of other émigré groups, split, and its overall effectiveness declined. It formally disbanded in 1862.

31. Helena Więckowska, "Wstęp," in Lelewel, *Listy emigracyjne,* Vol. II, p. vii. See also Lelewel, "Letter to Walenty Zwierkowski in Versailles," 15 March 1835, *Listy emigracyjne,* Vol. I, letter no. 238, p. 320. Also letters no. 241, 243, 246, 247, 256, 263, and 269, pp. 323, 326, 329, 331, 344, 351, and 359.

32. Stefan Kieniewicz and Witold Kula (eds.), *Historia Polski,* Vol. II, part iii, pp. 118–121.

33. Witold Łukaszewicz, *Szymon Konarski: 1808–1839* (Warszawa: "Książka," 1948), pp. 73–75. The program of the organization is reprinted here.

34. Helena Więckowska, "Wstęp," in Lelewel, *Listy emigracyjne,* Vol. II, p. vii. Also Aleksander Gieysztor et al., *History of Poland* (Warsaw: Polish Scientific Publishers, 1968), pp. 480–481.

35. Lelewel, in his letters to Walenty Zwierkowski, 16 January 1836 to 6 February 1837, i.e., one year, does not mention Konarski, indicating that he was not communicating with the emissary. See Lelewel, *Listy emigracyjne,* Vol. II, letters no. 291–373, pp. 2–106.

36. Kieniewicz and Kula (eds.), *Historia Polski,* Vol. II, p. 122.

37. Joachim Lelewel, *Mowy i pisma polityczne: Polska Dzieje i rzeczy jej* (Poznań: Nakładem Księgarni J. K. Żupańskiego, 1864), XX, pp. 221–230.

38. *Ibid.,* pp. 222–223.

39. *Ibid.,* p. 224.

40. *Ibid.,* pp. 224–225.

41. *Ibid.,* p. 226.

42. *Ibid.,* pp. 226–229.

43. Lelewel, "Letter to Leon Chodźko in Paris," October 1835, *Listy emigracyjne,* Vol. I, letter no. 281, p. 375. Also Lelewel, "Letter to Leon Chodźko in Paris," 10 April 1836, *Listy emigracyjne,* Vol. II, letter no. 303, p. 17.

44. Joachim Lelewel, *Dzieje Polski potocznym sposobem opowiedziane,* wydanie do użytku zastowowane i opowiadaniem do roku 1848 dopełnione z 3 krajobrazami (Lwów: Druk Zakład Narodowy Im. Ossolińskich, 1849). This volume is a copy which includes Lelewel's *"Polska odradzająca się."*

45. Joachim Lelewel, *Polska odradzająca się: Dzieła,* opracowała Helena Więckowska (Warszawa: Państwowe Wydawnictwo Naukowe, 1961), VIII, p. 30.

46. *Ibid.,* p. 161.

47. *Ibid.*

48. *Ibid.*, pp. 123-124.
49. *Ibid.*, p. 34.
50. Above, p. 000ff.
51. Lelewel, *Polska odradzająca się: Dzieła*, VIII, pp. 123-124. The italics are mine.
52. *Ibid.*, pp. 165-166.
53. Ignacy Chrzanowski, *Joachim Lelewel: Człowiek i pisarz*, edited by Stanisław Pigoń (Warszawa: Spółdzielnia Wydawnicza "Czytelnik," 1946), p. 128.
54. Helena Więckowska, "Komentarz I," in Lelewel, *Polska odradzająca się: Dzieła*, VIII, pp. 205-207.
55. Lelewel, *Mowy i pisma polityczne: Polska dzieje i rzeczy jej*, XX, p. 571.
56. *Ibid.*, p. 572.
57. *Ibid.*, p. 577.
58. *Ibid.*, pp. 578-579.
59. *Ibid.*, pp. 579-580.
60. *Ibid.*, p. 580.
61. *Ibid.*
62. *Ibid.*, p. 581.
63. *Ibid.*, pp. 281-285.
64. *Ibid.*, pp. 281-288. Poland as the Christ among nations was a theme in Polish romantic poetry, too. It stemmed from Adam Mickiewicz's *Księgi narodu polskiego i pielgrzymstwa polskiego* (*Books of the Polish Nation and of Polish Pilgrimage*, 1832) and *Dziady* (*Forefather's Eve*, 1833).
65. Lelewel, *Mowy i pisma polityczne: Polska dzieje i rzeczy jej*, XX, p. 284.
66. *Ibid.*, pp. 285-349. In the years 1839-1842, Lelewel became involved in a series of inefficacious political projects. His scholarly endeavors suffered as well. In his autobiography, he recalled the difficulties he experienced in finding an audience for his histories and mentioned economic difficulties. See Lelewel, *Dzieła*, I, pp. 96-101. Also Cygler, *Działalność polityczno-społeczna Joachima Lelewela*, pp. 178-195.
67. Lelewel helped to create the *Zjednoczenie Emigracyji Polskiej* (1837-1846), a new, left émigré organization. The Act of Foundation (Brussels, 29 November 1838), reflected Lelewel's influence. Approximately 2,000 émigrés joined, and branches were established in Lyon, Poitiers, Paris, Versailles, London, and Brussels. The purpose of the organization was to choose a chief authority to represent the Polish émigrés and to carry out programs on behalf of the Polish cause. No single person was chosen to head the organization. Instead, a Committee of Five was elected. This *Komitet Narodowy Polski* consisted of Lelewel (President, 1843), Walenty Zwierkowski (Versailles), Antoni Odynecki (Lille), Wiktor Tysza (Secretary), and Napoleon Szuniewicz (Editor of *Orzel Biały*, the organization's official publication). The

Komitet represented only a small segment of the Polish émigrés. The Democratic Society and Czartoryski's Hotel Lambert continued to function as separate entities. The *Zjednoczenie* disbanded in 1846. In April of that year, the right wing, led by Wincenty Tyszkiewicz, joined the Czartoryski faction. In July, the left wing, including Lelewel, joined the *Towarzystwo Demokratyczne Polskie* (the Democratic Society which he had criticized earlier). Lelewel maintained a formal membership in this organization, but he exerted no influence on it. See Cygler, *Działalność polityczno-społeczna Joachima Lelewela,* p. 216, p. 253, p. 261. See also Helena Więckowska, "Wstęp," in Lelewel, *Listy emigracyjne,* Vol. II, p. xi. Also Stefan Kieniewicz, *Samotnik Brukselski: Opowieść o Joachimie Lelewelu* (Warszawa: Wiedza Powszechna, 1960).

68. Lelewel, "Letter to Walenty Zwierkowski in Versailles," 3 July 1844, *Listy emigracyjne,* Vol. III, letter no. 746, p. 162.

69. Mikhail Bakunin, *The Confession of Mikhail Bakunin,* with the marginal comments of Tsar Nicholas I; translated by Robert C. Howes; introduction and notes by Lawrence D. Orton (Ithaca: Cornell University Press, 1977), p. 43.

70. Lelewel, "Letter to Walenty Zwierkowski in Versailles," 27 July 1844, *Listy emigracyjne,* Vol. III, letter no. 754, p. 175. Lelewel, "Letter to Walenty Zwierkowski in Versailles," 29 July 1844, *Listy emigracyjne,* Vol. III, letter no. 755, p. 175.

71. Bakunin, *The Confession of Mikhail Bakunin,* p. 43.

72. Lelewel, "Letter to Walenty Zwierkowski in Versailles," 29 July 1844, *Listy emigracyjne,* Vol. III, letter no. 754, p. 175.

73. *Ibid.,* p. 177. Lelewel, "Letter to Leon Chodźko in Paris," 13 August 1844, *Listy emigracyjne,* Vol. III, letter no. 755, p. 186. Lelewel, "Letter to Walenty Zwierkowski in Versailles," 16 March 1845, *Listy emigracyjne,* Vol. III, letter no. 816, p. 271.

74. Adam Leśniewski, *Bakunin a sprawy polskie w okresie wiosny ludów i powstania styczniowego 1863 roku* (Łódz: Zakład Narodowy Im. Ossolińskich, 1962), p. 146.

75. Bakunin, *The Confession of Mikhail Bakunin,* p. 52.

76. *Ibid.,* p. 53.

77. Lelewel, *Mowy i pisma polityczne: Polska dzieje i rzeczy jej,* XX, see, e.g., pp. 390, 413, 427, 429, 435, 461, and 470.

78. *Ibid.,* p. 427, p. 461.

79. *Ibid.,* p. 423, p. 427.

80. *Ibid.,* pp. 429–430.

81. *Ibid.,* p. 393. In the decade of the forties, the theme of Poland as Christ among nations was continued by Adam Mickiewicz in his lectures at the *College de France.* The theme was also expressed in the poetry of Juliusz Słowacki and Zygmunt Krasiński. František Palacký, in his *History of the Czech People* (1836–1848), attributed a similar "sense of mission" to the

Czechs. In the forties, the Slovaks, too, became nationally conscious. They received their ideas of cultural pan-Slavism and national mission from Kollár and Safařik, two leaders of the Czech national renaissance who were Slovaks by birth, and from the charismatic Ludevít Stúr. See Hans Kohn, *Pan-Slavism: Its History and Ideology*, 2nd edition, revised (New York: Vintage Books), pp. 27–55. Also Langer, *Political and Social Upheaval*, pp. 274–276.

82. Lelewel, *Mowy i pisma polityczne: Polska dzieje i rzeczy jej*, XX, p. 427.

83. *Ibid.*, p. 430.

84. *Ibid.*, p. 435.

85. *Ibid.*, p. 462.

86. *Ibid.*

87. *Ibid.*, pp. 478–481; pp. 482–485.

88. *Ibid.*, pp. 518–522. Lelewel sent W. Tyszka to Poznań and Galicia in mid-1844, but he did not know precisely what the situation in the homeland was because of inadequate communications. See Cygler, *Działalność polityczno-społeczna Joachima Lelewela*, pp. 203–205.

89. Lelewel, *Mowy i pisma polityczne: Polska dzieje i rzeczy jej*, XX, p. 526.

90. For details of the outbreaks of 1846 see Oscar Halecki, *Borderlands of Western Civilization: A History of East Central Europe* (New York: The Ronald Press, Co., 1952), pp. 309–313.

91. Lelewel, "Letter to Walenty Zwierkowski in Versailles," 26 February 1846, *Listy emigracyjne*, Vol. III, letter no. 912, p. 394. Lelewel, "Letter to Walenty Zwierkowski in Versailles," 18 November 1847, *Listy emigracyjne*, Vol. III, letter no. 927, p. 413.

92. Cygler, *Działalność polityczno-społeczna Joachima Lelewela*, pp. 233–234.

93. Halicz (ed.), "Towarzystwo Demokratyczne w Brukseli 1847–1848 i działalność w nim Marksa, Engelsa, Lelewela," p. 100.

94. Cygler, *Działalność polityczno-społeczna Joachima Lelewela*, p. 233. Cygler argues convincingly that Lelewel neither understood nor was influenced by Marx's scientific socialism. He also disputes Marx's statement that Lelewel signed the *Communist Manifesto*.

95. *Ibid.*, p. 221. Cygler cites Jenny Marx's reminiscences of Marx and Engels. She recalled meeting old Lelewel wearing his famous blue working-man's smock.

96. *Ibid.*, p. 230, p. 243. Marx (and Engels) associated the imminent class struggle with the Poles' striving for national independence. He equated the national question with the question of democracy and the liberation of the oppressed class.

97. Nina Assorodobraj, "Notaty Karola Marksa z *Histoire de Pologne* Joachima Lelewela," *Archiwum Historii, Filozofii, i Myśli Społecznej*, IV (1959), p. 251.

98. *Ibid.,* pp. 252–263.

99. Cygler, *Działalność polityczno-społeczna Joachima Lelewela,* p. 278. Also Lelewel, "Letter to Karl Marx in London," 10 February 1860, *Listy emigracyjne,* Vol. IV, letter no. 1225, pp. 435–436.

100. Lelewel, "Letter to Walenty Zwierkowski in Versailles," 1–2 January 1848, *Listy emigracyjne,* Vol. III, letter no. 929.

101. Lelewel, "Letter to Walenty Zwierkowski in Kraków," 28 April 1848, *Listy emigracyjne,* Vol. III, letter no. 939, p. 435. Lelewel was invited to attend but was too ill to travel.

102. Cygler, *Działalność polityczno-społeczna Joachima Lelewela,* p. 243.

103. Lelewel, "Letter to Stanisław Worcell in Paris," 26 May 1848, *Listy emigracyjne,* Vol. III, letter no. 942, p. 438. Lelewel, "Letter to Walenty Zwierkowski in Wrocław," 6 June 1848, *Listy emigracyjne,* Vol. III, letter no. 944, pp. 440–441.

104. Joachim Lelewel, *Korespondencja z Karolem Sienkiewiczem* (Poznań: Nakładem J. K. Żupańskiego, 1872).

105. Lelewel, "Letter to Karol Sienkiewicz in Paris," 28 May 1857, *Korespondencja z Karolem Sienkiewiczem,* letter no. 13, pp. 25–26. Lelewel, "Letter to Karol Sienkiewicz in Paris," 17 April 1858, *Korespondencja z Karolem Sienkiewiczem,* letter no. 21, p. 28.

106. Lelewel, *Dzieła,* I, p. 112. Joachim Lelewel, *Geographie du moyen age* (Amsterdam: Meridian Publishing Co., 1961), 5 vols. This commemorative reprint appeared on the centenary of Lelewel's death. The originals were published in 1852–1857. The Newberry Library, Chicago, Illinois, has a set of the originals.

107. Cygler, *Działalność polityczno-społeczna Joachima Lelewela,* p. 261.

108. Lelewel, "Letter to T. Januszewicz in Paris," 7 January 1854, *Listy emigracyjne,* Vol. IV, letter no. 1061, pp. 171–173. Lelewel, "Letter to Walenty Zwierkowski in Paris," 1 April 1854, *Listy emigracyjne,* Vol. IV, letter no. 1074, pp. 196–197. Lelewel, "Letter to Walenty Zwierkowski in Paris," 25 April 1854, *Listy emigracyjne,* Vol. IV, letter no. 1076, pp. 199–200. Lelewel, "Letter to T. Januszewicz in Paris," 25 April 1854, *Listy emigracyjne,* Vol. IV, letter no. 1077, pp. 201–202. For Polish émigré politics and the Crimean War, see Cygler, *Działalność polityczno-społeczna Joachima Lelewela,* pp. 261–263; pp. 266–279.

109. Lelewel, "Letter to T. Januszewicz in Paris," 2 May 1854, *Listy emigracyjne,* Vol. IV, letter no. 1078, pp. 202–203.

110. Helena Więckowska, "Komentarz," in Lelewel, *Dzieła,* I, pp. 413–418.

❀ 7: Lelewel's Interpretations of Poland's History

1. Joachim Lelewel, *O potrzebie elementarnych dzieł historycznych: Dzieła,* opracowała Janina Bieniarzówna (Warszawa: Państwowe Wydawnictwo Naukowe, 1961), VII, p. 301.

2. Joachim Lelewel, *Przygody w poszukiwaniach rzeczy narodowych polskich: Dzieła,* opracowała Helena Więckowska (Warszawa: Państwowe Wydawnictwo Naukowe, 1957), I, p. 131.

3. Marian Henryk Serejski, "Miejsce Joachima Lelewela we wspólnej nauce historycznej," *Kwartalnik Historyczny,* LXVIII (1961), p. 864. Nina Assorodobraj, "Notaty Karola Marksa z *Histoire de Pologne* Joachima Lelewela," *Archiwum Historii, Filozofii i Myśli Społecznej,* IV (1959), pp. 249–273. Marx's notes on Lelewel's two volume *Histoire de Pologne* are included with Professor Assorodobraj's commentary. The originals are in the International Institute of Social History in Amsterdam. Photocopies are available at the Marx-Engels-Lenin Institute in Moscow.

4. Lelewel, *Dzieła,* I, p. 87.

5. *Ibid.,* p. 48. This history remained in manuscript form until 1863 when it appeared as Volume XIII of *Polska dzieje i rzeczy jej.* The 1863 edition was followed by others. See Helena Hleb-Koszańska and Maria Kotwiczówna, *Bibliografia utworów Joachima Lelewela* (Wrocław: Wydawnictwo Zakładu Im. Ossolińskich, 1952). It also appears as Volume VI of Lelewel's collected works. See Joachim Lelewel, *Historia Polski do końca panowania Stefana Batorego: Dzieła,* opracował Zygmunt Kolankowski (Warszawa: Państwowe Wydawnictwo Naukowe, 1962), VI, pp. 43–485. The editor gives a complete history of the evolution of the manuscript in his introduction to this volume.

6. Ignacy Chrzanowski, *Joachim Lelewel: Człowiek i pisarz,* edited by Stanisław Pigoń (Warszawa: Spółdzielnia Wydawnicza "Czytelnik," 1946), p. 96.

7. Lelewel, *Dzieła,* I, p. 51. The influence of the German historicists, e.g., Johann Gottfried von Herder and Barthold Georg Niebuhr is evident. For a discussion of these and other German historicists see Friedrich Engel-Janosi, *The Growth of German Historicism* (Baltimore: The Johns Hopkins Press, 1944).

8. These Slav characteristics of freedom and citizenship developed in the primitive Slav communities in contrast to characteristics of despotism, feudalism, and social hierarchies which developed in those nations influenced by the Roman Empire. See Franciszek Bronowski, "Idea gminowładztwa w historii powszechnej J. Lelewela," *Kwartalnik Historyczny,* LXVIII (1961), pp. 879–885.

9. Joachim Lelewel, *Śpiewy historyczne Juliana Ursyna Niemcewicza pod względem historii uważane: Dzieła,* VII, pp. 263–271. Also Joachim Lelewel, "Letter to Walerian Pietkiewicz in Tours," 10 June 1834, *Listy emigracyjne Joachima Lelewela,* wydała i wstępem poprzedziła Helena Więckowska (5 vols., Kraków: Nakładem Polskiej Akademiji Umiejętności, 1948–1956), Vol. I, letter no. 200, pp. 278–279.

10. Lelewel, *Dzieła,* VII, p. 264.

11. *Ibid.,* pp. 263–265.

12. *Ibid.,* pp. 265–269.

13. Joachim Lelewel, *Historia Polski do końca panowania Stefana Batorego: Dzieła*, VI, p. 192, p. 199, p. 210.
14. *Ibid.*, p. 211.
15. *Ibid.*, p. 269, p. 354.
16. *Ibid.*, p. 369.
17. *Ibid.*, pp. 211–215.
18. *Ibid.*, pp. 361–376.
19. *Ibid.*, pp. 299–312.
20. *Ibid.*, pp. 374–375.
21. The problem of Poland rising only to be destroyed by the end of the eighteenth century was not dealt with in his history to the end of the reign of Stefan Batory, but it was discussed in *Panowanie króla polskiego Stanisława Augusta.*
22. Józef Dutkiewicz, "Komentarz," in Joachim Lelewel, *Panowanie Stanisława Augusta: Dzieła*, opracował Józef Dutkiewicz (Warszawa: Państwowe Wydawnictwo Naukowe, 1961), VIII, p. 463. The edition included in Volume VIII of *Dzieła* is the 1859 edition.
23. Lelewel, "Przedwstęp do wydania trzeciego," *Panowanie Stanisława Augusta: Dzieła*, VIII, p. 267.
24. *Ibid.*, p. 267, p. 272.
25. *Ibid.*, pp. 268–270.
26. Dutkiewicz, "Komentarz," in Lelewel, *Dzieła*, VIII, pp. 465–466.
27. Lelewel, *Panowanie Stanisława Augusta: Dzieła*, VIII, p. 418.
28. *Ibid.*
29. *Ibid.*, p. 421.
30. *Ibid.*, p. 420.
31. *Ibid.*, pp. 420–421.
32. *Ibid.*
33. *Ibid.*, p. 421.
34. *Ibid.*, p. 418.
35. *Ibid.*, pp. 277–278.
36. *Ibid.*, pp. 419–420.
37. *Ibid.*, p. 422.
38. Joachim Lelewel, *Historyczna paralela Hiszpanii z Polską: Dzieła*, opracował Marian H. Serejski (Warszawa: Państwowe Wydawnictwo Naukowe, 1961), VIII, p. 216.
39. *Ibid.*, pp. 223–224.
40. *Ibid.*, p. 226ff.
41. *Ibid.*, p. 243.
42. *Ibid.*, pp. 243–245.
43. *Ibid.*, p. 248.
44. *Ibid.*, p. 256.
45. Lelewel, *Dzieła*, I, p. 57.

46. Joachim Lelewel, *Pielgrzyma w Dobromilu czyli nauk wiejskich roz-biór z uwagami nad stanem wiejskim w Polszcze i ulepszeniem oświaty jego: Dzieła*, VII, pp. 273–279.

47. *Ibid.*, p. 281.

48. Lelewel, *Dzieje Polski potocznym sposobem opowiedziane: Dzieła*, VII, p. 51.

49. Janina Bieniarzówna, "Wstęp," in Joachim Lelewel, *Dzieje Polski potocznym sposobem opowiedziane: Dzieła*, VII, p. 18.

50. Lelewel, *O potrzebie elementarnych dzieł historycznych: Dzieła*, VII, p. 305.

51. *Ibid.*, p. 306.

52. *Ibid.*, pp. 306–307.

53. Lelewel, *Dzieje Polski potocznym sposobem opowiedziane: Dzieła*, VII, p. 39.

54. *Ibid.*

55. *Ibid.*, p. 162.

56. *Ibid.*, p. 68, p. 124.

57. *Ibid.*, pp. 86–87; p. 127.

58. *Ibid.*, pp. 202–203.

59. *Ibid.*, p. 316, p. 352, p. 371.

60. *Ibid.*, pp. 101–102, p. 335.

61. *Ibid.*, p. 203.

62. *Ibid.*

63. *Ibid.*, pp. 202–203.

64. Lelewel, *Dzieła*, I, p. 108. His contributions to the study of numismatics are discussed by Marian Haisig, "Znaczenie Lelewela dla numismatyki Europejskiej," *Kwartalnik Historyczny*, LXVIII (1961), pp. 939–946. His most significant contribution to the study of geography is a multivolume work published 1852–1857. See Joachim Lelewel, *Geographie du moyen age* (Amsterdam, Holland: Meridian Publishing Co., 1961), 5 vols.

65. The first national history which he wrote in exile, *Polska odradzająca się*, appeared in 1836. Since it was intended to be a political polemic rather than a serious piece of scholarship, it is discussed by the present author in the previous chapter. See above, p. 92ff.

66. Lelewel, *Dzieła*, I, pp. 92–93.

67. Joachim Lelewel, *Histoire de Pologne: considérations sur l'état politique de l'ancienne Pologne et l'histoire de son peuple* (Paris: A La Librairie Polonaise, 1844), II.

68. Joachim Lelewel, *Betrachtungen über den politischen Zustan des chemaligen Polens und über die Geschichte seines Volkes* (Leipzig: Druk von F. A. Brockhaus, 1845).

69. Joachim Lelewel, *Uwagi nad dziejami Polski i ludu jej: Polska dzieje i rzeczy jej* (Poznań: Nakładem J. K. Żupańskiego, 1855), III, p. 27.

70. Marian H. Serejski, "Miejsce Joachima Lelewela we wspólnej nauce historycznej," p. 864. Also Nina Assorodobraj, "Notaty Karola Marksa z *Histoire de Pologne* Joachima Lelewela," p. 251.

71. Lelewel, *Uwagi nad dziejami Polski i ludu jej: Polska dzieje i rzeczy jej*, III, p. 28.

72. Lelewel, *Dzieła*, VIII, pp. 32–33.

73. Lelewel, *Uwagi nad dziejami Polski i ludu jej: Polska dzieje i rzeczy jej*, III, p. 253.

74. *Ibid.*, p. 33.

75. *Ibid.*, pp. 39–40.

76. *Ibid.*, p. 42.

77. *Ibid.*

78. *Ibid.*, p. 49, p. 75, p. 133, p. 274.

79. Lelewel, *Dzieje Polski potocznym sposobem opowiedziane: Dzieła*, VII, p. 52, p. 75, p. 103, p. 148.

80. Chrzanowski, *Joachim Lelewel: Człowiek i piszarz*, p. 153. Marian H. Serejski, *Joachim Lelewel: Z dziejów postępowej myśli historycznej w Polsce* (Warszawa: Państwowe Wydawnictwo Naukowe, 1953), p. 47.

81. Lelewel, *Uwagi nad dziejami Polski i ludu jej: Polska dzieje i rzeczy jej*, III, p. 32.

82. *Ibid.*, p. 31.

83. *Ibid.*, p. 73.

84. *Ibid.*, pp. 67–69, p. 73.

85. *Ibid.*, pp. 73–74.

86. *Ibid.*, pp. 131–132.

87. *Ibid.*, p. 132.

88. *Ibid.*, p. 272.

89. *Ibid.*

90. *Ibid.*, pp. 272–273.

91. *Ibid.*, p. 273.

92. *Ibid.*, p. 253.

93. *Ibid.*, pp. 253–254.

94. *Ibid.*, p. 173.

95. *Ibid.*, p. 164.

96. *Ibid.*, pp. 164–165.

97. Joachim Lelewel, *Prawność czyli prawnota narodu polskiego: Polska dzieje i rzeczy jej* (Poznań: Nakładem J. K. Żupańskiego, 1864), XX, pp. 569–581.

98. Above, p. 87ff.

99. Lelewel, *Uwagi nad dziejami Polski i ludu jej: Polska dzieje i rzeczy jej*, III, p. 167.

100. *Ibid.*, pp. 188–190.

101. *Ibid.*, p. 108.

102. *Ibid.*, p. 221; pp. 227–232.

103. *Ibid.*, pp. 230–247.

104. *Ibid.*, p. 255.

105. *Ibid.*, p. 273.

106. *Ibid.*, p. 275.

107. *Ibid.*, p. 277.

108. *Ibid.*, p. 279.

109. *Ibid.*, p. 301.

110. *Ibid.*, p. 308.

111. *Ibid.*, p. 321.

112. *Ibid.*, p. 325.

113. *Ibid.*, p. 328; p. 441.

114. *Ibid.*

115. *Ibid.*, p. 349.

116. *Ibid.*, p. 391.

117. *Ibid.*, p. 429.

118. *Ibid.*, pp. 363–364. The estrangement between the Cossacks and Poland was the result of a long chain of events beginning with the Union of Lublin (1569) which merged Poland and Lithuania in a single state. Among the factors which contributed to the estrangement were: the introduction of serfdom and the imposition of heavier obligations on peasants by the Polish szlachta; the practice of Polish landowners of administering their estates through Jewish intermediaries (this led to anti-Semitism); the aggressive policies of the Roman Catholic Church.

119. Lelewel, *Uwagi nad dziejami Polski i ludu jej: Polska dzieje i rzeczy jej,* III, p. 373.

120. *Ibid.*, p. 374, p. 379. The policy of the Polish government was contradictory and inconsistent toward the Cossack army.

121. *Ibid.*, pp. 301–305.

122. *Ibid.*, p. 384. Provisions were also included for the admission of Muscovy into the federation, but the Union of Hadziacz (1657) remained a dead letter as Muscovy's interests in the Ukraine intensified. The Union of Hadziacz was superseded by the earlier Treaty of Perejasław (1654) which was signed by Boghdan Chmielnicki and Alexis, Tsar of Muscovy. The text of this treaty is not preserved. Russian and Ukrainian historians differ in their interpretations of its meanings. See Francis Dvornik, *The Slavs in European History and Civilization* (New Brunswick: Rutgers University Press, 1962), pp. 475–483. The Russian tsar used the treaty as a pretext for invading Poland. Wars between the Polish *Rzeczpospolita* and Muscovy over possession of the Ukraine continued sporadically from 1654 to 1689 and resulted in the ultimate division of the Ukraine in two. See Oscar Halecki, *A History of Poland* (Chicago: Henry Regnery Co., 1966), pp. 157–161.

123. Lelewel, *Uwagi nad dziejami Polski i ludu jej: Polska dzieje i rzeczy jej,* III, pp. 299–300.

124. *Ibid.*, pp. 307–310.

125. *Ibid.*, p. 321.
126. *Ibid.*, p. 433.
127. *Ibid.*, p. 468.
128. *Ibid.*, p. 469.

🕮 8: General Observations and Conclusions

1. William Leslie Blackwell, "Alexander I and Poland: The Foundations of his Polish Policy and Its Repercussions in Russia, 1801–1825" (unpublished Ph.D. dissertation, Department of History, Princeton University, 1955), p. 175.

2. *Ibid.*, p. 176.

3. William J. Rose, "Lelewel as Historian," *The Slavonic Review,* XV (July, 1936), p. 652, quoting Joachim Lelewel.

4. Joachim Lelewel, *Historyka: Wybór pism historycznych,* opracowała Helena Więckowska (Wrocław: Wydawnictwo Zakładu Narodowego Im. Ossolińskich, 1950), p. 39.

5. Lelewel, quoted by Helena Więckowska in "Wstęp," *Wybór pism historycznych,* p. xxx.

6. Joachim Lelewel, *Przygody w poszukiwaniach rzeczy narodowych polskich: Dzieła,* opracowała Helena Więckowska (Warszawa: Państwowe Wydawnictwo Naukowe, 1957), I, p. 84.

7. R. F. Leslie, *Reform and Insurrection in Russian Poland: 1856–1865* (London: The Athlone Press, 1963), p. 5.

8. Joachim Lelewel, *Mowy i pisma polityczne: Polska dzieje i rzeczy jej* (Poznań: J. K. Żupański, 1864), XX.

9. Lelewel, *Dzieła,* I, p. 86.

10. Peter Brock, "Polish Socialists in Early Victorian England: Three Documents," *The Polish Review,* VI (Winter, 1961), p. 34.

11. Marian H. Serejski, "Miejsce Joachima Lelewela we współczesnej nauce historycznej," *Kwartalnik Historyczny,* LXVIII (1961), p. 859.

12. *Ibid.*, p. 861.

13. Lelewel, *O piśmiennych pracach: Dzieła,* I, p. 130.

14. *Ibid.*

15. *Ibid.*

16. *Ibid.*

17. Lelewel, *Uwagi nad dziejami Polski i ludu jej: Wybór pism historycznych,* pp. 124–126.

18. Joachim Lelewel, *Z uwag nad dziejami Polski i ludu jej: Dzieła,* opracowała Nina Assorodobraj (Warszawa: Państwowe Wydawnictwo Naukowe, 1964), II, p. 878.

19. Ignacy Chrzanowski, "Lelewel," in *Great Men and Women of Poland,* edited by Stephen P. Mizwa (New York: The Macmillan Co., 1941), pp. 59–62, quotes Lelewel who is the object of criticism from both the aristocrats and democrats of the Great Emigration.

20. Joachim Lelewel, *Polska odradzająca się: Dzieła,* opracowała Helena Więckowska (Warszawa: Państwowe Wydawnictwo Naukowe, 1961), VIII, pp. 165–166.

21. Lelewel, *Do dzieći polskich: Dzieła,* VIII, p. 30.

22. Lelewel, *Polska odradzająca się: Dzieła,* VIII, pp. 33–35.

Selected Bibliography

❀ Primary Sources

Collected Works:

Lelewel, Joachim. *Dzieła*. Komitet redakcyjni: J. Adamus *et al.* M. H. Serejski, redaktor naczelny. Warszawa: Państwowe Wydawnictwo Naukowe, 1957–1969, 9 vols.

———. *Polska dzieje i rzeczy jej*. Poznań: Nakładem J. K. Żupańskiego, 1855, 6 vols.

———. *Polska dzieje i rzeczy jej*. Poznań: Nakładem J. K. Żupańskiego, 1859–1864, 20 vols.

Correspondence:

———. "Cztery nieznane listy emigracyjne z lata 1832, 1851, 1860." Wydał Władysław Bandura. *Biuletyn Biblioteki Jagiellonskiej*, 13 (1963), pp. 19–23.

———. "Do T. Bulharyna dziesięć listów z 1822–1830. Ogłosil Stanisław Ptaszycki. *Gwiazda-Kalendarz Petersburgski* (1881).

———. *Korespondencja Joachima Lelewela z Karolem Sienkiewiczem*. Oddruk z Rocznika Towarzystwa Historyczno-Literackiego w Paryżu na rok 1870. Poznań: J. K. Żupański, 1872.

———. *Korespondencja Joachima Lelewela z Tytusem hr. Działyńskim*. Wydał Dr. Zigmunt Celichowski. Poznań: Nakład Biblioteki Kornickiej czcionkami drukarnia Kuryera Poznańskiego, 1884.

———. List do Frańciszka Malewskiego z 3 II 1830. Opracował Bogdan Horodyski. *Przegląd Bibliograficzny*, 29 (1961), pp. 113–126.

———. Listy do Karola Świdińskiego z 28 stycznia 1826, 12 września 1829, i 7 stycznia 1829 (! 1830). Ogłosila Danuta Kamolowa. *Przegląd Historyczny*, 54 (1963), pp. 480–486.

———. *Listy do rodzeństwa pisane*. Poznań: J. K. Żupański, 1878–1879, 2 vols.

———. *Listy emigracyjne Joachima Lelewela*. Wydała i wstępem poprzedziła Helena Więckowska. Kraków: Nakładem Polskiej Akademii Umiejętności, 1948–1956, 5 vols.

_____. *Nieznane listy Joachima Lelewela z lat 1831–1846*. Wydała Janina Berger-Mayerowa. Katowice: Sląski Instytut Naukowy, 1961.

Works not included in the Collected Works:

_____. *Antiquités de pologne, de litvanie et de slavonie expliquees par Joachim Lelewel*. No. 1. *Notice sur la Monnai de Pologne* (Insérée dans *La Pologne Illustree*). Paris: Librairie Polonaise, 1842. Bruxelles: P. J. Voglet, Libraire, 1842.

_____. *Badania starożytności we względzie geografji: część naukowa*. Wilno i Warszawa: Nakładem i Drukiem Józefa Zawadzkiego, 1818.

_____. *Bibliograficznych ksiąg dwoje*. Wilno: Nakładem i Drukiem Józefa Zawadzkiego, 1823–1826, 2 vols.

_____. *Betrachtungen über den politischen Zustan des chemaligen Polens und über die Geschichte seines Volkes*. Leipzig: Druk von F. A. Brockhaus, 1845.

_____. *Całoroczne trudy Komitetu Narodowego Polskiego*. Paryż: Drukarnia A. Pinard, 1831–1833, 4 vols.

_____. *Część bałwochwalcza Sławian i Polski*. Poznań: Nakładem J. K. Żupańskiego, 1855.

_____. *Dzieje Litwy i Rusi aż do unji z Polską w Lublinie zawartej*. Wydanie drugie przejrzane i poprawione. Poznań: Nakładem i Drukiem W. Stefanskiego, 1844.

_____. *Dzieje Polski które stryj synowcom swoim opowiedział*. Wydanie szóste. Wrocław: Z. Schletter, 1849.

_____. *Dzieje Polski potocznym sposobem opowiedziane*. Wydanie do użytku zastosowane i opowiadaniem do roku 1848 dopełnione. Z 3 krajobrazami. Lwów: Druk Zakładu Narodowego Im. Ossolińskich, 1849.

_____. *Études numismatiques et archéologiques*. Premier volume: *Type Gaulois, ou Celtique*. Bruxelles: P. J. Voglet, Imprimeur-Libraire, 1841.

_____. *Geographie du moyen age*. Reprint of the 1852–1857 edition. Amsterdam: Meridian Publishing Co., 1961, 5 vols.

_____. *Geschichte Polens unter Stanislas August, 1764–1795*. Braunschweig: Verlag von Friedrich Biemeg, 1831.

_____. *Gilbert de Lannoy i jego podróże*. Poznań: J. K. Żupański, 1844.

_____. *Histoire de Pologne*. Paris: A La Librairie Polonaise, 1844, 2 vols.

_____. *Kilka statutów polskich warianty lub text wyjątek z pierwszego tomu Ksiąg Bibliograficznych*. Wilno: Nakładem i Drukiem Józefa Zawadzkiego, 1823.

_____. *Myśli z powodu pisma M. Kubrakiewicza pod tytulem Uwagi nad Konstytucją 3go Maja 1791 roku co do prawa własności gruntu*. Paryż: I. Gessern i A. Pinard, 1833.

_____. *Observations sur le type du moyen-âge de la monnaie des Pays-Bas, mémoir extrait d'un ouvrage intitulé numismatique due moyen-âge*. Bruxelles: [Imprimeur de E. Laurent], 1835.

————. *Odkrycia Kartagówi Greków na oceanie Atlanchim.* Reprint of the 1831 edition. Amsterdam: Meridian Publishing Co., 1964.

————. *Pamiętnik z roku 1830-1831.* Przedmową i przypisami zaopatrzył Janusz Iwaszkiewicz. Warszawa: Biblioteka Polska, 1924.

————. *Pisma rozmaite.* Poznań: Nakładem Księgarni J. K. Żupańskiego, 1863.

————. "Porównanie Karamzina z Naruszewiczem." Ogłosił w języku rosyskim (tłumaczył T. Bułharyn) pt. "Razsmotrenie *Istorii Gosudarstva Rossiskago* soc. g. Karamzina," *Severnyi Arkhiv* 1822, nr. 4, 1823, nr. 8, 1824, nr. 9, 11-12.

————. *Wybór pism historycznych.* Opracowała Helena Więckowska. Wrocław: Wydawnictwo Zakładu Narodowego Im. Ossolińskich, 1950.

————. *Wybór pism politycznych.* Wyboru dokonali i przypisami opatrzyli Wł. Bortnowski i J. Danieliewicz. Pod redakcją i ze wstępem M. H. Serejskiego. Warszawa: Książka i Wiedza, 1954.

Other Primary Sources:

Bakunin, Mikhail A. *The Confession of Mikhail A. Bakunin; with marginal comments of Tsar Nicholas I.* Translated by Robert C. Howes. Introduction and notes by Lawrence D. Orton. Ithaca: Cornell University Press, 1977.

Borkowski, Karol. *Pamiętnik historyczny o wyprawie partyzanskiej do Polski w roku 1833.* Lipsk: F. A. Brockhaus, 1862.

Bułharyn, Tadeusz. *Listy do Joachima Lelewela z 1821-1830.* Poddał Prot Lelewel. *Biblioteka Warszawska.* Warszawa: Gebethner i Wolff, 1877, volume 1, pp. 222-231.

Chodźko, Leon (ed.). *La Pologne historique, littéraire, monumental et illustrée.* Third edition. Paris: Au Bureau Central, 1843.

————. *Recueil des traites, conventions et actes diplomatiques concernant la Pologne: 1762-1862.* Paris: Amyot, éditeur, 1862.

Czubek, Jan (ed.). *Towarzystwo Filomatów Korespondencja: 1815-1823.* Kraków: Nakładem Akademii Umiejętności, 1913, 5 vols.

Domejko, Ignacy. *Moje podróze: Pamiętniki wygnańca.* Vol. 1 Przygotowała do druku, opatrzyła przedmową i przypisami Elżbieta Helena Nieccowa. Wrocław: Zakład Narodowy Im. Ossolińskich, 1962.

Heltman, Wiktor, Janowski, J. N. *Demokracja polska na emigracji.* Przedmową i przypisami opatrzyła Helena Rzadkowska. Warszawa: Książka i Wiedza, 1965.

Kieniewicz, Stefan, Mencel, Tadeusz, Rostocki, Władysław. *Wybór tekstów źródłowych z historii Polski w latach 1795-1864.* Warszawa: Państwowe Wydawnictwo Naukowe, 1956.

Konarski, Szymon. *Dziennik z lat 1831-1834.* Wrocław: Polska Akademia Nauk, 1973.

Lafayette, Marie Joseph. *Memoires, correspondance et manuscrits du Général Lafayette.* Publiés par sa famille. Tome sixieme. Paris: H. Fournier Aine, Editeur, 1837.

Lelewel, Prot. *Pamiętniki i diariusz domu naszego.* Przygotowała do druku i opatrzyła przypisami Irena Lelewel-Friemannowa. Wrocław: Zakład Narodowy Im. Ossolińskich, 1966.

Lewak, Adam (ed.). *Le Général La Fayette et la cause polonaise: lettres-discours-documents.* Varsovie: Gebethner and Wolff, 1934.

Lewicki, Adam (ed.). *Pamiętniki spiskowców i więźniów Galicyjskich w latach 1832-1846.* Wrocław: Zakład Im. Ossolińskich, 1954.

Łodyński, Marian (ed.). *Materiały do dziejów państwowej polityki bibliotecznej w Księstwie Warszawskim i Królestwie Polskim (1807-1831).* Wrocław: Zakład Narodowy Im. Ossolińskich, 1958.

Łukaszewicz, Witold, and Lewandowski, Władysław (eds.). *Postępowa publicystyka emigracyjna 1831-1864. Wybór Zródł.* Seria II *Materiały zródłowe do dziejów polskich walk narodowy zwolenczych,* Tom VI. Redaktor naczelny Henryk Jabloński. Wrocław: Zakład Narodowy im. Ossolińskich, 1961.

Mazzini, Giuseppe. *Scritti IV. Politica III.* Edizione Nazionale degli scritti di Giuseppe Mazzini, 1906-1909, 6 vols. Imola: Cooperativa typografico Paolo Galeati, 1908.

Melegari, Dora. *Le jeune Italie et la jeune Europe: lettres inédites de Joseph Mazzini a Louis-Amédeé Melegari.* Paris: Librairie Fischbacher, 1908.

Mickiewicz, Adam. *Dzieła.* Cześć I and II. W opracowaniu Stanisława Pigonia. Kraków: Drukarnia Narodowa, 1953-1954.

_____. *Dzieła.* Vol. I. Warszawa: Społdzielnia Wydawnicza "Czytelnik," 1955.

_____. *Korespondencja.* Tom 1-2. Paryż: Księgarnia Luxsemburgska, Rouge, Dunon, i Fresne, 1870-1872.

Mochnacki, Maurycy. *Powstanie narodu polskiego w roku 1830-31.* Drugie wydanie. Wrocław: Nakładem Zygmunta Schlettera, 1850, 2 vols.

Le Moniteur universel, journal officiel de l'Empire française (Paris, France), 1831-1833.

Mościcki, Henryk (ed.). *Promieniści, Filomaci, Filarci.* Wydanie trzecie poprawione i uzupełnione. Warszawa: Gebethner i Wolff, 1934.

Le National (Paris, France), 1831-1833.

Russia. Arkheograficheskaia komissiia. *Documents servant a éclaircir l'histoire des provinces occidentales de la Russie ainsi que leurs rapports avec la Russie et la Pologne.* St. Petersburg: E. Pratz, 1865.

Sarrons, B. *Memoirs of General Lafayette and of the French Revolution of 1830.* London: Richard Bentley, New Burlington Street, 1832, 2 vols.

Sokolowska, Stefania. "Materialy do historii węglarstwa polskiego z czasów Wielkiej Emigracji," *Przegląd Historyczny,* 65 (1974), pp. 159-169.

Szaniecki, Jan O. *Dola i niedola Jana Olrycha Szanieckiego: Korespondencja* z Joachimem Lelewelem. Wydał i wstęp poprzedził Stanisław Posner. Warszawa: E. Wende, 1912.

Świdiński, Konstanty. "Do Joachima Lelewela listy z 8 stycznia 1826 i 29 pazdżiernika 1829." Ogłosiła Danuta Kamolowa. *Przegląd Historyczny*, 59 (1963), pp. 480–486.

Wyspiański, Stanisław. *Dzieła zebrane*. Redakcja zespólna pod kierownictwem Leona Płoszewskiego *et al.* Vol. III: *Lelewel; Legion*. Kraków: Wydawnictwo Literackie, 1958.

Zwierkowski, Walenty. *Rys powstania walki i działań polaków 1830–1 skreślony w dziesęć lat po wypadkach na tułactwie we Francji.* Przygotował do druku wstępem, przypisami i indeksami opatrzył Władysław Lewandowski. Warszawa: Książka i Wiedza, 1973.

♞ Secondary Works

Askenazy, Szymon. *Rosya-Polska, 1815–1830*. Lwów: Nakładem H. Althenberga, 1907.

Assorodobraj, Nina. "Historyki Lelewela," *Kwartalnik Historyczny*, LXVIII (1961), pp. 967–991.

————. "Notaty Karola Marksa z *Histoire de Pologne* Joachima Lelewela," *Archiwum Historii, Filozofii, i Mysli Spólecznej*, IV (1959), pp. 249–273.

Basevich, Abram Moiseyevich. *Ioakhim Lelevel': Pol'skii revoliutsioner, demokrat, uchen'ii.* Moscow: Izdatel'stvo sotsial'no-ekonomicheskoi literatury, 1961.

Batowski, Henryk. "Ocena polskiego sławianofilstwa. Dekabryści a niepodległość Polski. Polacy a Słowianie południowi," *Kwartalnik Historyczny*, LXIV (1957), pp. 47–49.

————. "The Poles and Their Fellow Slavs, 1848–1849," *The Slavic and East European Review*, XXVII (1948–49), pp. 404–413.

Bieliński, Józef. *Królewski Uniwersytet Warszawski: 1816–1831.* Warszawa: Skład Główny w Księgarni Gebethnera i Wolffa, 1907–1911, 2 vols.

————. *Uniwersytet Wileński: 1579–1831.* Kraków: Druk W. L. Anczyca i Spółki, 1899–1900, 3 vols.

Black, J. L. "M. P. Pogodin: A Russian Nationalist Historian and the 'Problem' of Poland," *Canadian Review of Studies in Nationalism*, I (1973), pp. 60–69.

Blackwell, William Leslie. "Alexander I and Poland: The Foundations of his Polish Policy and its Repercussions in Russia, 1801–1825." Unpublished Ph.D. dissertation, Princeton University, 1959.

Block, Cesław. "Aid of the English People to Poland in 1831," *Acta Polonaie Historica*, XIV (1966), pp. 117–123.

Bobińska, Celina. *Ideologia rewolucyjnych demokratów polskich w latach sześćdziesiątych XIX wieku.* Warszawa: Państwowe Wydawnictwo Naukowe, 1956.

Bortnowski, Władysław. *Powstanie listopadowe w oczach rosjan.* Lódz: Instytut Historyczny, 1964.

———. "Stanowisko Joachima Lelewela wobec rosyskiego ruchu rewolucyjnego," ZNUŁ *Nauki Humanistyczno-Społeczne*, 24 (1962), pp. 65-77.

———. *Walka o cele powstania listopadowego.* Lódz: Zakład Narodowy Im. Ossolińskich, 1960.

Breunig, Charles. *The Age of Revolution and Reaction, 1789-1858.* New York: W. W. Norton and Co., 1970.

Brock, Peter. "Polish Democrats and English Radicals, 1832-1862, A Chapter in the History of Anglo-Polish Relations," *Journal of Modern History*, XXV (1953), pp. 142-154.

———. "Polish Socialists in Early Victorian England: Three Documents," *The Polish Review*, VI (Winter, 1961), pp. 33-52.

———. "Socialism and Nationalism in Poland: 1840-1846," *Canadian Slavonic Papers*, IV (1959), pp. 121-146.

———. "The Political Program of the Polish Democratic Society," *The Polish Review*, XIV (Spring, 1969), pp. 89-105.

Bronowski, Franciszek. "Idea gminowładztwa w historii powszechnej Joachima Lelewela," *Kwartalnik Historyczny*, LXVIII (1961), pp. 879-887.

———. "Idea narodu w twórczości Joachima Lelewela w latach 1806-1830," *Roczniki Historyczne*, XXVI-XXVIII (1960), pp. 171-194.

———. "Recenzja Abrahama M. Basewicza, *Joachim Lelewel, polskij rewolucioner, demokrat, uczenyi*," *Kwartalnik Historyczny*, LX (1963), pp. 489-490.

Bujarski, George. "Polish Liberalism 1815-1830: The Question of Cosmopolitanism and National Identity," *The Polish Review*, XVII (Spring, 1972), pp. 3-37.

Chrzanowski, Ignacy. *Joachim Lelewel: człowiek i pisarz.* Do druku przygotował i przedmową poprzedził Stanisław Pigoń. Kraków: Spółdzielnia Wydawnicza "Czytelnik," 1946.

———. *Tajemnica ostatnich dni Joachima Lelewela w świetle zródel.* Warszawa: Drukarnia Kasy Im. Mianowskiego, 1937.

Coleman, A. P. "Language as a Factor in Polish Nationalism," *The Slavic Review*, XIII (July, 1934), pp. 155-176.

Cygler, Bogusław. *Działalność polityczno-społeczna Joachima Lelewela na emigracji w latach 1831-1861.* Gdańsk: Gdańskie Towarzystwo Naukowe, 1969.

———. "Joachim Lelewel wobec polskich ziem północnych i zachodnych," *Zapiski Historyczne*, XXXI (1972), pp. 81-94.

Droz, Jacques. *Europe Between Revolutions: 1815-1848.* Translated by Robert Baldick. New York: Harper and Row, 1967.

Dutkiewicz, Józef. *Francja a Polska w 1831 r.* Lodz: Łodzkie Towarzystwo Naukowe, 1950.

———. "Historiografia Powstania Listopadowego," in Barbara Grochulska *et al.* (eds.). *Wiek XIX: Prace ofiarowani Stefanowi Kieniewiczowi w 60* rocznicę urodzeń. Warszawa: Państwowe Wydawnictwo Naukowe, 1967, pp. 211–224.

———. "Lelewel a nasze wychowanie polityczne," *Kwartalnik Historyczny,* LXVIII (1961), pp. 999–1002.

Dvornik, Francis. *The Slavs in European History and Civilization.* New Brunswick: Rutgers University Press, 1962.

Engel-Janosi, Friedrich. *The Growth of German Historicism.* Baltimore: The Johns Hopkins Press, 1944.

Eyck, Gunther F. "Mazzini's Young Europe," *Journal of Central European Affairs,* XVII (January, 1958), pp. 356–377.

Feldman, Wilhelm. *Dzieje polskiej myśli politycznej w okresie porozbiorowym (próba zarysu).* Vol. I. Kraków: "Książka," 1913.

Fitzsimmons, Matthew A., Pundt, Alfred G., and Nowell, Charles E. (eds.). *The Development of Historiography.* (The Stackpole Social Science Series) Harrisburg: The Stackpole Co., 1954.

Frost, Thomas. *The Secret Societies of the European Revolution: 1776–1876.* London: Tinsley Brothers, 1876, 2 vols.

Gadon, Lubomir. *Emigracja polska. Pierwsze lata po upadku powstania listopadowego.* Kraków: Społka Wydawnicza Polska, 1901–1902, 3 vols.

———. *Wielka emigracja w pierwszych latach po powstaniu listopadowym.* Wstępem poprzedził Marian Kukiel. Wydanie drugie. Paryż: Księgarnia Polska [1960].

Gąsiorowska, Natalja (ed.). *W stulecie wiosny ludów.* Warszawa: Państwowy Instytut Wydawniczy, 1948–1951, 4 vols.

Gieysztor, Aleksander *et al. A History of Poland.* Translated by K. Cęklaska. Warsaw: Polish Scientific Publishers, 1968.

Gloger, Zygmunt. *Geografia historyczna ziem dawnej Polski.* Kraków: Spółka Wydawnicza Polska, 1900.

Gooch, G. P. *History and Historians in the Nineteenth Century.* New York: Peter Smith Co., 1949.

Grabski, Andrzej F. "Badania nad Joachimem Lelewelem w Polsce współczesnej (1945–1960)," *Kwartalnik Historyczny,* LXVIII (1961), pp. 884–890.

———. "Działalność Joachima Lelewela w Tow. Warszawskim Przyjaciół Nauk (1808–1815–1831)," *Kwartalnik Historyczny,* LXVIII (1961), pp. 947–967.

———. "Sprawozdanie z sesji naukowej Uniwersytetu Łódzkiego w stuleci śmierci Joachima Lelewela," *ZNUŁ Nauki Humanistyczno-Społeczne,* 24 (1962), pp. 155–162.

Haisig, Marian. "Znaczenie Lelewela dla numismatyki Europejskiej," *Kwartalnik Historyczny,* LXVIII (1961), pp. 939–946.

Halecki, Oscar. *A History of Poland.* Chicago: Henry Regnery Co., 1966.

———. *Borderlands of Western Civilization: A History of East Central Europe.* New York: The Ronald Press Co., 1952.

_____. "Problems of Polish Historiography," *The Slavonic Review*, XXI (March, 1943), pp. 223–239.

_____. "What is Realism in Polish History," *Journal of Central European Affairs*, III (October, 1943), pp. 322–327.

Hales, E.E.Y. *Mazzini and the Secret Societies: The Making of a Myth*. London: Eyre and Spotteswoode, 1956.

Halicz, Emanuel (ed.). "Towarzystwo Demokratyczne w Brukseli 1847–1848 i działalność w nim Marksa, Engelsa, Lelewela," *Z Pola Walki*, IV (1961), pp. 100–127.

Handelsman, Marceli. *Adam Czartoryski*. Warszawa: Nakładem Towarzystwa Naukowego z Zasiłku Prezydium Rady Ministrów i wydziału Nauki Ministerstwa Oświaty, 1948–1949, 2 vols.

_____. "Joachim Lelewel: Próba characterystyki twórczości," *Przegląd Historyczny*, XXXIV (1937–1938), pp. 332–337.

_____. *Rozwój narodowości nowoczesnej*. Warszawa: Nakład Gebethnera i Wolffa, 1923–1926, 2 vols.

Hayes, C.J.H. *The Historical Evolution of Modern Nationalism*. New York: Stratford Press, Inc., 1931.

Hepner, Benoit P. *Bakounine et le panslavisme révolutionnaire*. Paris: Libraire Marcel et Cie, 1950.

Hleb-Koszańska, Helena and Kotwiczówna, Maria. *Bibliografia utworów Joachima Lelewela*. Wrocław: Wydawnictwo Zakładu Narodowego Im. Ossolińskich, 1952.

Horodyski, Bogdan. "Lelewel o prasie Warszawskiej," *Przegląd Biblioteczny*, 29 (1961), pp. 113–126.

Kaczmarczyk, Zdzisław. "Zagadnienie periodyzacji historii Polski u Joachima Lelewela," in Janusz Pajewski (ed.). *Z badań nad pracami historycznymi Joachima Lelewela*. Poznań: Drukarnia Uniwersytetu im. Adama Mickiewicza, 1962, pp. 25–32.

Kalembka, Sławomir. *Wielka emigracja: Polskie wychodżstwo polityczne w latach 1831–1862*. Warszawa: Państwowe Wydawnictwo "Wiedza Powszechna," 1971.

Kamiński, Aleksander. *Polskie związki młodzieży: 1804–1831*. Warszawa: Państwowe Wydawnictwo Naukowe, 1963.

Kamiński, Konstanty. "Polacy w Belgii w latach 1832–1863," *Przegląd Humanistyczny*, 6 (1977), pp. 113–127.

Karasińska, Irena. "Lelewel w Warszawie," *Stolica*, 22 (1964), pp. 6–7.

Kasnik, Aleksandra Helena. *Między Francją a Algierią: Z dziejów emigracji polskiej, 1832–1856*. Wrocław: Ossolineum, 1977.

Kieniewicz, Stefan. *Konspiracje Galicyjskie: 1831–1845*. Warszawa: Książka i Wiedza, 1950.

_____. "Le Développement de la conscience nationale polonaise au XIXe siecle," *Acta Poloniae Historica*, 19 (1968), pp. 37–48.

_____. "Les Émigrés polonais en Algérie (1832–1856), *Acta Poloniae Historica*, XI (1965), pp. 43–70.

————. *Samotnik Brukselski: Opowieść o Joachimie Lelewelu.* Warszawa: Wiedza Powszechna, 1960.

————. *Sprawa włościańska w powstaniu styczniowym.* 1st edition. Wrocław: Zakład Im. Ossolińskich, 1953.

Kieniewicz, Stefan and Kula, Witold (eds.). *Historia Polski* Vol. II, part iii: 1831–1864. Opracował W. Długoborski, J. Jedlicki, S. Kieniewicz, W. Łukaszewicz, S. Sreniowski. Warszawa: Państwowe Wydawnictwo Naukowe, 1959.

Kohn, Hans. *Nationalism: Its Meaning in History.* Princeton: D. Van Nostrand Co., Inc., 1955.

————. *Pan-Slavism: Its History and Ideology.* 2nd edition. Revised. New York: Vintage Books, 1960.

————. *The Idea of Nationalism: A Study of its Origins and Background.* New York: The Macmillan Co., 1944.

Koht, H. "The Dawn of Nationalism in Europe," *American Historical Review,* LII (1947), pp. 265–280.

Korzon, Tadeusz. "Działalność naukowa Joachima Lelewela," *Kwartalnik Historyczny,* XI (1897), pp. 257–309.

Kotarbiński, Tadeusz. "Przedmówienie na otwarciu sesji Lelewelowskiej Polskiej Akademii Nauk," *Kwartalnik Historyczny,* LXVIII (1961), pp. 853–854.

Kowalska, Aniela. "O kontaktach Lelewela z Filomatami i Prasą Warszawską," *Przegląd Humanistyczny* (1962), pp. 127–141.

————. *Mochnacki i Lelewel: Współtwórcy życia umysłowego Warszawy i kraju, 1825–1830.* Warszawa: Państwowy Instytut Wydawniczy, 1971.

————. "Przyczynek do działalności popularyzatorskiej i poselskiej Joachima Lelewela (1829–30)," ZNUŁ *Nauki Humanistyczno-Społeczne,* 27 (1962), pp. 85–102.

Koźmiński, Karol. *Lelewel.* Toruń: Ludowa Spółdzielnia Wydawnicza, 1967.

Kraushar, Aleksander. *Towarzystwo Warszawskie Przyjaciół Nauk: 1800– 1832: Monografia historyczna osnuta na źródłach archiwalnich.* Kraków: G. Gebethner i Spółka, 1902–1906, 8 vols.

Kridl, Manfred, Wittlin, Józef, and Malinowski, Władysław (eds.). *The Democratic Heritage of Poland: For Your Freedom and Ours.* London: Allen and Unwin, Ltd., 1944.

Krzyżanowski, Julian. "Stanisław Wyspiański (1869–1907)," *The Polish Review,* IV (Autumn, 1957), pp. 23–32.

Kukiel, Marian. *Czartoryski and European Unity: 1770–1861.* Princeton: Princeton University Press, 1955.

————. "Lelewel, Mickiewicz, and the Underground Movements of the European Revolution (1816–1833)," *The Polish Review,* V (Summer, 1959), pp. 59–76.

————. "Uwagi i przyczynki do genezy rewolucji listopadowej i wojny w 1831 r.," *Teki Historyczne,* IX (1948), pp. 311–321.

Labuda, G. "Twórczośc Joachima Lelewela w poglądach historyków," in Janusz Pajewski (ed.), *Z badań nad pracami historycznymi Joachima Lelewela.* Poznań: Drukarnia Uniwersytetu im. Adama Mickiewicza, 1962, pp. 7–24.

Langer, William F. *Political and Social Upheaval: 1832–1852.* New York: Harper and Row, 1969.

Lednicki, Wacław. *Life and Culture in Poland as Reflected in Polish Literature.* New York: Roy Publishers, 1944.

_____. "Panslavism," in Felix Gross (ed.). *European Ideologies.* New York: The Philosophical Library, 1948.

_____. "Poland and the Slavophil Idea," *The Slavic and East European Review,* VII (1928), pp. 128–140.

Leslie, R. F. "Left-Wing Political Tactics in Poland 1831–1846," *The Slavic and East European Review,* XXXIII (1954), pp. 120–139.

_____. *Polish Politics and the Revolt of November 1830.* London: The Athlone Press, 1956.

_____. *Reform and Insurrection in Russian Poland, 1856–1865.* London: The Athlone Press, 1963.

Leśniewski, Adam. *Bakunin a sprawy polskie w okresie wiosny ludów i powstaniu styczniowego 1863 r.* Łódz: Zakład Narodowy Im. Ossolińskich, 1962.

Leśnodorski, Bogusław. "Badacz i historyk," *Nowe Drogi,* V (May, 1961), pp. 81–95.

_____. *Les Jacobins Polonais.* Paris: Sociétés des études Robespierrists, 1965.

Lewak, Adam. "Ideologia polskiego romantyzmu politycznego a Mazzini," *Przegląd Historyczny,* XXXVII (1948), pp. 311–321.

_____. "The Polish Rising of 1830," *The Slavic Review,* IX (December, 1930), pp. 350–361.

Lewalski, Kenneth F. "Lelewel's Third Exile: Alternatives for Relocation," *The Polish Review,* XXIII (1978), pp. 31–39.

Łepkowski, Tadeusz. "Ocena powstania listopadowego. Chłopy w powstaniu. Ujęcie spraw wojskowych. Rola Skrzyneckiego. Problem zdrady. Rok 1831 w tradycji narodowej," *Kwartalnik Historyczny,* IV–V (1957), pp. 188–207.

_____. *Warszawa w powstaniu listopadowym.* Wydanie drugie przejzane i uzupełnione. Warszawa: Wiedza Powszechna, 1965.

Łukaszewicz, Witold. *Szymon Konarski (1803–1839).* Warszawa: Spółdzielnia "Książka," 1948.

_____. "Wielka emigracja (1831–1862). Obozy ideologyczne, polityka, publicystyka," *Prace Polonistyczne,* IX (1951), pp. 147–188.

_____. "Wpływ masonerii, karbonaryzmu i Józefa Mazziniego na polska myśł rewolucyjna w latach poprzedzających wiosne ludów," in Nina Gąsiorowska (ed.). *W stulecie wiosny ludów 1848–1948,* Vol. III, Part II. Warszawa: Państwowy Instytut Wydawniczy, 1951, pp. 169–289.

Maternicki, Jerzy. *Warszawskie śródowisko historyczne, 1832–1869.* Warszawa: Państwowe Wydawnictwo Naukowe, 1970.

Mazour, Anatole G. *Modern Russian Historiography.* 2nd edition. Princeton: Van Nostrand Co., Inc., 1958.

————. *The First Russian Revolution 1825: The Decembrist Movement, Its Origins, Development, and Significance.* Stanford: University Press, second printing, 1963.

Michalski, Jerzy. *Z dziejów Towarzystwa Przyjaciół Nauk.* Warszawa: Nakładem Towarzystwa Naukowego z zasiłku Ministerstwa Szkolnictwa Wyższego, 1953.

Mizwa, Stephen (ed.). *Great Men and Women of Poland.* New York: The Macmillan Co., 1942.

Mocha, Frank. "The Karamzin-Lelewel Controversy," *The Slavic Review,* 31 (1972), pp. 592–610.

Morley, Charles. "The European Significance of the November Uprising," *Journal of Central European Affairs,* XI (1952), pp. 407–416.

Nadolski, Andrzej. "Joachima Lelewela wkład do archeologii," *Kwartalnik Historyczny,* LXVIII (1961), pp. 931–938.

Nowodworski, Witold. *"Bibliograficznych Ksiąg Dwoje" Joachima Lelewela: Studium historyczno-bibliograficzne na tle epoki.* Wrocław: Zakład Im. Ossolińskich Wydawnictwo, 1959).

Owińska, Anna. "Sprawa Polska i liberalne niemcy w latach 1832–1833," *Przegląd Zachodny,* 13 (1956), pp. 225–266.

Pajewski, Janusz (ed.). *Z badań nad pracami historycznymi Joachima Lelewela: Referaty i głosy dyskusyjne z sesji naukowej UAM zorganizowanej ku uczczeniu setnej rocznicy śmierci.* Poznań: Uniwersytet im. Adama Mickiewicza. Prace wydziału filozoficzno-historycznego, seria historia, nr. 9, 1962.

Pietraszkiewiczówna, Stanisława M. *Dzieje Filomatów w zarysie.* Kraków: Skład Główny w Księgarni G. Gebethnera i Społki, Druk W. L. Anczyca i Społki, 1912.

Pigoń, Stanisław. *Z dawnego Wilna: Szkice obyczajowe i literackie.* Wilno: Wydawnictwo Magistratu M. Wilna, 1929.

Plamenatz, John. *The Revolutionary Movement in France, 1815–1871.* London: Longmans, Green, and Co., 1952.

Popkov, Boris. *Pol'skii uchen'ii i revoliutsioner Ioakhim Lelevel'.* Moscow: Izdatel'stvo "Nauka," 1974.

Reddaway, W. F., Penson, J. H., Halecki, O., Dyboski, R. (eds.). *The Cambridge History of Poland.* Cambridge: University Press, 1959, 2 vols.

Riasanovsky, Nicholas V. *Nicholas I and Official Nationality in Russia, 1825–1855.* Berkeley: University of California Press, 1967.

Rogger, Hans. *National Consciousness in Eighteenth Century Russia.* Cambridge: Harvard University Press, 1960.

Rose, William J. "Hugo Kołłątaj, 1750-1812," *The Slavic Review,* XXIX (December, 1950), pp. 48-65.

———. "Lelewel as Historian," *The Slavic Review,* XV (July, 1936), pp. 649-662.

———. "Polish Historical Writing," *The Journal of Modern History,* II (December, 1930), pp. 569-585.

———. "Realism in Polish History," *Journal of Central European Affairs,* II (October, 1942), pp. 233-249.

———. *The Rise of Polish Democracy.* London: G. Bell and Sons, Ltd., 1944.

Rosin, Ryszard. "Ziemie zachodnie i północne w pismach Joachima Lelewela," ZNUŁ *Nauki Humanistyczno-Społeczne,* 27 (1962), pp. 103-110.

Rostocki, Władysław. "Ogólna ocena Księstwa Warszawskiego; jego ustrój polityczny W. Ks. Konstanty w latach 1815-1830. Lelewel i Mochnacki w dobie powstania listopadowego," *Kwartalnik Historyczny* (1957), pp. 142-144.

Serejski, Marian Henryk. "Joachim Lelewel (1786-1861)," *Acta Poloniae Historica,* VI (1962), pp. 35-54.

———. *Joachim Lelewel, 1786-1861: Sa vie et son oeuvre.* Traduit par Stanisław Lazar. Warszawa: Zakład Narodowy Im. Ossolińskich Wydawnictwo Polskiej Akademii Nauk, 1961.

———. *Joachim Lelewel: Z dziejów postępowej myśli historycznej w Polsce.* Warszawa: Państwowe Wydawnictwo Naukowe, 1953.

———. *Koncepcja historii powszechnej Joachima Lelewela.* Wydanie 1. Warszawa: Państwowe Wydawnictwo Naukowe, 1958.

———. "Miejsce Joachima Lelewela we współczesnej nauce historycznej," *Kwartalnik Historyczny,* LXVIII (1961), pp. 855-879.

———. "Ocena historiografii," *Kwartalnik Historyczny,* LXIV (1957), pp. 145-146.

———. "Próba charakterystyki ideologicznej postawy Lelewela jako historyka," *Przegląd Historyczny,* XL (1949), pp. 53-71.

———. *Przeszłość i terażnejszość; szkice i studia historiograficzne.* Wrocław: Zakład Narodowy Im. Ossolińskich, 1965.

———. *Studia nad historiografią Polski.* Wrocław: Drukarnia Naukowa, 1953.

———. "Upadek Polski a idea 'odrodzenia' narodu w historiografii polskiej końca XIX wieku," *Przegląd Historyczny,* LXIII (1972), pp. 413-423.

———. *Zarys historii historiografii polskiej.* Wyd. 2. Łodz: Państwowe Wydawnictwo Naukowe, 1954-1956-1959.

Skowronek, Jerzy. "Powstanie listopadowe i Wielka Emigracja," *Almanach Polonii 1980.* Warszawa: Wydawnictwo Interpress, 1979, pp. 73-79.

Skurnowicz, Joan S. "Joachim Lelewel: A Polish Émigré's Anti-Tsarist Politics, 1831-1833," *Laurentian University Review,* X (November, 1977), pp. 31-46.

Słowikowski, Tadeusz. *Joachim Lelewel, krytik i autór podręczników historii.* Wydanie 1. Warszawa: Państwowe Wydawnictwo Naukowe, 1974.

———. *Poglądy na nauczanie historii w Polsce w wieku XVIII oraz dydaktyczna koncepcja Joachima Lelewela.* Kraków: Państwowe Wydawnictwo Naukowe, 1960.

Smoleński, Władysław. "Patriotyzm historiografji polskiej w czasach porozbiorowych," *Przegląd Historyczny,* XXII (1919–1920), pp. 176–185.

———. *Szkoły historyczne w Polsce.* Z przedmową Aleksandra Rambowskiego. Warszawa: Drukarnia Artystyczna Saturnia Sikorskiego, 1898.

Smolka, Stanisław. "W drodze do Petersburga (z życia Lubeckiego) III spotkanie z W. Ks. Konstantym," *Przegląd Historyczny,* II (March–April, 1906), pp. 222–246.

Sokolnicki, Michel. *Les Origins de l'emigration polonaise en France 1831–1832.* Paris: Felix Alcan, éditeur, 1910.

Spitzer, Alan B. *Old Hatreds and New Hopes: The French Carbonari Against the Bourbon Restoration.* Cambridge: Harvard University Press, 1971.

Stecka, Marja. "Układy T-wa Demokratycznego z Młodą Polską (1834)," *Przegląd Historyczny,* XXII (1919–1920), pp. 156–175.

Szacki, Jerzy. *Ojczyzna, naród, rewolucja: problematyka narodowej polskiej myśli szlachecko-rewolucyjnej.* Warszawa: Państwowy Instytut Wydawniczy, 1961.

Śliwiński, Artur. *Joachim Lelewel: Zarys biograficzny lata 1786–1831.* Warszawa: Wydawnictwo M. Arcta, 1919.

———. *Joachim Lelewel: Zarys biograficzny lata 1786–1831.* Wydanie drugie przejrzane i uzupełnione. Warszawa: Wydawnictwo Kasy Im. Mianowskiego-Instytutu Popierania Nauki, 1932.

———. *Powstanie listopadowe.* Wydanie nowe. Londyn: Wydawnictwo Świątowego Związku Polaków z Zagranicy, 1946.

———. "Z Paryża do Brukseli (Karta z życia Joachima Lelewela)," *Przegląd Historyczny,* XXIV (1924), pp. 84–96.

Talmon, J. L. *Romanticism and Revolt: Europe 1815–1848.* London: Thames and Hudson, 1967.

Treichel, Irena. *Pierwszy polski podręcznik bibliotekarski.* Z przedmową Heleny Więckowskiej. Wrocław: Nakład Biblioteki Uniwersyteckiej w Łodzie, 1957.

Tymieniecki, K. "Lelewel jako badacz dziejów chłopów i obrońca sprawy chłopskiej," *Kwartalnik Historyczny,* LXVIII (1961), pp. 887–899.

Tyrowicz, Marian. *Towarzystwo Demokratyczne Polskie: 1832–1863: Przywódcy i kadry członkowskie.* Warszawa: Książka i Wiedza, 1964.

Valkenier, E. K. "Soviet Impact on Polish Post-War Historiography, 1946–1950," *Journal of Central European Affairs,* II (January, 1952), pp. 372–396.

———. "Sovietization and Liberalization in Polish Post-War Historiography," *Journal of Central European Affairs,* XIX (July, 1959), pp. 149–173.

Venturi, Franco. *Roots of Revolution: A History of the Populist and Social-ist Movements in Nineteenth Century Russia.* Translated from the Italian by Francis Haskill. London: Weidenfeld and Nicolson, 1960.

Ward, Sir A. W., Prothero, Sir G. W., and Leathes, S. (eds.). *The Cambridge Modern History.* Vol. X: *The Restoration.* New York: The Macmillan Co., 1934.

Weill, G. J. *Histoire du parti républicain en France (1814–1870).* Paris: Librairie Felix Alcan, 1928.

Weintraub, Wiktor. "Adam Mickiewicz the Mystic Politician," *Harvard Slavic Studies,* I (1953), pp. 137–178.

_____. *The Poetry of Adam Mickiewicz.* Leiden: Mouton and Co., 1954.

Więckowska, Helena. "Joachim Lelewel na emigracji," *Przegląd Historycz-ny,* XXXIV (1937–1938), pp. 322–331.

_____. "Lelewel w opinii historyków polskich," *Kwartalnik Historyczny,* LXVIII (1961), pp. 899–912.

Wołoszyński, Ryszard. *Polsko-rosyjskie związki w naukach społecznych, 1801–1830.* Warszawa: Państwowe Wydawnictwo Naukowe, 1974.

Zajewski, Władysław. "Ideologia i rola polityczna *Nowej Polski* w powstaniu listopadowym," *Przegląd Historyczny,* XLIX (1958), pp. 681–699.

_____. "Sprawa reformy rządu w czerwcu 1831 r.," *Przegląd Historyczny,* LI (1961), pp. 635–662.

_____. "W sprawie genezy rewolucji listopadowej 1830 r.," *Przegląd His-toryczny,* L (1959), pp. 852–856.

Zakrzewski, Jan. "Czasopiśmiennictwo polskie na emigracji," *Przegląd His-toryczny,* IV (May–June, 1907), pp. 82–97.

Zawadzki, Tadeusz. "Joachim Lelewel jako badacz dziejów świata starożyt-nego; Próba charakterystyki," *Przegląd Historyczny,* XLIII (1952), pp. 177–194.

Zdrada, Jerzy. "Joachim Lelewel o początkach cenzury w Królestwie Pol-skim," *Przegląd Historyczny,* LIX (1968), pp. 287–293.

Ziffer, Bernard. *Poland: History and Historians: Three Bibliographical Es-says.* New York: Mid-European Studies Center, 1952.

Żaczek, Wacław. "Joachim Lelewel w Czechach i Słowacji," *Kwartalnik Historyczny,* LXVIII (1961), pp. 913–930.

Index

The following abbreviations are used: d. = death; r. = reign.

era of, 103, 129; European, 138; and nationalism, 131

Rome, 2, 35, 36, 37

Rose, William J., British historian, 8, 170n

Rotteck, Karl von, German historian, 3

Rousseau, Jean-Jacques, 118, 127

Rożycki, Karol, 87

Rus, one of three legendary brothers and founders of the Slav race, 115

Russia, *see* Russian Empire

Russian Empire, western provinces, 20, 29, 30, 33, 52, 54, 63, 71, 77, 84, 97, 131, 147n, 150n; Enlightenment influence, 31; Russia, 38, 64, 70, 85, 87, 100, 170n; Polish lands, 41, 58, 71–2, 90, 102, 133; central provinces, 42; mentioned, 40, 43, 50, 51, 55, 78, 79, 80, 81, 116; *see also* Byelorussia, Lithuania, Podolia, Ruthenia, *Rzeczpospolita,* Ukraine, Volhynia

Russo-Turkish War (1828–29), 56

Ruthenia (Rus), 64, 71, 77–8, 127, 132

Rząd Narodowy (National Government) (1831), reforms, 30, 69; established, 64; defeated militarily, 68, 69, 72; and Joachim Lelewel, 70, 93, 131–2; *see also* November uprising of 1830, National Assembly of 1831

Rzeczpospolita (Commonwealth), 10, 52, 74, 77, 83, 91, 127, 140n, 169n; *see also* Poland

Safařik, Paul Joseph, and Slovak national renaissance, 163n

Saint Bartholomew Day Massacres (1572), 9

St. Petersburg, 40, 42, 45, 49, 56, 62, 63, 112

St. Petersburg Society of Friends of Learning, 40

Sand, Karl, *Burschenschaften,* 31–2

Sandomir, 45

Sarrons, B., secretary to Lafayette, 156n

Saśicki, Stefan, priest, Joachim Lelewel's teacher at the *Collegium Nobilium,* 12

Savoy expedition (1834), 86, 90

Scandinavians, 16, 38

Schelling, Friedrich von, German idealist philosopher, 31

Schlözer, August Ludwig von, theory of Germanic origins of Lithuanians, 16; criticized by Joachim Lelewel, 18–9, 146n

Schlüsselburg Prison, 55

Schroek, J. (d. 1808), German historian, 143n

Scythians, 16

Sejms (Diets), Chęcińsk, 121; Piotrków, 121; Radom, 121; Wiślicki, 121; of 1659, 127; *see also* Diets, Congress Kingdom of Poland

sejmiki, see dietines

Serejski, Marian Henryk, studies of Joachim Lelewel, 6, 7, 120, 139n, 142n, 146n, 165n, 166n, 168n, 170n

Severnyi Arkhiv (*The Northern Archive*), 40

Siberia, 42, 55, 95

Sienkiewicz, Karol, émigré, intellectual, 9; member, *Towarzystwo Historyczne-Literackie,* 102; correspondence with Joachim Lelewel, 140n, 141n, 164n

Skarbek, Fryderyk, 49

Skrzynecki, Jan, command of Polish military forces (1831), 86; head, Belgian army (1833–44), 86

Slav Congress, 101–02

Slavs, 17–8, 37–8, 40, 99, 100, 118

Slav virtues, mentioned, 48, 122–23, 136; *duch narodowy* (national spirit), 64–6, 107, 121, 124; *duch obywatelski* (spirit of citizenship), 48, 121; *narodowość* (nationalness), 17, 37, 39, 61, 89, 113, 115; *obywatelstwo* (citizenship), 2, 39, 107, 109, 112, 115, 117, 118, 120, 121, 122, 126, 165n; *ojczyzna* (fatherland), 19, 66, 89; *pomyślność* (well being or welfare), 22; *równość* (equality), 92, 117, 119, 120; *wolność* (freedom), 2, 22, 23, 38, 39, 80, 91–2, 107, 108, 109, 112, 117, 119, 120, 165n

Slovaks, 163n

Śląsk, 123

Słowacki, Euzebiusz, member, faculty, University of Wilno, 15

Słowacki, Juliusz, Polish romantic poet, 15; and Polish messianism, 162n

Smoleńsk, 78

Société Democratique Internationale, 100, 101, 158n

Société Philomatique de Paris, 32

Society for the Improvement of Youth in Learning and Science, *see Towarzystwo Doskonalającej się Młodzi w Naukach i Umiejętnościach*

Society of Friends of Learning, *see Towarzystwo Przyjaciół Nauk*

Society of Jesus, *see* Jesuits

Society of Lovers of Learning, *see* So-